Opening
Carnegie Hall

Opening Carnegie Hall

The Creation and First Performances of America's Premier Concert Stage

Carol J. Binkowski

*To Judy,
With heartfelt thanks!
Best wishes now
and always!!!
Love,
Carol*

McFarland & Company, Inc., Publishers
Jefferson, North Carolina

ALSO BY CAROL J. BINKOWSKI

Joseph F. Lamb: A Passion for Ragtime
(McFarland, 2012)

Frontispiece: The new Music Hall in 1891
(courtesy Carnegie Hall Archives).

Photographs are from the author's collection unless otherwise noted.

LIBRARY OF CONGRESS CATALOGUING-IN-PUBLICATION DATA

Names: Binkowski, Carol J.
Title: Opening Carnegie Hall : the creation and first performances
of America's premier concert stage / Carol J. Binkowski.
Description: Jefferson, North Carolina : McFarland & Company,
2016. | Includes bibliographical references and index.
Identifiers: LCCN 2016008511 | ISBN 9780786498727
(softcover : acid free paper) ∞
Subjects: LCSH: Carnegie Hall (New York, N.Y.) | Concerts—
New York (State)—New York. | Music—New York (State)—
New York—19th century—History and criticism.
Classification: LCC ML200.8.N52 B56 2016 | DDC 780.78/7471—dc23
LC record available at http://lccn.loc.gov/2016008511

BRITISH LIBRARY CATALOGUING DATA ARE AVAILABLE

ISBN (print) 978-0-7864-9872-7
ISBN (ebook) 978-1-4766-2398-6

Front cover: the new Music Hall in 1891 (courtesy Carnegie
Hall Archives)

Printed in the United States of America

*McFarland & Company, Inc., Publishers
Box 611, Jefferson, North Carolina 28640
www.mcfarlandpub.com*

For Pop,
with gratitude and thanks for your
inspiration, encouragement, and love

"This is no ordinary structure."
—*Andrew Carnegie*

Table of Contents

Acknowledgments

Writing this book was a unique journey. Along the way, I met many wonderful people; without them, the following pages might never have existed.

Deepest thanks to Carnegie Hall's incomparable archivist Gino Francesconi for generously sharing his time, resources, and exceptional insights about the early days of this iconic musical landmark. This was valuable not only from a research perspective but also from a human one, providing me with a deeper understanding of the people who were at the heart of its history. I am truly grateful, as well, for his contribution of the beautiful foreword to this book.

My sincerest gratitude to Marie Gangemi, archivist for the Oratorio Society of New York, for kindly granting me generous time and access to the singular materials in the organization's collection. Her vast knowledge of the Society's history and her keen observations on its place within the cultural heritage of the city brought the musical past vividly alive.

Additional thanks to Kathleen Sabogal and Samantha Nemeth at Carnegie Hall and to David Ralph of the Oratorio Society of New York for their kindness and welcome assistance.

To all of the superb staff at the New York Public Library for the Performing Arts, Music Division, Research and Special Collections—a resounding thank you for untiring patience in helping me discover and retrieve a wealth of valuable materials.

Special appreciation goes to Carolyn Waters at the New York Society Library; Jessica Lautin and Morgen Stevens-Garmon at the Museum of the City of New York; Gabe Smith at the New York Philharmonic Archives; and the helpful staffs at the Library of Congress, the New-York Historical Society Library, and the New York Public Library's Main and Mid-Manhattan branches. Additional thanks to Paula Kepich and Gil Pietrzak at the Carnegie Library of Pittsburgh; Thomas Lisanti at the New York Public Library; and Alexandra Henao at Budget Print Center in Bloomfield, New Jersey.

I am especially grateful to each of the friends who offered words of encouragement during the research and writing of this book. They were spoken at just the right moment and were more valuable than their speakers will ever know.

As always, heartfelt thanks to my family for their support on this and all of my projects—my father, A. Robert Knobloch; my husband, Richard Binkowski; and my daughter, Daria Binkowski.

Although I am not affiliated with or sponsored by Carnegie Hall, I am certainly appreciative of their gracious assistance. I have tried to present the facts in this book as accurately as possible and to the best of my ability. Any errors or omissions are mine alone and are definitely unintentional.

Foreword

by Gino Francesconi

When Carol Binkowski emailed me in September 2014 that she wanted to write a book on the founding of Carnegie Hall and its inaugural five-day Music Festival, my first reaction was less than encouraging. The Carnegie Hall Archives were not established until 1986. By that time, much of the Hall's documented history had been lost. Nearly 30 years later, the Archives team has made considerable progress filling in the gaps, documenting more than 51,000 events that have taken place at the Hall—including the 1891 opening Music Festival— but a portion of the day-by-day activity of our earliest history still eludes us for the time being.

Did that stop Carol? Not at all! Instead she combed and examined every piece of documentation that does exist; some of it readily available and some not easy to access at all. When I would make a recommendation to visit a collection or archives, she had already been there. I enjoyed her questions and thoroughness. She added two and two and got an adventure. The result is an enjoyable first in-depth look at each of the five days of the Music Festival, what led up to it, the color and atmosphere of the period, and the people who set Carnegie Hall on its journey to becoming one of the most famous concert halls in the world.

Gino Francesconi is the director of the Archives and Rose Museum at Carnegie Hall.

Introduction

A young woman approached the gleaming ebony piano at the center of the stage, her blue gown shimmering faintly under the warm glow of lights. Low murmuring from the audience abruptly turned to a hush, then silence altogether—only to be broken a moment later by the first crisp, clear notes of Bach. It was a scene that lingered—my first visit to Carnegie Hall.

Earlier that afternoon, my family was stunned to receive complimentary box-seat tickets for this concert from a local piano showroom. Each weekend, we had been spending time at such places, many of them then located in New York's West 57th Street area. We hoped to find "the" appropriate grand piano to replace my well-worn console model. Coincidentally, this particular firm was supplying a piano for that evening's concert—a debut recital by an unknown, out-of-town performer—and it was hoping to fill a representative portion of the seats in the massive main hall. Several hours later, my parents, my grandmother, and I settled in to enjoy the grandeur, the excitement, and the exquisite sound of it all—and from box seats, no less.

Until then, just the name "Carnegie Hall" held a mythical status in my mind—a place reserved only for famous performers and savvy, elite audiences. I couldn't have been more wrong. The name of the young woman onstage that evening was in no way familiar, especially when compared to those of many performers advertised on the posters outside. She came from a place far from West 57th Street—Colorado, to be exact. Her audience that evening was small, tiny clusters of individuals scattered throughout the vast space. Nevertheless, on that special occasion, she had the opportunity to live her dream of making a debut on one of the world's most famous—or perhaps the most famous—of concert stages. She was able to share her music with the audience, no matter how modest in size

3

it might have been. We were able to enjoy her music with the others in that small crowd—old, young, rich, poor, musically attuned or not. This place was for everyone, symbolizing worthwhile achievements and the realization of dreams. It was not beyond the realm of possibility for anyone to be there—performers and audiences alike. This gave me much to think about.

From the very beginning of its existence, Carnegie Hall was unique. Initially conceived as a home that would be suitable for large choral and symphony groups, it quickly became available to a wide array of individuals and musical organizations—both classical and otherwise. Non-musical events of all kinds were held there, as well. Carnegie Hall was for the enjoyment, education, and enrichment of everyone—a philosophy that has held for well over a century despite the glamour and awe-inspiring nature of its name.

However, during the Gilded Age into which it was born, the creation of this same concert hall seemed improbable on many counts. This was at the heart of what interested me at first. I have always been drawn to such accounts: their details cut across time and space, offering inspiration that is relevant to everyone. Carnegie Hall—originally called the Music Hall—was the fond dream of a talented and enterprising conductor and musician, an immigrant who came to America in 1871 to build a new career for himself and a new life for his family. That man was Leopold Damrosch, founder of both the Oratorio and Symphony societies of New York. These groups had been "making do" for years, performing in a number of venues that were not suitable in a variety of ways. New York did not lack concert halls, but many of them came with challenges. The spaces were either too large or too small or geared to one specific purpose—opera, popular variety, solo recital, and the like. Sometimes there were especially poor acoustics or multiple conflicts in scheduling rehearsals and performances. The list of problems was long. In order to present choral and orchestral concerts of true quality, something had to be done. That was when Damrosch began to dream of a new hall—a real home where his groups could perform at their best and share fine music with their audiences the way it was meant to be heard. Unfortunately, he did not live to see his dream realized. It did not, however, die with him.

Damrosch's son Walter was an extremely young conductor. He knew how much his father's musical groups had meant to him and what a loss it would be if all he had worked for fell apart. Therefore, he bravely carried through all of Leopold Damrosch's outstanding musical commitments upon his death—and they were many. Soon, he also assumed the role of conductor for both the Oratorio and Symphony societies. Walter Damrosch was only twenty-three years old when thrust into this well of enormous responsibility, an overwhelming situation by any standards. More than this, he also championed his father's dream of a new concert hall, an idea that now seemed even more improbable. Just as improbable was the young Damrosch's friendship with millionaire Andrew Carnegie and his wife, Louise—the result of a chance meeting on an ocean journey. Yet this friendship grew and prospered. Carnegie was a leading philanthropist who supported the building of libraries and educational institutions. Concert halls were not necessarily the first on his list. He did, however, love oratorio music, and the timing of his meeting with Damrosch was fortunate for all. Carnegie had just gotten married and his wife was not only a music lover but also a longtime member and supporter of the Oratorio Society. Naturally, Walter Damrosch introduced the subject of a new concert hall as their acquaintanceship grew. Although concert halls were not at the top of Carnegie's potential recipients, he was still a forward thinking individual. The possibilities of the new hall that he and Damrosch discussed over time became more intriguing. Carnegie envisioned it as a place that would not only perfectly accommodate musical groups such as the Oratorio and Symphony societies but also non-musical ones—additionally serving as a platform for "all good causes." Eventually, plans for the new concert hall moved forward.

Still, more improbabilities were added to the plot of this narrative. For one, there was the setting chosen for the new building—a piece of property removed from the clusters of existing concert and entertainment venues of the era. There were those, including many distinguished members of the musical community, who believed that this potential site alone would doom the project to failure. Why would audiences elect to travel to a concert or other event in a neighborhood where stables and saloons dotted the landscape and where the dust of blacksmiths' shops rose in the air? And why did New York need another concert hall anyway? Nevertheless, the plans for the building still continued at full speed, and these doubters were eventually proven wrong.

Next on the list of eyebrow-raising events was Andrew Carnegie's choice of the architect for the project. Why would a millionaire such as Carnegie—with his vast network of contacts and experience in supporting philanthropical building projects—assign this critical role to someone who had never before designed a concert hall? And yet—and again improbably so—William Burnet Tuthill, a fine young architect who was also an accomplished amateur cellist and singer, would eventually rise to fame through his exceptional and acoustically astounding design of the new building.

Still, it was one thing to create a concert hall and another to gain enough audience members to fill its near three thousand or so seats for an opening week Festival—and beyond. What were the chances of drawing a decent sized crowd? There would be music lovers, especially those who had supported the Oratorio Society and the Symphony Society in the past. Of course, curiosity seekers would be added to this number. However, would these groups together be enough to resemble a real audience for the five-day opening festivities that were being planned? The answer was a resounding "yes," particularly when famed composer Peter Ilyich Tchaikovsky entered into the equation. He also represented another improbable portion of the narrative. His reply to an invitation to come to New York and conduct some of his works at the opening Festival might well have been to decline. There were several reasons for this possibility. He had never traveled as far as America before. Added to this, his conducting activities had recently been curtailed due to difficulties with his arm. However, he accepted—and New York welcomed him with open arms. Opening Festival audiences were filled to overflowing, and tickets to the concerts were among the hottest items up for sale in the musical world during that season.

There were many supporting characters to this narrative, too—famed opera singers, piano manufacturers, virtuoso solo performers, board members for the new hall, local business owners, participants in musical groups—even the U.S. secretary of state. Some of them are well remembered to this day. Others are names in the pages of history books. Each one played a part, though, and each one had a unique personal account, as well.

These people, places, and events were all a part of the early days of Carnegie Hall. The improbable factors turned into ones of great possibility. The end result was not only successful but also rippled over time into one of great benefit for generations to follow.

I have always been intrigued by the history and people behind specific places. This history is everywhere, just waiting to be uncovered. All it takes is a small yet intriguing detail to begin a journey of discovery: the name of a former resident etched on the brass plaque of a city brownstone; a sign at the entrance to the rolling lawns of a park created in honor of someone vaguely recollected; or a construction date over a century old embedded in a building's ornate exterior. Even a little casual browsing in the library or, as is more common these days, a few clicks on some Internet information sites can yield some fascinating results. Suddenly, that brownstone, or park, or building is teeming with people and past events. They give the place a new meaning that is far from ordinary. Behind those exteriors are accounts of inspiration, achievement, scandal, and heartbreak. The people and events are many times woven into the present or, at the very least, can offer much food for thought. In effect, the buildings and places themselves come alive.

For me, Carnegie Hall is one of those places that demanded a further look into the past. However, there is so much history that emanates from its very walls that it would take many volumes to even begin to address it. I wanted to know how it began. Some group didn't just proclaim, "Let's build a concert hall," and it was done. Surely it wasn't always a place associated with the famous—or was it? At first, I wanted only to concentrate on the opening week's Festival, the time when Tchaikovsky's name was definitely in the foreground. But almost immediately, I discovered that, as always is the case, there was enormously intriguing background to go with it—the chance meeting of the Carnegies and Walter Damrosch on a ship bound for Europe; the inner workings of New York's cultural scene of the day, ranging from its opera intrigues to its competitive piano manufacturers; the plight of choral and orchestral groups hunting for appropriate places to perform. These were just for starters. In addition, the history reached back further in time to the arrival of Leopold Damrosch in America and his creation of two outstanding musical groups. The general subject of the opening of Carnegie Hall and what preceded it soon turned out to also have the potential to fill a number of volumes, as well, despite certain gaps in information that were the result of the passage of time.

Still, the part of the history most fascinating to me revolves around the people, and this is what I chose to focus upon. Their experiences bring this place to life, and even though they are long gone, they still inspire. Despite the many improbabilities that existed, their combined ability to have created this beautiful and iconic place known worldwide deserves recognition. Without them, Carnegie Hall would not have existed as we know it. In the following chapters, I have done my best to portray these remarkable individuals and the surrounding events that led to the building and opening of Carnegie Hall. There are some details included about the business, administrative, and construction ends of the project; however, they are relatively few and brought in only as they relate to the central narrative. The main scope and theme is focused on the people. Time-wise, the book ranges from the fortuitous meeting of the Carnegies and Walter

Damrosch in April of 1887—with necessary background history that predates this—through the opening Festival week held in May of 1891. Although there have been several fine histories of Carnegie Hall written over past years, at this point there are none to my knowledge that dwell exclusively on this time period. My research into the subject began with collections at special libraries and historical societies as well as with pertinent internet sources. Beyond this, the archival collections at Carnegie Hall and the Oratorio Society were both exceptionally helpful and fascinating. The original programs, clippings, and memorabilia were especially valuable as were my conversations with the archivists who were the most knowledgeable individuals that any author could have hoped for.

There are some writers who are able to cover all aspects of even a small segment of history in the most complete manner possible, leaving no stone unturned—I am not among this group. There is more to be said about these early days. In years to come, I am sure that additional information from the time period will come to light—some diaries or photographs, perhaps, that might now be lingering in an attic somewhere; a valuable book or two misplaced in a library; or some cherished mementos that will surface in a dusty antique shop far from West 57th Street. As these items are discovered and as other researchers and authors continue to delve into the existing resources about Carnegie Hall's heritage, there will no doubt be other works written about this segment in time and presented with different perspectives than mine. All of this is to the good—it will consistently add to the knowledge and understanding of a vibrant place and its history.

I do not know what became of that pianist from Colorado—whether she continued in her concert career or not, whether she remained in music or not. In the years that followed, however, she surely would have recalled the thrill of walking onstage for her debut on that world-famous stage. Witnessing this moment enriched my own life. Not only did I have the opportunity to hear a beautiful recital presented in a beautiful space, it was a first—introducing me to Carnegie Hall and its capacity to embrace great music of all kinds and to offer infinite possibilities to everyone, onstage and off, no matter what their circumstances. Andrew Carnegie remarked that this was "no ordinary structure." He was correct.

• ONE •

Beginnings

On the evening of April 22, 1887, a horse-drawn carriage pulled away from the quiet Manhattan residence located at 35 West 48th Street.[1] Its passengers were a newly married couple. The pair had exchanged their vows at 8:00 p.m. before a handful of family members and distinguished guests in the front drawing room of the bride's mother's home. Tasteful arrangements of palms, wreaths, and, especially, roses—red, white, and Catharine Mermot varieties—spilled over doorways and arches and generously filled assorted baskets, adding a touch of festivity to the space.[2]

The thirty-year-old bride did not wear an elaborate or traditional wedding gown but, instead, chose a "heavily braided"[3] traveling suit of gray wool.[4] The garment was tastefully well-made and had been ingeniously designed for multiple uses—extra collar, cuffs, and bodice for regular wear and an insert stitched with "gold embroidery on red ground"[5] for special occasions. This was a practical young woman who was already planning for the versatile needs of her new married life.

The groom, age fifty-one, was also conservatively dressed with a "four-button black cutaway coat"[6] and trousers that were dark to match. His dignified and understated attire reflected the tone of the occasion itself. There were no attendant bridesmaids or groomsmen, and the lack of fanfare at this event was obvious.

There were a number of reasons for the simplicity of the wedding, and at the heart of it was a lingering grief. Both the groom's mother and brother had passed away in the fall of the previous year. The groom, himself, had also been seriously ill during that time. A lavish affair would have been inappropriate on all counts. In addition, it seemed preferable not to attract any attention on the part of the press or curiosity seekers to what was intended to be a quiet, private event.

By 8:50 p.m., less than an hour after the simple yet respectful Universalist Church ceremony had concluded, congratulations had been offered, and—as the press later reported—"Pinard furnished a simple collation"[7]—the couple was on their way to the *Fulda*. This was the steamship that would take them on their honeymoon trip to England and Scotland. It was docked at the Bremen pier in Hoboken and was scheduled to depart the following morning at 6:00 a.m.[8]

The *Fulda*, part of the North German Lloyd line, was a top-of-the-rank steamship that had been in operation for only a few years. Its reviews, however, were outstanding. Its first-class passengers, in particular, could delight in its luxurious interior. The glowing woodwork and well-designed decorative appointments were akin to works of art. Guests could catch their reflections in the many elegant mirrors sparkling under the unique new electrical lighting. Tasteful carpeting and upholstery added more than just a touch of refinement. Here, it was easy to relax and savor the company of fellow travelers in the beautiful salons and to enjoy the journey at hand. The ship's technical features were no less superior. It was sturdy and fast, praised for its "staying powers"[9] in the face of any challenges that the weather at sea might present. Its reputation was of the highest caliber in every category. This was a desirable way to travel abroad and, judging by the number of ships in this fleet, quite a popular one. It had been called "the crack German liner" during this era.[10]

The bride and groom—attended by a maid and a servant—were booked into particularly choice quarters and could look forward to enjoying their voyage in comfort. They had reserved the captain's room as well as that of the general officer,[11] a practice not unusual at the time.

This was not only the beginning of their honeymoon journey but also of their journey into married life, and it was on board the *Fulda* that millionaire steel magnate Andrew Carnegie and his bride, Louise Whitfield Carnegie, would also cultivate a new and lasting friend. Together, these three individuals would take the first step on another journey—a magnificent musical one that would eventually impact New York, the country, and the world.

The fellow passenger and future friend of the Carnegies was twenty-five-year-old musician and conductor Walter Damrosch. His ultimate destination was Frankfort, Germany, where for several months he intended to pursue intensive conducting studies with the world-renowned Hans von Bulow.

In addition to his fame as a conductor and virtuoso pianist, von Bulow was a widely recognized interpreter of Beethoven. The young Damrosch wanted, in particular, to concentrate on studying and analyzing the symphonies of Beethoven[12] with this master conductor. Despite a busy schedule, von Bulow accepted this eager student, the son of an old friend and beloved musical colleague from years gone by. The two would spend several months doing a close reading of all nine Beethoven symphonies—"bar by bar, phrase by phrase"[13]—discussing each score's many technical components, interpretive elements, and related artistic considerations. The ultimate goal for Damrosch was to gain a deeper understanding of these symphonies in order to better conduct them himself in the future. Damrosch was not new to conducting, but he was willing to keep learning and improving, particularly at this pivotal juncture in his career. The time spent in Germany was to prove worthwhile and of long-lasting value to the young man. Several months after returning from his trip, he received high marks from a reviewer for his interpretation of Beethoven's *Fifth Symphony*, an example of the value of his recent studies, the report was quick to note.[14]

Now, although their destinations and purposes for traveling were widely divergent—the Carnegies on their leisurely wedding trip and Damrosch on an intensive musical mission—they would have the opportunity to spend some social time together on board ship. Aside from this chance meeting on the *Fulda*, though, their connection was not a totally random one. The three had a mutual link—the Oratorio Society of New York. Walter Damrosch was the conductor of the group. The new Mrs. Carnegie was a longtime supporter, and Mr. Carnegie was on its Board of Directors. However, there had been little occasion for their paths to cross until this time, and many years later, Damrosch stated that he only first met Andrew Carnegie on this voyage.[15]

Carnegie had known the young man's father, Leopold Damrosch, the founder and former conductor of the Oratorio Society. He talked of him "with great affection and respect" and had once invited him to a dinner for the poet Mathew Arnold.[16] Although Leopold Damrosch had passed away two years previously, the lasting effects of his contributions were still quite evident in New York musical circles—particularly for the Oratorio Society and its members and, especially, for his son. His legacy was a common bond for the three travelers and would, in turn, serve as a springboard for their own future additions to the cultural landscape.

Leopold Damrosch had been a famed musician and conductor in Germany where the family lived in Breslau until 1871. Although a serious musician, he received a degree in medicine at the insistence of his family, doing his best to respectfully honor their wishes. Upon graduating, however, he chose to pursue a full-time career in music instead—it was his

consuming passion. Damrosch subsequently spent three years as first violinist in the orchestra at Weimar under the direction of Franz Liszt, who
later became godfather to his son, Franz (Frank). Richard Wagner was
also a good friend and godfather to another son, Richard, who, unfortunately, died in infancy.[17] Walter was born later.

The Damrosch household in Germany was always filled with music
and musicians. Leading figures visited the family at their home in Breslau—Liszt, Wagner, Tausig, Clara Schumann, and von Bulow, to name a
few.[18] Later on, Walter Damrosch would follow in this tradition when he
had his own family. Visitors were numerous, and his daughter once commented that she and her sisters always "heard music in our home."[19]

Leopold Damrosch ultimately built a successful orchestra in Breslau,
featuring numerous visiting soloists. Musical opportunities, though, were
still not plentiful there, and the city did not place a high enough value on
artistic pursuits. As a result, it was difficult for a musician to make a decent
living and to support a family. In addition, political and social unease
within the country did not enhance the general atmosphere. It was time
for a change.

In 1871, after presenting a successful final concert in Breslau featuring
Beethoven's *Ninth Symphony*,[20] Leopold Damrosch left for New York
where he had been invited to direct the *Mannergesangverein* Arion, a
prominent German choral society.[21] Here was the promise of a more musically welcoming atmosphere and a brighter future for him and his family.

More than two decades before Leopold Damrosch came to the United
States, German immigrants had already become a substantial presence in
New York as well as in other major American cities. They were recognized
for their well-organized, active musical groups—particularly their male
choral societies. Music was an important common denominator in this
culture. The performance of good music was an uppermost goal for these
singing organizations, but there was a significant social component built
into them as well. The groups provided a comforting ethnic bond in a
challenging new environment and, at the same time, offered an opportunity to preserve the culture and traditions their members held dear. These
groups organized large choral festivals and, eventually, their American
counterparts followed suit. The members of these societies, including
large numbers of amateur singers, acquired much skill in music and
became knowledgeably well versed in choral literature. Over the years,
the work of an ever-widening selection of composers was also able to be
performed.[22]

The Arion Society in New York was one of the most significant of these groups. They came into existence when a handful of individuals split from the Deutsche Liederkranz, an already established organization. When the Arion was searching for a superior musician to direct them, they approached Leopold Damrosch with an offer at the suggestion of music publisher Edward Schuberth, an individual with ties to both Germany and New York. When Damrosch accepted, the Society was thrilled to have such a high caliber musician as their director. He was said to be the foremost European individual to have established himself permanently in this type of position in the U.S. at that time. Their gratitude was such that they found housing for Damrosch and his family on East 35th Street and did everything in their power to set it up and help them move in.[23]

Since the Arion Society had been in existence since 1854,[24] Leopold Damrosch assumed his new position as part of a well-established organizational structure which was within a familiar cultural frame of reference. His would be a highly visible position with opportunities to expand from there within New York's continually blossoming musical world. He remained as the group's conductor until 1883[25] when the talented conductor Frank Van der Stucken was to take over the post.[26]

As soon as Damrosch was settled in New York, he arranged for his wife, sister-in-law, daughters, and two young sons—Walter and Frank—to join him. They sailed on the *Hermann*, a ship that was part of the North German Lloyd line,[27] the fleet that the *Fulda* was to join during the following decade. By the time his family arrived, Damrosch was already building a thriving career as both a violinist and conductor in his newly adopted country and was succeeding admirably. His energy and determination would serve as a fine role model and inspiration for his sons in the following years.

Leopold Damrosch was an innovator who was destined to leave an indelible mark on New York's musical scene. He worked tirelessly in its cultural world but, even more than this, he actively championed the works of Wagner, Liszt, and Berlioz. Among the "impassioned fighters" for "the new ideals" that he felt their music represented,[28] he was also responsible for giving the United States premieres of works by many composers.

One of Leopold Damrosch's most lasting accomplishments was his creation of two new musical organizations that added to New York's cultural variety and richness. Both were to have a lasting impact that would long survive their founder and would contribute greatly to New York's growth as a serious artistic center. The first was the Oratorio Society of New York, the organization that had grown so close to the hearts of the three travelers on the *Fulda*. At its inception in 1873, it was an eighteen-voice choral group with Leopold Damrosch serving as their musical director and conductor.[29]

The story behind the formation of this group—and the suggestion to form it—has numerous variations. One version states that Damrosch created the group in the home of banker and music enthusiast Elkan Naumburg and his wife Bertha, who was said to have provided the name for the group.[30] Other versions say that the Russian pianist Anton Rubinstein had already urged Damrosch to begin his own choral group[31]—a remark that came close on the heels of Damrosch's unsuccessful move to include women as regular members in the Arion Society. This would have broken the all-male singing society tradition, a move that they were not willing to make at the time although, as such, their repertoire choices were more limited.[32]

Additional reports speak of Morris and Marie Reno, neighbors of the Damrosch family who were to figure in their lives for decades. Critic H. E. Krehbiel, in his book about the early years of the Oratorio Society, indicated that it was Marie Reno who suggested to Leopold Damrosch the forming of a choral group.[33] Years later, Andrew Carnegie would publicly confirm that it was, indeed, Mrs. Reno who was responsible for the idea.[34] Damrosch, though, was the ultimate driving force behind founding of the Oratorio Society—a group that was to continue into the twenty-first century, gaining the honor of being New York's "second oldest cultural organization."[35] In addition, this was a group that would figure prominently in the lives of the Carnegies as well as of the entire Damrosch family.

A meeting was officially held at the Damrosch home to formally organize the Society. In addition to Leopold Damrosch and his wife Helene, there was her sister Marie. The assemblage also included music publisher Gustav Schirmer and his wife, the Naumburgs, and the Renos. Morris Reno became the long-term Treasurer and was later referred to by a Damrosch family biographer as "the workhorse"[36] of the group. The president for the first year was Columbia College president Frederick A.P. Barnard—an individual who was, ironically, deaf.[37]

The Oratorio Society expanded rapidly and soon began presenting serious concerts. Unlike the Arion, Liederkranz, and others like it, this was not an all-male group, an element that broadened the scope of its potential repertoire and defined the group socially and culturally in a different way. Its first concert—which included repertoire by Bach, Mozart, Palestrina, Handel, and Mendelssohn—was held in the Knabe piano warerooms.[38] Leopold Damrosch firmly believed that it was essential for musicians, particularly young individuals, to have a thorough grounding in

Bach and Handel oratorios.[39] Over time, he continued with numerous such ambitious programs, including a production of Handel's *Samson* with orchestra as well as a performance of that composer's *Messiah*.[40] The presentation of this latter work was to become an annual tradition.

At the outset, both Walter Damrosch and his mother were members of the Society's chorus.[41] Helene Damrosch (nee von Heimburg) had been an active musician in Germany. A founder of Leipzig's Riedel Chorus in 1854 and an opera singer at Weimar while Franz Liszt was director, she was one of the first artists to sing the role of Ortrud in Wagner's *Lohengrin*.[42] She was surely a fine asset within her husband's new Oratorio Society, and their son praised her "glorious voice" as she worked to lead the group's soprano section.[43] Her sister, Marie Heimburg, along with Marie Reno, were also singers with the Society.

The Oratorio Society increased in membership rapidly from the very beginning with Leopold Damrosch as its well respected musical director, an individual who was able to elicit the best from his singers. He also chose challenging, quality repertoire that resulted in performances of substance and, at the same time, enhanced the deep musical knowledge and skills of the members. The Oratorio Society also attracted supporters and subscribers from a number of quarters, including some high-profile individuals. Louise Whitfield, before she became Mrs. Andrew Carnegie, was one of them. "A life member"[44] of the Society and its ardent supporter, she was "a rapt listener"[45] at performances of the *Messiah, Elijah*, and other such works.

Of course, there were challenges. Forming a choral society was one thing; building it and keeping it going was quite another. Later, Walter Damrosch admitted that in a city the size of New York, the "many temptations and distractions"[46] could have a deep effect on rehearsal attendance. Aside from this, everyday responsibilities of any given group's members could stand in the way of their ability to offer the total commitment that would have been the ideal. The subject of regular attendance was not considered lightly. Eventually, those who were not present for a significant amount of time were dropped from the roster.[47] Yet Damrosch's ability to draw loyalty and the best musical quality from the members of his group surmounted these challenges, and the Society continued to grow in number.

Leopold Damrosch was an increasingly busy man. In 1878, he formed the Symphony Society of New York, offering direct competition to the Philharmonic Society that, until this time, had been the only major orchestra in the city. Although Leopold Damrosch had conducted the Philharmonic for one season, the more well-established Theodore Thomas was ultimately named its permanent conductor—the result of a number of factors and a move that helped to generate a sense of future rivalry between the two men and their groups. This was not necessarily a bad thing. Now, audiences in the city had two major orchestras to hear and enjoy.

Early on, though, Thomas was not pleased with Leopold Damrosch's popularity, and the two had an encounter in a music shop one day that reflected this attitude and, subsequently, became a legendary tale. It was the first meeting of the two. Thomas greeted Damrosch and complimented him on his fine musical reputation. On the heels of this pleasantry, though, he quickly added a warning: "Whoever crosses my path I crush."[48] Thomas believed that there was room for only one orchestra in New York and that he alone should be the one holding the baton.

This was far from enough to deter the energetic Damrosch, who continued to build his career, develop his groups, and introduce fresh repertoire to the public. Known for his diverse selection of orchestral and choral works, he also went outside the boundaries of the typically all-Germanic programming so popular during the era, despite his close association with this musical tradition. His admiration for all good quality music was far-ranging, and he offered a showcase for it, as well.

Inevitably, the competition between Damrosch and Thomas became more marked, particularly at large festivals. Neither man was reticent to vie for public favor. Thomas was well respected, left an indelible mark on the city's musical life over many years, and led the critically superior group—although orchestral comparisons were difficult since the Symphony Society was still new and upcoming. Damrosch, however, demonstrated a better knack for garnering the support of local patrons—a talent that his son Walter inherited. Eventually, Thomas continued his career in Chicago,[49] a good opportunity for him and one in keeping with his objectives. In the meantime, New York was able to follow the competition between these conductors with interest.

Leopold Damrosch began turning over more musical responsibilities to his son, Walter, as he became older and more experienced. They ranged from developing a piano reduction based on the orchestral score of Berlioz's *Requiem* to leading portions of the New York Festival Chorus and the Newark Harmonic Society in rehearsals for a "monster" music festival in 1881.[50] Walter Damrosch also accompanied all of the Oratorio Society's rehearsals on the piano or the organ.[51]

It was obvious that Leopold Damrosch respected his son's talents and wanted to help him grow into a top-quality musician and conductor. Along these lines, he next urged Walter to go to Europe to be introduced to the famed composer/conductors who were his old friends—Franz Liszt and Richard Wagner.[52] Their music, particularly that of Wagner, would figure significantly in the young Damrosch's musical career later on.

Walter Damrosch made the journey. He was awestruck upon meeting these two famous men, despite their close relationship with his father— or perhaps because of it. He was fortunate to have had the chance to spend time with Liszt and thought highly of him both musically and personally. After overcoming an initial "great trepidation,"[53] he became comfortable in the man's presence. Several years later, when Walter Damrosch returned to Germany to conduct a portion of *Sulamith*, a cantata written by his father, Liszt was present and quite well pleased to hear this performance,[54] a distinct honor for the young man. He eventually had a chance to pay tribute to his father's old friend posthumously several years later, not long before his voyage on the *Fulda* in 1887, when he presented the complete U.S. premiere of Liszt's oratorio *Christus.* This was in memory of the composer who had died the previous year.[55]

Walter Damrosch also met Wagner, who received him "with kindness."[56] He then attended one of the first productions of *Parsifal* in Bayreuth—a work he admired immensely, confessing that it "made a tremendous impression"[57] on him. Wagner subsequently provided Walter with a manuscript copy of the finale to the first act of the work for his old friend, Leopold Damrosch, who was such a champion of both Wagner as well as of German opera. Of course, this gift was an immense gesture of friendship and something that thrilled the young man to bring home to his father.[58]

Over time, the concerts and rehearsals and festivals continued in New York. In 1884, Leopold Damrosch took on yet another enormous project in his busy schedule—introducing German repertoire to the Metropolitan Opera. Managing and conducting this season successfully turned the fledgling company around and placed Damrosch in an even higher place of visibility on the cultural scene. New York musical life—and Leopold Damrosch—moved on at a frenetic pace. Both father and son kept up with the momentum, working together on many projects. Walter Damrosch was always there for his father; "his faithful son and companion," commented opera singer Marianne Brandt.[59] Despite this support, however, Leopold Damrosch's schedule was still a crushing one, yet he pursued it with whole-hearted passion for the groups and the music he loved so well—the oratorio, the symphony, the German opera, the festivals, the tours. It seemed impossible that one man could do so much. He was assuredly enthusiastic. He was continually ready to begin new projects. He seemed indefatigable. Unfortunately, this was not the case. He fell ill from what many agreed might have been the result of overwork, and he did not recover. Leopold Damrosch died in 1885 at the age of 52.

There was a huge outpouring of grief upon Damrosch's passing. He had touched the lives of large numbers of performers and audiences and had made an enormous impact on the musical world. Wherever there was serious music, it seemed that Leopold Damrosch had been a part of it. His symphony orchestra could hold its own on the concert scene. He had introduced German opera into the regular repertory in New York. And, especially, his beloved Oratorio Society had grown to 500 members and, in a few short years, would be a significant catalyst for a major addition to the city's musical landscape.

Damrosch's funeral services were held at the Metropolitan Opera House. His Symphony Society performed funeral music from Wagner's *Gotterdammerung.* His Oratorio Society sang a selection from Bach's *St. Matthew Passion.* Henry Ward Beecher spoke movingly of how much Damrosch had accomplished—how he had "raised music ... higher ... in this nation."[60] There were numerous additional eulogies and fitting musical tributes.

Of course, the family of Leopold Damrosch was left grief-stricken. Walter Damrosch and his father were especially close, and this loss left a tremendous void for him—both personally and professionally. He loved and respected the man and certainly knew how much the musical groups had meant to him. He could not let all that his father had treasured and worked so hard to realize fall apart.

As a result, Walter Damrosch immediately took on the admirable, if not Herculean, task of honoring all his father's outstanding conducting commitments, both in New York and on tour. These commitments were numerous. He had already commendably conducted *Die Walkure* and *Tannhauser* at the Met when his father had taken ill, and yet, as one newspaper observed, he was quite young to assume such a responsible role so quickly.[61] He was only twenty-three years old. However, Walter Damrosch was determined to preserve his father's legacy. Shortly after Leopold's death, he stepped in to lead a previously planned tour, bringing the opera group cross country and conducting a performance of *Tannhauser* during a Chicago blizzard. The performance began extremely late—long after curtain time. Nevertheless, the audience waited until the group's arrival and was enthusiastic in their response to the performance.[62]

Not long afterward, Damrosch also accepted the offer of the positions as permanent conductor for both the Oratorio and Symphony societies, attempting his best to uphold the traditions of both groups. These combined responsibilities were enormous. Over time, some critics were harsh in their reviews of him pointing out his youthful lack of experience coupled with his swift appointments to these positions when there were other, more seasoned individuals who might have been considered. Some continued to criticize Damrosch for years, including noted music critic Henry T. Finck of the *Evening Post.* At one point, Finck was brought into a superior's office and asked if he couldn't "let up a little on Damrosch."[63] Nevertheless, there were many others who liberally praised the young conductor's efforts and his noble desire to continue all of his father's musical missions.

The truth was that Walter Damrosch was the natural choice to immediately step into place in all of these groups—that is, if things were expected to continue reasonably smoothly. He knew the repertoire, had been closely tutored by his father, and had been given a hands-on role at rehearsals and performances for quite a while. He also felt a keen responsibility to keep things going out of respect for his father and his contributions to the growing New York music scene, one which he, too, had grown to love. And it would have been financial disaster both for the groups and for the Damrosch family if the season could not continue as planned. There was little choice but to go on. Fortunately, Walter Damrosch also possessed a great deal of energy and enthusiasm for music and musicians; was not afraid of working hard; and, also, continually tried to build his knowledge and skills.

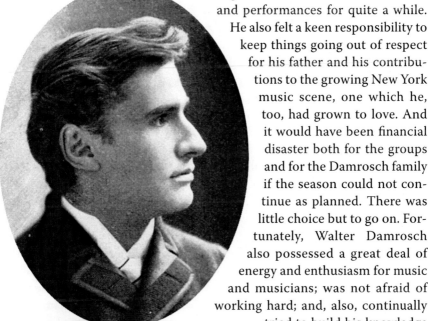

The young conductor Walter Damrosch, who kept his father's dream of a new concert hall alive.

As critical to him as his many new musical duties,

Walter Damrosch was also committed to keep alive one of his father's fondest dreams: to work toward the creation of a new concert hall in New York City that could be a suitable home and performance space for the Oratorio Society as well as for the Symphony Society. This was never far from his mind while on the *Fulda* and during subsequent seasons. It was clearly apparent to him, as it had been to his father, that a new concert hall was necessary to meet the increasing needs of both groups. With a new performance space, they could realize their full potential and provide audiences with truly superior concert experiences.

Since their creation, both organizations needed to rehearse and perform in whatever space was available to them—regardless of size, acoustics, or practicality on any level. And there was little in existence that was suitable for their particular requirements. Building a new concert hall, however, would require considerable fundraising efforts. The Oratorio Society had started a fund, but this was a challenging and long-term project. Substantial support from interested benefactors would also help, but this could take much time to realize—if it had a chance of success at all.

Yet now, Walter Damrosch found himself on the steamship *Fulda* with Andrew Carnegie, an individual who certainly had the philanthropic inclinations and financial resources to move the idea of a new concert hall from a dream into the realm of possibility. He was already on the Boards of both the Oratorio and Symphony societies. And it was not an insignificant detail that the new Mrs. Carnegie was a longtime, committed supporter of the Oratorio Society and, in the bargain, a passionate music lover. The Carnegies were also well aware of Leopold Damrosch's contributions to the cultural scene in New York and cognizant of his son's burgeoning efforts to keep it all afloat. Now these three individuals had time to spend together during their voyage and could discuss any subject they chose—including musical groups and their relevant issues and challenges.

By the time the *Fulda* sailed in 1887, the nation's cities had become increasingly charged with energy and growth. New York was a center in this trend. Immigrants from abroad continued to flock to America. With increasing urbanization and the rise of new industries and their associated opportunities, people from other parts of the country also gravitated to the city. In the aftermath of the Civil War, a shift in emphasis had begun to take place, and there was an awakening of the possibilities inherent in industry, business, invention, and culture. Cities were a critical part of it all. From groundbreaking innovations to new landmarks, big changes and additions to city life were already capturing the attention of the public.

From electricity to transportation and from the Brooklyn Bridge to the Metropolitan Museum of Art, the face of New York was changing and a new world was emerging with it. There was much to see, to do, and to experience.

Serious music was gaining greater respect, although it still had room to grow. In terms of orchestras, the New York Philharmonic had been the major group in existence the longest—in business since 1842. With the addition of the Symphony Society in 1878, the public had more performances to choose from and, thus, had the opportunity to hear more fine orchestral music—familiar repertoire as well as new compositions that were being introduced with greater frequency. Sometimes, though, it took audiences a while to become used to these newer works.

The one season that Leopold Damrosch had conducted the New York Philharmonic (1876–1877) had been less than successful. At that time, he introduced a portion of Wagner's *Siegfried.* It was not enthusiastically received. However, by the time the Symphony Society was becoming established and performing on a regular basis, audiences had become more receptive to the Wagnerian sound.[64] Leopold Damrosch included this composer's works on his programs, and, at the same time as Wagner's operas became more appealing to the public, they enjoyed hearing instrumental works drawn from them. These became a part of the regular repertoire.

Opera had also attained importance in the city, particularly among the rich. In this segment was a new group of millionaires, individuals who had made fortunes by recognizing available opportunities in industries that ranged from railroads to steel mills and from finance to manufacturing. Those who had amassed these fortunes had the means to build beautiful houses, buy superb carriages, select the finest of clothing and housewares, and invest in all of the other lovely items that displayed their wealth. Their mansions were also beginning to be a part of the developing landscape on Fifth Avenue. When this was not enough, they immersed themselves in culture to show that in addition to lavish possessions, they also had refinement. To this end, they turned their attention to the arts. Money could not buy happiness, but it could go a long way toward buying culture—or, at least, its outer trappings. And what better place to be seen as a supporter of great culture and to visibly display wealth, finery, and prominence than at the opera?

The Academy of Music on 14th Street had long been an opera stronghold with the richest of patrons regularly attending and enjoying longterm subscriptions to their cherished box seats. This group represented wealthy families with well established fortunes, such as the Belmonts. The new millionaires, however, were another story. Individuals in this latter group were disdained by the old guard and were not granted the precious box seats they felt that they deserved—no matter how much money they offered in return for a subscription. These newcomers, although quite rich, were thought to be lacking in refinement.

This was not the first time that there had been social conflict in the world of opera. Decades before, the Astor Place Opera had catered to prominent citizens, its own box seating going to the well-dressed upper tier of society. Otherwise, the smaller numbers of gallery seats for the general public boasted a view obstructed by a large crystal chandelier. Financial mismanagement, though, rendered this house a failure before social inequities became a larger problem. The Academy, on the other hand, found itself in an era that placed it uncomfortably in the spotlight of social issues.

The manager of the house, Colonel James H. Mapleson, had a reasonable grasp on the administration of the Academy of Music opera enterprise. A shrewd man, he was willing to go the extra mile to import superb talent for his stage and to ensure the happiness and financial satisfaction of these performers. They, in turn, would keep his elite audiences happy. His stars included Adelina Patti whose father, ironically, had once managed the ill-fated Astor Place company.[65] Yet Mapleson could not control larger forces at work concerning the box-seating issue. The old money and the new would soon be at odds. The new millionaires coveted the prestige and high visibility of the Academy's box seats, and they took their lack of success in obtaining them as a personal affront. They also had the funds to do something about it.

In response to this perceived snub, William Henry Vanderbilt, Jay Gould, and a few others spearheaded the building of the Metropolitan Opera House. This institution was created to run in direct competition with the Academy. At the Met, the new millionaires could have the premiere seating and the visible prestige that they craved. Here, too, was an enormous opera house, outdoing its rival in a number of ways. It opened in the 1883–1884 season and was completed just in time for the curtain to rise. In a move that was adroitly timed, opening night was scheduled for the same evening as that of the Academy. The rest was history. By the time that the Carnegies and Walter Damrosch met aboard the *Fulda* a few short years later, the Academy of Music had deteriorated into a popular entertainment venue, thus proving the power of the newly rich magnates to make their mark on culture. Colonel Mapleson eventually conceded failure and closed the doors on opera there. He famously confessed, "I cannot fight Wall Street."[66]

There were problems with this new Metropolitan Opera House, though, and it did fall short on musically aesthetic levels. First, the architect had not been well matched to the project. His experience was in designing churches, and the resultant acoustical scheme and placement of the orchestra pit left much to be desired. Beyond this and despite the splash of its glittering opening, the first season was overall not a success.[67] Enter Leopold Damrosch with a plan to introduce German opera to the Met. By this time, New York was more willing to enlarge its musical world and immerse itself in this segment of the genre. As a result, Damrosch was engaged for the 1884–1885 season to conduct German opera there, and his appearance helped to turn the tide for the organization.

Because of his work in the new opera house, Leopold Damrosch certainly knew the physical components of the space, and it was a natural thought for him to try and rent it for use by his own groups. On the surface, this was logical; but, in reality, the plan was studded with flaws. Although it was possible to engage the place at off-peak times, the stage was far too big and the acoustics inappropriate for anything aside from opera. It was just not a suitable performance hall for either oratorio or orchestral concerts.

Of course, there were other music-related venues. Numerous recital halls existed, particularly those connected to the continually growing number of piano companies in the city—Steinway, Chickering, and Knabe, to name a few. Since a great many households in America had a piano, the manufacturing business for this instrument had increased and, along with it, their considerable influence. During this era, owning a piano was a mark of respectability and of possessing a home that was stable and filled with culture and harmony. Piano sales soared, and solo recitals and small ensemble concerts soared with them.

Piano company concert halls were active places, offering not only recitals featuring their own instruments, but also a variety of other types of events. On the day of Andrew and Louise Carnegie's wedding, there were two performances advertised at Chickering Hall that offered a good example. The afternoon featured a piano recital by Mme. Madeline Schiller, and in the evening, the Yale Glee and Banjo clubs performed.[68] These halls were in demand. However, their spaces were not suitable for either large symphony or choral groups either. Size was a major issue— the halls were just too small. Added to this, the competition between the piano companies was not an insignificant factor. Therefore, if an individual or a group was lucky enough to rent one of the spaces available on a given date—suitability notwithstanding—the piano company itself might eagerly press them to publicly endorse their instruments. This resulted in additional pressure and complications for the renters.

Variety and ethnic music halls, theaters, and other such venues were not suitable either and were in continual use for their own purposes. Under the best of circumstances, rented halls had spatial limits, acoustical problems, difficulties with sightlines, complications with bookings, and generally ill-suited physical components for the type of performances offered by the Oratorio and Symphony societies.

New York conductors and musicians looked to Boston as an example of how a proper setting could impact the life of an orchestra or similar large musical group. The symphony orchestra in that city hired its players for thirty weeks during the year. They rehearsed daily and were paid weekly. But most notably, they had their own concert hall—a home for themselves.[69] Such a venue could do the same for an orchestra in New York. But it could also offer the Oratorio Society, a high-level avocational group with an enormous supporting membership, a fine place to perform and a means of increasing their enjoyment of the music as well as that of their audiences. The question became: if Boston could have a music hall, why not New York?

Backers for such a project were certainly necessary. There were those who might have been enthusiastic about this type of music, but they did not have a large amount of money to donate. On the other hand, some of the wealthy with substantial funds at their disposal were preoccupied more exclusively with other interests. Andrew Carnegie, however, was an entirely different type of wealthy individual—unique in his well-defined and genuine philanthropic ideals. Of the many individuals whom Walter Damrosch might have encountered on his voyage, Carnegie was perhaps the most appropriate and empathetic at this particular juncture in time.

Born in Dumfermline, Scotland, in 1835, Carnegie had truly humble beginnings in the weaver's cottage where his family lived. Although they were poor, they placed great value on reading and education. Unfortunately, opportunities to take advantage of these pursuits were scarce. However, when Carnegie was a child, the family immigrated to Allegheny, Pennsylvania. Scotland had been experiencing some hard times, and this move seemed promising and one that Carnegie's mother especially encouraged.

Soon, the young Carnegie began working as a telegraph messenger. Delving into his work with characteristic enthusiasm, he did his best and learned as much as possible. His attitude and approach did not go unnoticed and attracted promotions into increasingly more responsible jobs. Although Carnegie did not have much formal education, he was an avid reader and took advantage of whatever opportunities were available to borrow and read books. Throughout his life, he highly praised the value of libraries and passionately believed that reading had great power to educate and broaden the horizons of any individual. The young man's skills and experience with the telegraph jobs eventually gained him posts within the railroad industry, and he continued to advance in his work. He also began saving and investing his money wisely. Such ingenuity eventually helped him to create his famous and highly lucrative empire in the steel and iron industry. His was a true rags-to-riches story, and Carnegie became one of the wealthiest and most successful individuals of his era.

Unlike others who had acquired great wealth during this time, Carnegie had a strict code of values when it came to money, strongly believing that it was his responsibility to distribute much of his acquired fortune for the good of others during his lifetime, not afterward—"the proper administration of wealth"[70] being a principle to which he scrupulously adhered. True, he lived comfortably and did not insist that his family adopt a Spartan lifestyle, yet he had little personal need to hoard or display his riches.

Carnegie practiced what he preached since, over time, there were a large number of recipients of his generosity. His favorite projects were public libraries and educational institutions. Increasingly throughout his life, he liberally funded these. In keeping with this emphasis on the importance of literary and intellectual pursuits, he also became a prolific writer. One of his most popular works, "The Gospel of Wealth" brought him marked recognition. He also enjoyed the company of literary figures such as Mark Twain, as well as of those who held political offices and possessed high ideals. Here was a truly self-made man and one with a practical and generous code of philanthropy.

While Andrew Carnegie was generous with his money in support of building projects such as libraries, he felt that once these places were completed, the institutions in question needed to be self-sustaining in supporting and maintaining their operations.[71] With this in mind, he would give an outright monetary gift but also gave the recipients the gift of a sense of accomplishment as they worked to keep their institutions afloat and thriving as well as a vital part of the community.

Not only was Carnegie unique in his beliefs about the distribution of money, but he also had strong ideas about what was important otherwise in life. He had faith in the power of a good attitude, citing his optimistic nature as being important and stating that "a sunny disposition"[72] was of high value—above fortune—and could be cultivated and used to advantage.[73] This was essential to him as he progressed in all of his successful endeavors. Carnegie also remained loyal to his immediate family, understanding the sacrifices that they had made and the hardships that they had endured. This was extremely important to him. Even in his middle years, he was especially respectful of his mother, ensuring that she had the care and attention that she needed as she grew older and in more frail health. Feeling that she was, in a large part, responsible for his success since she had fostered the move from Scotland to the U.S. in the first place,[74] he believed that he owed her much in return. This loyalty, noble though it was, also led to some complications, especially pertaining to the third individual on the *Fulda* journey—Mrs. Louise Carnegie.

Andrew Carnegie's marriage to Louise Whitfield was no sudden move. He had courted the young woman for six years. She came from a fine New York family and had numbered Teddy Roosevelt and his sister Corinne as childhood friends. Carnegie's mother, though, did not look upon the match fondly. Many believed she thought that this potential marriage—or any marriage for that matter—would distance her from her son. Her health was not good in her later years and this, too, added to her dependence on him.

Andrew Carnegie, the benefactor of the Music Hall that would eventually bear his name (courtesy Carnegie Library of Pittsburgh).

Andrew Carnegie and Louise Whitfield, though, were well matched and complemented each other, building a solid friendship over time. They both enjoyed reading, and her biographers stated that their true courtship began with a book—Sir Edwin Arnold's *The Light of Asia*. This they read and discussed in detail together, finding much enjoyment in their subsequent talks about the work, further deepening their friendship.[75] They both loved horseback riding; it was a frequent pastime for them as a couple. There was no doubt that both were family oriented. Louise was close to her mother and grandmother. Therefore, she understood this feeling of family responsibility that Carnegie exhibited toward his own mother. Like Mrs. Carnegie, Louise's mother had experienced health issues, too, although she was not a person to stand in the way of her daughter's life and happiness.

Louise Carnegie always enjoyed going to theater and music events in her youth, many times accompanied by her sister, Stella Whitfield. They frequented all types of musical presentations—from opera to oratorio. They attended the Academy of Music in its heyday, but became devotees of the Met when it opened. Along the way, Louise also "became a Wagnerian."[76] Her love of music, according to her biographers, was among the "strongest ... links" between her and husband.[77] It was several years before the couple quietly became engaged and then subsequently married. Carnegie referred to his future wife in his autobiography as "the perfect one."[78]

The new Mrs. Carnegie totally supported her husband's philanthropical pursuits and, to this end, signed a pre-nuptial agreement foregoing inheriting the bulk of his huge estate. She was not coerced into this but, instead, readily agreed, believing in the high ideals that it represented.[79] This did not mean, however, that Carnegie neglected his wife's financial security. From the beginning of their marriage and well into the future, Carnegie ensured that she would be well set. During the evening of their wedding, the couple spent several quiet minutes in a sitting room at which time he formally presented an agreement providing securities that would yield her $20,000 annually for whatever purpose she chose. Added to this was his wedding gift to her—a house at 5 West 51st Street in Manhattan, neighboring that of the Vanderbilts.[80]

These were the three individuals who grew close on the *Fulda*, far from the hectic pace of New York City. They forged a lasting friendship during the voyage, and the Carnegies became quite fond of Damrosch. Before they parted at the end of their journey, the Carnegies invited him to visit them in several months, as soon as he finished his studies with von Bulow. They were planning on an extended holiday at Kilgraston House in Scotland and genuinely wanted to see Damrosch again. The feeling was mutual.

The Carnegies continued on their wedding trip—first in England and then in the place that was close to the new husband's heart—Scotland. Before the couple settled in for their stay at Kilgraston, Louise not only had the chance to visit Dumfermline where he grew up, but she also was able to meet some of his relatives from his uncle's family—the Lauders.[81] Louise Carnegie was happily enthralled with Scotland and wrote to her mother, saying "how lovely this place is."[82] Even after arriving at Kilgraston, the Carnegies still took many side trips, including additional forays into Dumfermline as well as to other locations for special events. Once more, Louise Carnegie's letters contain enthusiastic details about many of these excursions. One unusual event stands out—a stop at nearby Kinghorn where the couple, along with the American politician James G. Blaine, were guests at a unique park opening and statue unveiling of Russian czar, Alexander III. Both gentlemen offered speeches on the occasion.[83]

In the meantime, Walter Damrosch continued on to Frankfort where he presented himself to his father's old friend Hans von Bulow and began his studies of the Beethoven symphonies. The time was well spent. Having been thrust into the limelight at an extremely early age, these studies helped him to learn, gain confidence, and define himself as a conductor. Afterward, he commented that von Bulow had provided him with the "courage to go my own way."[84] This mentorship had been a successful enterprise musically and personally.

Damrosch made good on his promise to visit the Carnegies after his time in Germany was over. He arrived to a sincere and friendly welcome in Kilgraston, amidst its gardens of lovely strawberries and gooseberries, the scent of the Highlands always in the air, and a costumed Piper sounding traditional reels and songs on awakening and at dinnertime.[85] It was a fine place for a respite after his intensive work in Germany. In addition to being able to spend time with his hosts there, Damrosch enjoyed meeting the Blaine family who were also guests at the castle.

A well-known and popular political figure, James G. Blaine had run against Grover Cleveland for president in 1884 and was defeated by a narrow margin. Now he and his wife and two daughters were on a lengthy holiday overseas. Andrew Carnegie very much admired Blaine, especially pointing out his fine storytelling abilities and "bright sunny nature."[86] Damrosch found the entire family to be intriguing and congenial company, growing quite fond of their companionship. He had never known a statesman before and was taken with Blaine's dignity and his wife's impressive knowledge of many subjects. Having been immersed in music for his entire life, Damrosch was fascinated with the opportunity to establish an association with people who were totally removed from his artistic sphere.[87] It was an enriching experience for him. He also found Blaine's daughter Margaret particularly enjoyable to talk with, and they soon developed a sociable friendship.

During this holiday, Carnegie and Damrosch had the chance to take long walks and to go fishing together. Their conversations touched on education, books, music, and many other topics. Damrosch remembered Carnegie's eloquence years later—sometimes forgetting a "possible trout" on his fishing pole when describing his future plans and possible bene-factions.[88] The two had many things to share, discuss, and learn from each other. In many ways, they had much in common, although it may not have appeared so on the surface. Both men were a blend of the old world and the new. Each had spent his childhood in another country, experiencing poverty in different ways, and had come to America at a young age, even-tually building careers through hard work according to their individual circumstances and talents. They also both felt a deep responsibility to honor and respect their immediate families.

As always, Carnegie enjoyed talking about the power of libraries to further education. As a boy, his love of books had been greatly responsible for enlarging his world, and he could not place enough emphasis on their importance. He well remembered that while working as a messenger in his youth, a certain Colonel James Anderson opened his four-hundred-volume library to young local working men each Saturday. They could borrow a book and return it the following week. This left a deep impres-sion upon him, opening up new vistas and contributing to his lifelong pursuit of learning.[89] Damrosch also enjoyed books and reading, partic-ularly highlighting his fondness for Homer's *Iliad* and *Odyssey,* among others that he became familiar with at an early age. As a child, he was so taken with Homer that he began acting out scenes from his works with props of pasteboard and furniture.[90] Many years later, Damrosch's daugh-ter commented on this love of literature, remembering that her father urged his children to read Shakespeare aloud.[91]

Damrosch greatly believed in education just as Andrew Carnegie did. He expressed this in his own unique manner. During his stay at Kilgraston, he enjoyed entertaining the guests on the piano, performing excerpts from Wagner's *Nibelungen* Trilogy and explaining various portions of the text and the music. These evenings marked a turning point for him. He very much enjoyed presenting these informal talk-recitals and in the decades to come, he continued to develop them further, educating wider and wider audiences. He later commented that this time at Kilgraston was the basis for a very important part of his career throughout his life.[92] The lecture-recitals that grew from this experience earned him widespread appreciation and fame, and he was to become an effective educational force in music through his public talks, radio programs, and related activities. Later, even Henry T. Finck, never reluctant to criticize Damrosch's conducting, praised his speaking abilities and said that his comments on the musical programs were among "the best things about them."[93]

Inevitably, Carnegie and Damrosch discussed music. They had each naturally cultivated the music related to their own particular heritage. Damrosch, of course, exhibited his expertise in the music of Beethoven and Wagner, as evidenced in his talks and performances for the guests at Kilgraston. Some of Carnegie's interests in music had a different focus. He enjoyed oratorios and mentioned having his "taste for music ... aroused"[94] as a youth while attending gatherings of the Swedenborgian Society of Pittsburgh where he also sang in the choir. Intrigued by the excerpts from oratorios in their hymnal, his favorites were "the gems of Handel's."[95] His true musical love, however, was for the Scottish folk songs. They were a part of his heritage. He was passionate about these songs and could sing numerous works by memory.[96] He was especially fond of the bagpipes, as well.

Carnegie also enjoyed and appreciated the sound of the organ and felt that this king of instruments held an important place in both religious and community life. Because of his fondness for the organ, Carnegie donated funds for the building of more than 7,000 instruments during his lifetime.[97] He first began by giving financial support for this purpose to the Swedenborgian chapel in Allegheny City, the place where he had attended services with his father in his youth and where he gained his initial knowledge of the oratorio form. He felt that a church setting was often the first introduction to serious music for the working classes, and the presence of an organ on the premises was a vital component to many aspects of the life of its congregation. Carnegie later commented that hearing regular organ music could be a "substitute for family prayers."[98] He loved the sound of the organ so much that for a while, he woke daily to renditions of his beloved Scottish folk music played by a hired organist.[99] Coincidentally, Walter Damrosch had been organist and music director for a time at the famed Plymouth Church in Brooklyn[100] where Henry Ward Beecher had been pastor. He also accompanied the Oratorio Society on both piano and organ during the time his father was its conductor.

Although Andrew Carnegie certainly understood the value of the musical arts, he did not emphasize them in the same way as he did literature or science.[101] Yet his interest grew stronger in the work of the Oratorio and Symphony societies to the point that he eventually agreed to be "their president and chief financial supporter."[102] Perhaps this was the result of his marriage to Louise and his growing friendship with Walter Damrosch, although Andrew Carnegie was always open to expanding his horizons.

The subject of a new concert hall for New York had moved to the forefront by this time. Although Carnegie could still not bring himself to elevate this to the same importance as a library, he became more sympathetic to the idea during his and Damrosch's many walks and fishing expeditions. Yet, as Walter Damrosch commented years later, they initially had "many, sometimes heated, discussions"[103] on the subject. Carnegie believed that an enterprise such as a concert hall should generate the revenue through public patronage in order to be self-sustaining after an initial gift of money had been made for the building. Damrosch felt that continuing subsidies would show the institution's emphasis on its artistic mission, as opposed to only the generation of profit.[104] And so, the debates continued.

The following season, Damrosch was once again pleased to be invited along with a group of people to go on a coaching trip hosted by the Carnegies. By now, he was thought of as "an established friend of the Carnegie couple."[105] Andrew Carnegie's business partner, Henry Phipps, was part of the group as was the Reverend Charles H. Eaton, the minister who had performed the Carnegie's wedding ceremony. The Blaine family was also invited. Together, they would all spend several weeks touring the countryside in England and Scotland.

The journey was an exceptionally memorable one. They took off as a nearby genial crowd gathered to wish them a good trip—a trip with lunch hampers always at the ready for a tree-shaded picnic and a country inn awaiting at each day's end. The happy party visited Walter Scott's home as well as the ruins of Linlithgow, the castle where "Mary Queen of Scots was born,"[106] and savored the cathedral towns in the eastern portion of Britain.[107] They eventually arrived at the Macpherson family's celebrated and historic Cluny Castle—with its "turreted white granite"[108] and thousands of acres of beautiful land. Here, Louise Carnegie wrote glowingly to her mother once more about a countryside dotted with heather and ripe with gushing waterfalls, mountain brooks, and picturesque bridges.[109]

As the traveling party neared their destination, they sounded a horn to signal their approach. A salute of guns responded. Cottagers waved joyously as the party grew closer, and Macpherson himself greeted them play-

A piano composition inscribed to the Carnegie couple, published during the year of their marriage and return from their trip abroad (courtesy Carnegie Library of Pittsburgh).

ing the bagpipes.[110] It was here they would stay for what Walter Damrosch referred to as "a summer of delights."[111] This was also to be a summer of eclectic musical activities. A piper was there to awaken the household each morning—a Scottish custom.[112] The Carnegies sang Scottish ballads, admittedly enhancing Damrosch's musical world as he learned to enjoy and appreciate the qualities of this music.[113] During this summer, he taught Macpherson to play "Yankee Doodle"[114] on the bagpipes and coached Louise Carnegie in singing.[115] In the evenings, Damrosch would play Beethoven and Wagner for the group on the "excellent Broadwood piano."[116] According to Mrs. Blaine, his was the last candle still burning in the evening as he played from his opera scores.[117]

Just as they had done at Kilgraston, Carnegie and Damrosch continued with their walks and trout fishing expeditions at "some lonely loch among the hills."[118] Discussions about the possibility of a music hall intensified. Andrew Carnegie became more confident of the value of this project. He had accepted the presidency of both Oratorio and Symphony societies and was increasingly involved with each. He knew both their needs as well as their potential. Eventually, Damrosch wrote to his brother Frank to tell him that the groups would soon have their concert hall, asking him to pass this word along to Morris Reno.[119]

The chance meeting of the Carnegies and Walter Damrosch on the *Fulda* had blossomed into what would be a lifelong friendship. And it also resulted in what Damrosch later said was to be New York's "proper home" for music,[120] especially for the Oratorio and Symphony societies. Upon their return to New York, Andrew Carnegie began organizing people and resources in earnest. The practicalities of the project were just beginning. Leopold Damrosch's dream of a new concert hall would finally become a reality.

Just prior to that memorable summer in Scotland—on May 5 of 1888—a beautiful monument to Leopold Damrosch was dedicated in Woodlawn Cemetery. It had been placed there as the result of the combined efforts of the Arion, Oratorio, and Symphony societies. Six hundred were in attendance and among the musical selections presented were several chorales from *St. Matthew Passion*, sung by the Oratorio Society. Andrew Carnegie spoke.[121] And this event took place three years to the exact day prior to the official opening of the new music hall—the place of which Leopold Damrosch had so fervently dreamed.

• Two •

Building

William Burnet Tuthill was fascinated with acoustics. So was Richard Wagner. Tuthill's focus on the subject was first superbly demonstrated at a New York concert performance of Wagner's *Parsifal* in 1886, an event which took place two years before Andrew Carnegie agreed to fund the new music hall. Tuthill and his acoustical acumen would eventually find lasting fame through Carnegie's famous building project. Wagner's attention to acoustical issues had surfaced earlier in the decade, also with *Parsifal*. His fixation with perfection in this and related artistic concerns would eventually generate notoriety of a different sort. However, it also inadvertently helped to bring the matter of acoustics—as well as appropriate performance venues—into a brighter spotlight.

When his last opera, *Parsifal*, was premiered at the *Festspielhaus* in Bayreuth on July 26 in 1882, Wagner deemed the acoustics and the setting perfect for the work. The design of the hall, the placement of the orchestra, and the particularly beautiful transmission of sound rendered the performance superior in every way—so much so that Wagner declared this the only place in which *Parsifal* should ever be staged and performed in its entirety. Although there were those who suggested that this declaration was as much financially driven as it was aesthetically conceived, none could say that Wagner had not made his wishes clear. After his death the following year, his widow Cosima adhered to them with single-minded precision.[1]

This dictum presented immediate problems since American audiences had become increasingly high on Wagner as the 1880s progressed. Given the fact that *Parsifal* was the composer's final work—and not permitted to be produced outside of Bayreuth in the bargain—it took on the trappings of forbidden fruit. The American press had helped set this frenzy in motion by covering the German premiere nonstop. Predictably, plans to offer up allowable portions of the music itself flew quickly to the draw-ing board. Leopold Damrosch was at the head of the line. In 1882, after his son returned from meeting Wagner with manuscript in hand for the Finale to Act I, the elder Damrosch promptly included this music in a November 4 concert at the Academy of Music. On the same night, Theodore Thomas presented his own audiences with music from Act III in a performance in Brooklyn.[2] The public was already engrossed in the continuing Damrosch-Thomas rivalry, and the events of November 4 stoked the fires of curiosity in this continuing saga and, at the same time, increased to the insatiable point a general appetite for more of the elusive *Parsifal*.

Wagner's appeal continued to soar in the U.S. and so did that of *Par-sifal*, particularly after the composer's death in 1883. On this occasion, both Leopold Damrosch and Theodore Thomas paid tribute to the man and his music—each conductor presenting selections from *Parsifal* in his own separate concert. Damrosch went one step further. He had already planned to include the *Good Friday Spell* from the work on his program and after learning of Wagner's passing, he subsequently added the funeral march from *Gotterdammerung*, thus broadening the scope of the tribute and further familiarizing the public with the works of the composer. Iron-ically, this same march would be performed at Damrosch's own funeral a short few years later. Theodore Thomas programmed the *Flower Maiden Scene* music from *Parsifal* in his own concert.[3]

The public's interest in Wagner—and in *Parsifal*—continued to esca-late, yet the opera was still not permitted to be performed in a fully staged production outside of the *Festspielhaus*. The ban was solidly in place. Wagner had declared Bayreuth perfect, and his widow held fast. In a literal sense, though, the German restrictions did not apply in the U.S., but gen-eral adherence to these constraints grew out of respect for the composer and his wife. And if by some chance a U.S. production was mounted, it would have been inappropriate for German singers to perform the work—even outside of their native land and after Wagner's death—thus flagrantly violating the restrictions upheld by Cosima Wagner on behalf of her late husband. If a space as perfect as Bayreuth, acoustically and otherwise, were in existence elsewhere, would things have been different? Possibly not, but it presented an intriguing question.

Despite the controversial restraints regarding performance of the work, steps were still taken to present *Parsifal* outside of Bayreuth. After all, the public was already familiar with some of the music and wanted more. It was inevitable that there would be a breakthrough at some point, and who better than Walter Damrosch to be in the middle of it? Damrosch rented the Metropolitan Opera House for an unstaged concert version of *Parsifal* to be presented on March 4, 1886.[4] This was the U.S. premiere of the work in its musical form only and, therefore, did not fall into the category of a fully staged work. It was not exactly complete in its musical form either. However, the importance of this event could not be minimized. It was significant and controversial to be sure, but it also opened the door a little wider for a full opera production in the future, although this would still be a long time coming. The concert performance featured both the Oratorio and Symphony societies under Walter Damrosch's direction. However, the evening was William Burnet Tuthill's moment to shine—his notable part in the event drawing attention to his expertise in acoustics, something that would in a few short years secure him a place in musical history.

As a talented and passionate amateur musician as well as a professional architect, Tuthill understood the important role of acoustics both in conveying a composer's intent and in maximizing the aesthetic possibilities of an artistic performance. He also fully realized that achieving a fine acoustical sound could be complicated. There were many subtly interwoven factors that needed to be considered: from the size and myriad components of the performance space itself to the very particular requirements of a specific composition. Given his musical and technical expertise, Tuthill was aware of the special acoustical challenges of *Parsifal*, just as Wagner had been, and he put his knowledge to use in this concert performance of the work.

Tuthill created a special hammer for the chimes. Then, he tuned the chimes himself. On the surface, this might have seemed a relatively small detail in a large and sweeping piece of music; but, in reality, it was an enormous factor in achieving a precisely nuanced effect in performance. The chimes or bells in *Parsifal* set a mood that is liturgical in character—a key element in building tension in the piece and in establishing its somber and religious tone. In addition, they figure significantly in maintaining dramatic, musical, and symbolic unity. *The Sun* took singular note of their importance in the concert, praising their tuning and resulting effective impact on the performance.[5] Tuthill's efforts illustrated his respect for Wagner's work while, at the same time, demonstrating his superior knowledge of the materials and conditions that affected its sound. It drew attention to his expertise and to the value of seriously considering acoustical issues. Tuthill's was a sufficiently unique enough accomplishment that evening to warrant special mention in his obituary forty-three years later.[6]

William Burnet Tuthill took to music early on. Born in Hoboken, New Jersey, in 1855, he learned the cello as a youth,[7] an instrument that he continued to play and enjoy throughout his life. Later, he formed the Wiederholen Quartet, a group of string players that included his brother Arthur on the viola.[8] This group rehearsed in his home weekly for over thirty years,[9] often performing informal concerts. Tuthill not only played the cello at these events, but he also saw to many of their associated details—even frequently hand painting "small watercolors" on the concert programs themselves.[10] This same attention to detail was characteristic of his approach to all endeavors.

It was Tuthill's admirable singing voice, though, that connected him to people who would be of paramount importance in his life. In 1879, he became a part of Leopold Damrosch's Oratorio Society,[11] still a relatively new organization but one that had already made a mark on the New York music scene. His joy in singing was also reflected in his membership in the choir at Calvary Baptist Church in Manhattan. It was there that he met his future wife, Henrietta Corwin, the organist for the church as well as the director of a women's choral organization known as Sorosis.[12] Active in music early on, at age 17 she had become an organist in her hometown of Newburgh, New York, and, subsequently, a piano accompanist for a Poughkeepsie choral group. Later, she often played with the Wiederholen Quartet when their repertoire required a pianist.[13] The couple married in 1881,[14] and music became a cornerstone of their family life. Together they instilled a love of music in their son, Burnet, born in 1888, who went on to become a composer.[15] The same year as their marriage, Tuthill became Secretary for the Oratorio Society, a position he was to hold for the ensuing thirty-six years[16] and one that would bring him into close contact with Leopold and Walter Damrosch and, eventually, with Andrew Carnegie. They would all figure significantly in his life.

In spite of his numerous and time-consuming musical pursuits, however, Tuthill was by profession an architect. Similar to his music, architecture was also a passion, not just a career. After graduating from City College in New York in 1875 and later receiving his master's degree from the same school, he continued his architectural studies in Richard Morris Hunt's atelier.[17] This proved to be both fine training as well as a valuable connection for the future.

Over the course of his career, Hunt was recognized for his work on many diverse projects that did not confine themselves to a single style and also took into serious account such factors as place, function, and relevance to surroundings. He inspired a number of architects who followed

in later years.[18] Hunt designed the city's first apartment building—the
Stuyvesant Apartments—as well as the Stevens House, noted for its "tech-
nological innovations" which included an elevator.[19] Recognized for his
design of the Great Hall and the Fifth Avenue façade of the Metropolitan
Museum of Art as well as of the New York Tribune building, his work also
encompassed a number of other historic edifices. Some were mansions
located in Newport, Rhode Island, and others lined New York's Fifth
Avenue—including those created for the Vanderbilts and the Astors. An
accomplished man, Hunt also founded the Municipal Art Society.[20]

   Tuthill's studies with Hunt provided a matchless opportunity for him
to learn and further his practical architectural knowledge while enhancing
his professional contacts within the field. During this era, many Americans
felt that they lacked the background equivalent to that offered at the premier center for architectural studies—Ecole des Beaux-Arts in Paris.[21] In
this regard, Tuthill was again fortunate since his mentor, Richard Morris
Hunt, happened to have been the first American to attend this institution.[22] Hunt modeled his fine American Architectural Atelier on this
French system in which he had received his own training.[23]

   Tuthill gradually ventured out on his own, opening an architectural
office and becoming established at 52 Broadway.[24] He maintained a collaborative association with Hunt, though, over the years. Along with
Hunt,[25] Tuthill was among the founders of the Architectural League of
New York,[26] a group dedicated to raising standards in the field and to
enhancing the professional development of its members. The League
believed that architecture was an art consisting of many diverse components[27]—a philosophy to which both men adhered. Tuthill was active in
the League and was a supporter and member of the jury of its first exhibition of architectural drawings in 1886. It was held at the Salmagundi
Club, a noted center for American art, as a part of one of their regular
shows.[28] The League's exhibition became an annual event, emphasizing
that architecture as a discipline did, indeed, encompass art in a broader
sense.

   Tuthill's career in architecture and his outside interests in music and
its related elements intersected. As proven by his work in the *Parsifal* performance, he was captivated by the art of acoustics, an emerging field at
that time, and he carefully examined its role from both architectural and
musical perspectives. As both a cellist and a singer, he was keenly aware
of the subtler elements of sound—from its creation to the components
that affected its dissemination in a given physical space. By the time that
Andrew Carnegie was coordinating plans for his new music hall project,

Tuthill had given much attention to the subject of acoustics. Based upon his association with the Oratorio Society, he was conscious of the deficits of a number of concert spaces as settings for the performances of large choral groups. Many did not do justice to the performers or their music. This issue was one that Tuthill would study further and ponder on both professional and artistic levels. His cumulative knowledge became highly regarded, and he later lectured frequently on the subject and wrote a work called *Practical Acoustics* that was published posthumously.[29]

Architects had long grappled with the elements of sound conduction when designing structures for performance venues. Although most of them acknowledged acoustics as an important issue, their understanding of it as an art and science was often ambiguous. The effective conception and design of a building's form, shape, and size were thought to be among the essential factors that affected sound, yet, as time progressed, it became evident that these were not the only considerations. The composition of materials used in construction as well as those selected for the completion of interior spaces was also critical. However, isolating the essential features of these materials and drawing precise conclusions about using them in specific combinations was not so easy.[30] And this was only a small portion of the entire picture. There were a number of other elements—some of them elusive—that entered into the total acoustical equation.

As New York and other urban areas aspired to make their mark as centers of serious music, particularly within a global context, these acoustical matters and their related questions became of increasing urgency. Yet acoustics was a study that still had far to go. In the majority of cases, imitation became the preferred and, understandably, the more comfortable of approaches. When undertaking a new building project for musical use, architects many times tried to replicate the acoustical design of successfully constructed European edifices. If it worked abroad they concluded, it would surely do the same at home. As a result, the Academy of Music in New York drew inspiration from the Berlin Opera House. Milan's La Scala opera house was the model for the Philadelphia Academy of Music. Additional cities did likewise, using various other structures as patterns.[31] The final product, however, was not always as effective as intended. Other factors needed evaluation. Duplication of an existing model was not always the best or most accurate of approaches for design.

Tuthill had a different understanding of the subject. He did not just want to mimic an existing structure. If sound was to be a major consideration, then he wanted to analyze all of the components that were a part of the production of this sound and match this information to the requirements of a prospective space. He could then assess what might or might not work and begin designing from that point. His serious background in music gave him a keener awareness of some of the subtler aspects of acoustics, superseding that of many in his profession.

In *Practical Acoustics*, Tuthill goes into great depth about the finite details of the subject. This work represents his years of accumulated study and reflects his ongoing thought-processes and well-considered approaches to both the art and science of acoustics. Tuthill felt it was critical to analyze all of the principles of architecture in addition to those pertaining to sound and physical motion. With this in mind, he outlined very specific information to be evaluated when designing a concert hall, specially emphasizing that the shape or size of the land on which the building would be placed should not determine the shape or proportions of the edifice itself. He clearly stated that a given sound should be able to be transmitted distinctly for one hundred feet—both being produced and heard without undue effort—and further stressed the importance of comprehending how this sound could be impacted by the shape and texture of nearby surfaces. Tuthill further emphasized that the study of sound waves—direct, indirect, and reflected sound as well as the length of its path and speed, among other factors—was crucial to understanding how to achieve a superior acoustical setting. Here was an individual who embraced detail and one who, over time, devoted much thought to the subject. His book would contain a number of precise drawings illustrating his points and, also, provided analyses of existing halls, their design, and acoustical set-ups.[32] Tuthill was a man who never took the importance of quality sound lightly.

Years before Tuthill penned this work about acoustics, Andrew Carnegie was acquainted with him through the Oratorio Society. Carnegie was a keen observer and had also been associated with the Society long enough to have become aware of Tuthill's professional and musical talents along with his personal character. His respect for him was clear. Andrew Carnegie chose William Burnet Tuthill to be the architect for the design of his new Music Hall.

To some, this might have been surprising. Carnegie could have had his choice of any established architect or architectural firm in the city or beyond—ones with long experience in designing musical and public spaces. Yet he chose a young architect who, until he was hired for this project, had never before designed a concert hall. Although he would later go on to lecture and write about acoustics and was in demand as a consultant to assist in correcting acoustical difficulties in various halls,[33]

William Burnett Tuthill was never to design another concert space. The Music Hall, eventually to be known as Carnegie Hall, would be his lasting masterpiece in the musical realm.

By the time that Tuthill was officially chosen as architect, Andrew Carnegie had already been active in overseeing many of the details that were required to get the new hall underway. On March 23, 1889, he hosted a meeting at his home with Tuthill, Stephen M. Knevals, Morris Reno, and Walter Damrosch all present. They would create the Music Hall Company "with a capital of $300,000"[34] and would incorporate the new concert hall. The filing of the articles of incorporation was planned for the following Monday.[35]

William Burnet Tuthill, architect of the Music Hall. He achieved lasting fame for the perfection of its acoustics (courtesy Carnegie Hall Archives).

In May, there was yet another meeting to select the Board of Directors for the Company. It was held at the law offices of Sherman W. Knevals at 34 Nassau Street,[36] whom, in addition to himself, Andrew Carnegie also appointed to the Board. Yale educated, Knevals was also a director of the Lawyers' Surety Company and the Associates Land Company.[37] Both William Tuthill and Walter Damrosch were also appointed as Board members.

The Board of Directors as a whole was comprised of a diverse group. Morris Reno was chosen as its president. Morris and Marie Reno had been neighbors of the Damrosch family during their early days in New York, and Leopold Damrosch and Reno had been good friends. They enjoyed playing chess together—"an awful lot of chess," Helene Damrosch once wrote to her sister—and were not unknown to debate topics in voices that could be heard clearly by the neighbors.[38] The two families shared a long-time association together.

Reno had immigrated from Germany and worked as a real estate broker during his earlier career in the U.S.[39] Long before the Music Hall project was begun, advertisements for various property auctions in Paterson, New Jersey, listed his name as a managerial contact for free excursions to this city to view villa plots of new homes with "charming views."[40] These trips included free luncheons prior to the sale of the properties and, intriguingly, several of them boasted free music as well.[41] One ad in particular promised an appearance by the well-known Seventh Regiment Band.[42]

In addition to his business acumen, Reno was obviously a music enthusiast, a fact that was borne out through his activities with a number of the city's groups over the years. He was connected with the Oratorio Society and Leopold Damrosch, having been on the ground floor of the organization when it was formed, and having functioned as Treasurer from its inception.[43] His responsibilities increased exponentially with time and the growth of the organization. By 1883, Oratorio Society advertisements were listing him as the Treasurer and prime contact for overseeing subscriptions when the Society performed at the Academy of Music.[44] He was concurrently the Corresponding Secretary for the Symphony Society of New York, also based at the Academy during the same season, and additionally acted as this organization's contact for ticket sales.[45] Reno had been involved in the Met's German opera productions as well.[46] His wife, S. Marie Reno, previously studied voice in Cologne and sang in the soprano section of the Oratorio Society. She was credited with suggesting the formation of a choral society to Leopold Damrosch.[47]

In addition to Reno as president, Andrew Carnegie chose a select group of other individuals to serve on the Board. Frederick William Holls was appointed as Secretary. Holls was a lawyer whose practice consisted of "a large German-American clientage" in the city.[48] Because of this, it is possible that the ethnic connection offered acquaintances with individuals in the many musically active groups within the German community, including the Damrosch family. Holls was busy on a number of fronts and in 1880, he was "prominent as a Republican campaign orator."[49] He was later to be a part of the country's delegation to the Peace Conference at The Hague. Coincidentally, Holls also sailed on the *Fulda* to Europe in April of 1887 on the same voyage as the Carnegies and Walter Damrosch.[50]

Stephen M. Knevals was named Treasurer. When the Symphony Society was originally incorporated in 1879, Knevals acted as Secretary of the group.[51] According to a contemporary business directory, he worked in the syrup trade. In an early written recollection of the downtown area, his firm is referred to as "Foote & Knevals," jobbers within the syrups and molasses industry.[52] As a youth, Frank Damrosch had been employed to do errands for the firm.[53] Knevals was previously a merchant tailor in New Haven, but his brother persuaded him to come to New York and change careers.[54]

A senior partner in his family's dry goods firm, John W. Aitken was also added to the Board roster. His family, similar to Andrew Carnegie's, was from Scotland. A graduate of Princeton, he also became a trustee of the Bowery Savings Bank.[55]

William S. Hawk, who served on the board of the Symphony, came from a family that was active in the hotel business and, as such, succeeded his uncle in the firm of Hawk and Wetherbee in the management of hotels. A charter member of the Hotel Association of New York City, established in 1878, he eventually became one of the proprietors of the Windsor Hotel where Andrew Carnegie and his mother had at one time resided. It is reasonable that Hawk and Carnegie would have become acquainted while the Carnegies lived at the hotel. Hawk had also been a good friend and former Ohio neighbor of William S. McKinley.[56]

John J. Wilson's name was only briefly mentioned. Appointed to the Board, he later resigned.[57] However, he is included in records as a stockholder[58] in the Music Hall Company and, therefore, maintained some connection with the project.

All the while a major question had turned into a more pressing one. Just where was this new music hall going to be located? In this, Andrew Carnegie looked to the future of musical, artistic, and social culture in New York—not to the past.

At the time the Music Hall project was underway, the cultural and entertainment world was clustered in the 14th Street area. One of the most notable fixtures of this neighborhood, having been located there since 1866, was Steinway Hall. Steinway pianos had already established a far-flung reputation for the superior quality of its instruments. In the years after coming to New York in 1853, this firm introduced many innovations in the design and construction of its pianos, subsequently winning a number of coveted awards—not to mention acclaim and visibility on an international level.[59]

The Steinway company was a family affair. Heinrich Engelhard Steinway built the firm and brought it from Germany to New York. Several of his sons joined him in business and carried on the tradition in subsequent years. Among these sons was Theodore, whose gift for refining and improving the mechanical components of a piano helped to advance the quality of the Steinway brand. Complementing Theodore's contributions was William, whose business and marketing acumen were behind making Steinway a "name" in the piano world.[60]

Although William Steinway did train and work in the mechanical end of the piano business, his talents for promotion and finance soon identified him for an entirely different role than that of his brother. He handled business matters, attracted the endorsements of renowned performers, and was fruitfully active in a large network of major commercial, artistic, and community organizations. One of his most visible achievements was overseeing the opening of Steinway Hall—the firm's beautiful concert venue. William Steinway was largely responsible for the company's fame.[61] He was a major presence in the musical world.

It was Steinway Hall, attached to the piano showroom, which showcased a tremendous array of artistic talent over the years—musically and otherwise. Events ranged from the silver anniversary of the New York Philharmonic Society to pianist Anton Rubinstein's debut in America to an appearance by Charles Dickens.[62] Steinway Hall was a major force in the 14th Street area. Hand in hand with this renowned piano manufacturer was Luchow's, the famous restaurant on 14th Street—also an established neighborhood landmark that served as a meeting place for many in the musical world. Victor Herbert later formed ASCAP on the premises. Steinway was king in this venerable eatery. It was no coincidence that members of his firm were treated well here. Early on, William Steinway had offered some financial help to August Luchow to help him get his business underway. Subsequently, Steinway and his executive staff frequented Luchow's on a daily basis to partake of their forty-five-cent lunch,[63] dining at their own special table. This connection was, of course, stellar advertising for all and certainly a favorable relationship for piano company and restaurant.

One of Steinway's major rivals also boasted a popular concert space—Chickering Hall. It was located slightly to the north at Fifth Avenue and 18th Street, but still within the general cultural district. Chickering Hall gained particular notice in the 1870s when Hans von Bulow performed there. His first concert on an American tour had been in Boston to premiere Tchaikovsky's *Piano Concerto No 1*

Head of the successful piano company and its famed concert hall, William Steinway was a key presence in the New York musical world.

in B flat Minor. The second, though, was a New York event on November 18, 1875, introducing Chickering's lovely new concert space via an all-Beethoven program that also featured von Bulow's old friend Leopold Damrosch at the podium. Von Bulow became testy during the course of his tour, however, at having to be a conspicuously "live" advertisement for the piano firm—these events having been a part of a series of his concerts sponsored by Chickering.[64] His attitude did not gain him fans, and it did not achieve what Chickering had hoped for, although any advertising was better than none. Endorsements were serious business in the piano world. Both Steinway and Chickering had a long-standing rivalry over who received the most endorsements as well as the most prestigious awards for their products. The resulting press kept both names in the news and, of course, helped to sell pianos.

Other piano manufacturers had their warerooms in the 14th Street environs, too: Sohmer Pianos on East 14th Street, Decker Brothers on Union Square, and Knabe on Fifth Avenue. The latter firm would figure prominently during the opening of Andrew Carnegie's new Music Hall. This was the heyday of the piano, the piano virtuoso, and the piano recital. The firms all made the most of it—their instruments, their concert spaces, and their influence all having an enormous impact on the city's cultural life. And many of them were clustered in the 14th Street area at that time.

The neighborhood featured every form of entertainment—from vaude-ville, to minstrel shows, to theater, to concerts, to operas. Music publishers were fixtures there, as well. Among them were pioneers who were sowing the seeds of Tin Pan Alley—M. Witmark & Sons, T.B. Harms, and Willis Woodward & Company. Venerable classical publishing firms were long established in the neighborhood—Oliver Ditson, Edward Schuberth, William A. Pond, and the famous G. Schirmer. *The Musical Courier* resided on Union Square, a publication that reported on many facets of the cultural world. Both the 7th and 22nd Regiment Bands had offices based in the vicinity. There were wine gardens and beer gardens, all with vast forms of entertainment. Critics and writers flocked to Brentano's Literary Emporium, a favorite place for their gathering.[65] Music stores, art galleries, artists' studios—were all located in the surrounding blocks. There were famous residents, as well, from the Biddle family of the piano firm to inventors William and George Andrews.[66] A new concert hall within a reasonable distance nearby would not have been totally surprising. This was, after all, an established center of New York's thriving cultural and entertainment scene.

And yet, signs of change were increasingly noticeable. The famous

Academy of Music that had once been a lynchpin of the area had been dealt a blow when the Metropolitan Opera House put down roots at Broadway and West 39th Street. Reverberations from this change affected 14th Street. More theaters and houses of entertainment were being built or were on the move, joining the Met in their new area and venturing beyond. This was progress. Still, when it was announced that Andrew Carnegie's Music Hall would be built on land parcels located on Seventh Avenue between 56th and 57th streets, some eyebrows were raised—whether at the specific location or at the venture away from the conventional cultural districts, it was hard to say.

It was true that museums had already opened up new vistas in Manhattan. The Metropolitan Museum of Art at Fifth Avenue and 82nd Street was open. The new American Museum of Natural History at Central Park West between 77th and 81st streets had also been firmly established. These were significant institutions forging new territory for the arts-minded. They needed large pieces of property, although each did have immediate proximity to the oasis of Central Park.

Residential areas had also broken new ground in recent years. The rich were building mansions on Fifth Avenue and were consistently moving northward. Among them were the Carnegies and the Vanderbilts. This area had already become an established enclave for the well-to-do. Pioneers in the building industry had even gone as far as West 72nd Street to construct the Dakota apartment building, completed in 1884. It was then considered to be in a remote part of the city—hence, the derivation of its name. It was, however, also close to the park. Once the first pioneers moved in, though, others soon followed.

Despite this trend toward expansion, there was still skepticism when Andrew Carnegie purchased the nine adjoining lots in several stages for his new Music Hall. This particular locale was different from some of the others. The land had once been part of an old farm originally owned by the Cosine family, its roots going far back in New York City history.[67] It was not many decades away from its rural roots when shacks and animals dotted the landscape. The area was also unremarkable in many ways as compared to the contemporary entertainment districts, fashionable residential streets, and great pioneering museums. There were still blacksmith shops in the environs, as well as a brewery and saloons.[68] The site was right near Dickel's Riding School, located on 56th Street between Sixth and Seventh avenues. It was the oldest riding school in New York[69] and, of course, had a number of accompanying stables nearby—not the only such ones in the neighborhood. When Andrew Carnegie bought the lots, the sidewalks might have been paved, but the streets were not. All of it raised questions from observers. Who would travel this far away from the accepted musical and cultural neighborhoods to hear a symphony or choral concert—especially to a place with the dust of blacksmiths lingering in the air? How would such a large venue fare financially, especially when its fine music and other events were intended for an audience from all walks of life? These and other questions arose. Veteran concert hall owners William Steinway and Charles F. Chickering believed that the new venture would not work.[70]

Although skeptics questioned the viability of the locale and the project, there was also a faint undercurrent of unease below the surface. Would a new space such as this dilute the popularity and success of existing ones? This was not an unfounded concern. If, by chance, the new hall did happen to be successful, then even the harshest of critics would have to at least privately consider the bigger picture. Even in an unusual location, there was still something attractive about a new concert space—the potential for grandeur and a look to the future. As to the subject of too many large halls—the impact of this remained to be seen.

Andrew Carnegie was not fazed by any of the questions or speculations. He was an innovator and an exceptionally shrewd one at that. He believed that a quality hall was necessary and if one existed that offered fine concerts and interesting events, then the audiences would come— despite the location. Time would prove him correct. He also understood the nature of the urban experience. A city would always expand, and what might have once seemed to be a drab or even remote locale one day would not be so the next. The *Musical Courier* offered its agreement, citing the city's growth trends that would soon render the new hall "sufficiently central"[71] as well as the surface and elevated transportational resources that already existed, making the location "easily accessible."[72] The publication further offered an intriguing insight, commenting that with the new hall New York would not again "endure the taunts"[73] of Boston and Cincinnati, cities that already had suitable concert spaces.

Andrew Carnegie was aware of an increasing trend in building. The same year that ground was broken for the Music Hall, other new structures were being raised for different purposes and in various city locations. *The New York Times* reported that in addition to Carnegie's new edifice, five other organizations were building or planning on building new quarters. From the Century Club, Republican Club, and Manhattan Athletic Club, to the Lenox Lyceum and the German Society, a number of new structures were being added to the existing landscape.[74] The city had growing pains, and construction was rushing to keep up. Now some new energy was being infused into once forgotten segments of neighborhoods.

A closer look at the area where the Music Hall would be located showed that it was not the cultural and social wasteland that some might have implied. It was not all stables and blacksmiths and saloons. There were already nearby dwellings, some in particular that attracted artists and others that appealed to those in comfortable circumstances. In the 1880s, a number of Queen Anne style town houses were built as residences between 147 and 151 West 57th Street, and artists had already discovered the area via the Sherwood Studios at Sixth Avenue and 57th Street, a part of the neighborhood since the beginning of the same decade. The Rembrandt Studio joined them at 152 West 57th Street—right next door to the new Music Hall's site.[75] The Osborne Apartment building was already a fixture at 201 West 57th Street and Seventh Avenue. Completed in 1885, the building stood tall against the generally low, sparse landscape. Thomas Osborne, a stone dealer with an eye for grandeur in a dwelling and a desire to rival the sensational features of the Dakota, made his mark in the neighborhood—it, too, was right across the street from the site of the new Music Hall. Its residents would include famed ad agency executive J. Walter Thompson[76] and actress Lillian Russell.[77] Aside from residences, there were other indicators that the neighborhood was attracting interest and had shown signs of continuing development. One particular example was Calvary Baptist Church. They had raised a fine new building and relocated to West 57th Street in 1883. The Tuthills met at this church when it was in their previous location in the 23rd Street area.

Although the vicinity was not as glittering as 14th Street, its chance to shine was not far in the future. It had potential, offering advantages that a man such as Andrew Carnegie had the ability to perceive. Characteristically, he moved forward with conviction in his plan to build.

Early in 1889, while Carnegie was evaluating possible sites for the concert hall, he would have certainly included members of the Board in various aspects of the process. In a commemorative record of the Oratorio Society for its 1888–1889 year, the librarian/historian for the group noted an episode that occurred at a rehearsal for the season's last concert—a time when there seemed to have been little visible progress toward the realization of the proposed concert hall. The singers were to be pleasantly surprised that evening. Walter Damrosch "arrived late, by a minute and a half, looking flushed ... with an apology for making the members wait so long." He knew they would offer him forgiveness "as he had been, with others, to secure the site for the 'Music Hall.'"[78]

Ledger entries from 1889 show the purchase of land on April 6 and April 8 for the respective amounts of $117,000 and $130,000.[79] On June 12 of the same year, the excavation of the lots upon which the Music Hall would be built was authorized.[80] On July 1, there was another entry for land purchase totaling $55,000.[81] Progress was definitely in the air.

The New York Times reported in mid–July of 1889 that the additional property bought by Andrew Carnegie would enable the new hall to be larger than first thought—the main entrance portion on 57th Street said to be 150 feet. Both the Seventh Avenue and 56th Street properties would have 175 and 25 foot spans, respectively. The article eagerly continued, divulging that the main hall alone would accommodate an estimated 3,300 seats, not to mention its versatile capacity to be transformed into a ballroom for non-concert occasions. There would be adjacent smaller halls and rooms as well as a multitude of attractive amenities.[82] These glowing details were enough to stir up a significant degree of curiosity and anticipation on the part of the public.

This progress went beyond the acquisition of land. Required goods and services were also being arranged. Smaller expenditures—although extremely necessary ones—were entered in the July ledger books. They represented funds paid for surveyors ($65), water-rent ($14), several sewer permits ($30 and $346.75), and other items.[83] By November, there was a financial statement in place for the building and equipment relating to the project that totaled $763,531.25.[84] Everything was moving forward with speed and resolve.

During this time, William Tuthill had been busy researching and planning the design of the new structure. He had seriously considered all factors and reviewed input from a number of sources. The question of acoustics was at the forefront—it had been one of the prime considerations in contemplating a new hall. One of the individuals Tuthill consulted on the subject was Walter Damrosch. His musical groups, particularly the Oratorio Society, had been the initial catalysts for the project. Damrosch had a fine grasp of music as performed in many types of venues in the U.S. and abroad. His input was valuable.

Years later, Tuthill's son, Burnet, reported that as a part of the information gathering process, his father also issued questionnaires to hundreds of concert halls worldwide. He wanted to obtain a broad range of details and ideas about structural and other factors that were critical to producing fine sounds in many different types of buildings.[85] Since there was an increasing emphasis on the global context of this concert space, Tuthill needed to dissect the many features that could make it equal to or even surpassing some of the existing great halls of the world. As more and more international musical figures were giving concerts in the U.S., a hall of the finest quality could attract even further numbers of these individuals to New York and put both the city and the country on a larger cultural map.

Tuthill also sought advice and assistance from other architects, particularly from Dankmar Adler of the firm of Adler & Sullivan. Adler, an accomplished architect who was known for his work in helping to rebuild Chicago after the 1871 fire, was responsible for the acoustical design of the Auditorium Theater there.[86] His associate, Louis Sullivan, was quoted as saying that Adler made acoustics an art, rather than only a science. He felt that "all science is sterile" unless looked upon in this much wider context.[87]

The firm of Adler & Sullivan was well respected, and their input was of substantial value to Tuthill. Their part in the design of the Music Hall is further corroborated by ledger entries for 1889. Between July and November of that year, there were entries of $1,500 and $1,800 paid to the firm. Additional amounts were recorded in 1891, 1893, and 1895.[88] Frank Lloyd Wright was once a draftsman for Adler & Sullivan and not only acknowledged their popularity as consultants for theatrical type structures,[89] but was also reported to have seen the Music Hall's plans in their office at one time,[90] further supporting the importance of their role during the process. This firm was named "associate architects" for the project,[91] and Tuthill initially insisted that it be listed in conjunction with an 1890 drawing of the Music Hall that was subsequently published.[92] In addition, Tuthill also consulted with his former mentor, Richard M. Hunt for input and advice. He was a "consulting architect."[93]

Tuthill first designed the main building but, in future years, he was responsible for additions, including studios. He opted for substance over showiness, choosing not to include a grand dome at the top of the structure—a feature that might have adversely affected the sound. He also allowed for walls that were several feet in thickness. These walls not only supported the building more than amply but were said to have contributed significantly to the building's famed acoustics. The curved interior as well as the lush wood and velvet treatments inside further added to the superior quality of the beautiful sound.[94] This lovely velvet absorbed extraneous echoes and noises, and the curved design of the boxes not only enhanced the audience sightlines from all perspectives, but also removed certain harsh acoustical elements that a more angular design would have, instead, only emphasized.[95] All of these treatments augmented the visual appeal of the interior, as well. However, these refinements were yet to come. First, the construction team and those associated with it needed to be assembled and their work plans organized and begun. Numerous individuals and firms were a part of the construction process, representing an elaborate network of required goods and services—from suppliers of building materials to specialists in artistic details.

Isaac A. Hopper was the builder in charge of the actual construction of the project. His company had a solid record of achievement, including the Emigrant Savings Bank downtown on Chambers Street as well as the Hotel Normandie, located at 38th Street and Broadway,[96] a site that would figure prominently during the Music Hall's opening Festival. Hopper's work on the new concert hall would go a long way toward ensuring his continued success in the building industry and beyond. Within two years of its opening, he was named as one of New York's "leading builders" and a potential candidate for Commissioner of Public Works.[97] In addition to being a contractor and builder, he was one of the founders and eventual president of Empire Savings Bank. Hopper was active in local politics for many years and a supporter of the Democratic party.[98] A number of entries are recorded for him in the 1890 and 1891 accounts of the Music Hall's ledgers, including outlays of various amounts for cash and other expenses noted in conjunction with his firm. Also, there were entries for shares of stock in his name.[99] It is possible that this was a partial payment arrangement, perhaps similar to the one provided to William Tuthill and others.

There are also ledger entries for Isaac Hopper's brother, John J. Hopper. They are dated from 1890 and 1891. He headed a firm specializing in foundations and heavy masonry,[100] eventually advertising himself as a "Civil Engineer and Contractor," and offering services for "general building construction."[101] Later he became one of the first contrac-

Isaac Hopper's firm handled the construction of the Music Hall.

tors to work on a portion of the New York subway system. A graduate of Dartmouth College, Hopper, similar to his brother, became active in politics.[102]

Among the many who contributed their expertise was the ventilating and steam heating engineer, Alfred R. Wolff. Working with top architects as a consultant in this area, the systems he designed were installed not only in the Music Hall, but also at St. Patrick's Cathedral, Bellevue Hospital, and in the homes of Andrew Carnegie and Cornelius Vanderbilt.[103] His ventilating system in the Music Hall received special praise.

Notices of payments to Johnson & Morris were also in the ledger books of 1890.[104] In the same specialized field as Wolff, this firm produced "steam heating and ventilating apparatus"[105] that was known for its reliability. George H. Morris eventually received an award from New York's Master Steam and Hot Water Fitters' Association for his excellent service over a period of twenty-five years. His presence in the New York Building Trades group was subsequently an active and highly regarded one.[106] Some years later, his firm also did work in conjunction with the building of the Henry Clay Frick residence on Fifth Avenue.[107]

Charles H. Davis, the electrical engineer, was an innovator. He operated as a consulting engineer in electric lighting and in a number of other areas—from power and railways plants to highways, working not only in New York, but also in Philadelphia and Boston. His electrical lighting for the Music Hall received continual praise from the press and audiences alike. The massive generators in the basement had extremely powerful dynamos that were buffered by a solid building foundation, thus preventing vibrations from interfering with sound in the Hall. Davis installed double-throw switch and unique wiring systems that were efficient, reduced repairs, and enhanced the entire operation.[108] The year following its opening, he would be the one to institute the "first concealed public electric lighting" at the Music Hall.[109]

The electrical lighting system overseen by Davis was a major and innovative feature of the Music Hall. It was beautiful as well as safe. This was a new method of illumination for public places that phased out the gaslights that had long been in vogue. The Lyceum Theatre, built in 1885 on Fourth Avenue near Twenty-Third Street, was the first to have electric lighting exclusively on the premises. Its installation, supervised by Thomas Edison,[110] was not only groundbreaking but also an additional boon to safety. It set the standard for new buildings to come. Now the Music Hall would have its own such system—aesthetically pleasing and a help in reducing the chances of fire.

Safety from fire was still of paramount concern in the late nineteenth century. A high percentage of theaters and halls, as well as other types of public structures, had been devastated by fire during the era. There was still much wood used in construction, and gaslight had been the favored means of illumination—a potent combination. Added to this was a still evolving series of fire codes. When combined, the stage was often set for disaster. Although many theatres were destroyed by fire—even the original Academy of Music burned down in 1866—these buildings were often empty when such episodes occurred. It took a tragedy, however, to bring the subject of fire safety into sharper focus. When Brooklyn's Conway Theatre burned at the end of 1876, there was a full audience in the house, and more than two hundred people were killed. The theater had much flammable material inside, inadequate exits, and no resources to extinguish even the smallest of flames. This tragedy prompted new fire codes and even more rigorous inspections.[111] Although other theaters and music spaces continued to burn after this incident, the Brooklyn fire was a turning point, introducing not only the improved codes but also raising awareness of fire safety on the part of officials, building designers, and the public. Later, the establishment of electrical lighting systems and the subsequent phasing out of gaslights in theaters was an important step toward safety. Hand in hand with this was a greater emphasis on choosing building materials that could aid in fireproofing. By the time that the new Music Hall was being built, this consideration was of prime importance.

The Guastavino Fire-Proof Construction Company contributed to the Music Hall's nicely designed fireproofing scheme. The clay tile used was lightweight, strong, attractive—and a marked deterrent to fire. Based upon centuries-old engineering techniques, the system allowed large building spaces to be filled with tiles that were bound together with Portland cement and plaster, a combination that produced higher quality results than previously used materials.[112] No expensive wooden framework was needed, and the tiles were thin with a high-load capacity. In comparison to stone vaulting, this system was highly economical and quick to install.[113] The floors, ceilings, and roof of the Music Hall were constructed using this method.[114] During the same era, the Guastavino firm also worked on such buildings as the Edison Electric Illuminating Company Building and the Arion Club.[115]

There were many other companies involved with the Music Hall project, illustrating its massive scope. Souvenir booklets name elevators installed by Otis Brothers & Company, ornamental iron done by Jackson Architectural Iron Works, and plumbing by Byrne & Tucker.[116] Ledger entries list Westerly Granite Company; the Durham House Drainage Company, for proper sanitary conditions; and Abendroth & Root,[117] manufacturers of water tanks and heaters and patented spiral pipes for water works.[118] These were but a few of the numerous firms involved in the entire project, and they represent the many systems and related equipment necessary for its completion.

Interior appointments were also essential. The Music Hall needed to be both comfortable and beautiful in addition to possessing fine structural features and systems. The Herters provided decorations for the space. This firm had long been established in New York as the finest of interior designers and custom furniture creators.[119] The Hall's ledger books in 1891 listed amounts of almost $22,000 in connection to the Herter Brothers firm.[120] In addition, there were entries for Andrews Manufacturing Company under the heading of furniture.[121] This firm was located at 74 and 76 Fifth Avenue and was known for its quality chairs. In the case of the Music Hall, they installed seating of superior quality that ensured comfort and sufficient space for audience members.[122]

Constructing a building as massive and complex as this one required the contributions of many individuals and firms, each possessing distinct specialties. Various entries in the ledgers reflected the requirement for all manner of materials and services of varying sizes. The larger entries are straightforward, such as those related to major construction. However, the smaller ones offer an insight into just how many not so obvious details needed to be addressed—lettering; sundries such as mason work; extra marble; skylight metal; and a time detector, among many more.[123] The list was long, and an intricate network of individuals and companies were represented.

Some of the key people received stock as partial payment for their services. William Tuthill was among them, although over the years he did receive monetary compensation for much work that he did on additions to the original edifice as well as for refinements to the existing one.[124] There was also the investment factor, and Andrew Carnegie himself retained stock for his monetary outlay on the project. Other stockholders generally listed in the ledgers included Morris Reno and other Board members, Walter Damrosch, Gustav Schirmer, John Crosby Brown (of the investment bank), Hugh T. Auchincloss, brewer George Frank Ehret, and banker Isaac Seligman, among additional others.[125]

As time passed, the construction process and related business matters continued to progress. In the midst of it all, a red-letter day arrived. May 13, 1890, was a busy one in New York. The newspapers advertised multiple numbers of events that the public could choose to attend during the day or in the evening. The Casino offered an afternoon concert—the first of a series of farewells presented by violinist Pablo de Sarasate and pianist Eugen d'Albert, both highly acclaimed musicians.[126] For those with a taste for sports, there was baseball to be enjoyed at the New Polo Grounds. Or one could choose an afternoon or evening trip to the Lenox Lyceum for an "Electrical Exhibition." Further possibilities were also attractive—a production of *H.M.S. Pinafore* at the Academy of Music, an evening of variety at Koster and Bial's Hall, or the show *Around the World* at Niblo's.[127] Chickering Hall was proud to be the site of a commencement concert presented by the greatly praised New-York College of Music, at which students performed on their various instruments and received medals for their accomplishments. A highlight was having the opportunity to play the Overture from Mozart's *Marriage of Figaro* in an orchestra directed by Frank Damrosch.[128] This was only a sampling of the many choices available on that day.

However, with all of the absorbing and worthwhile events advertised, the one that received the most attention took place at the site of the future Music Hall. There, the cornerstone for the new building was to be laid with a great amount of well-deserved fanfare. According to one account, five hundred individuals from numerous musical groups were on hand.[129] There were representatives from the Philharmonic Society, the Symphony Society, the opera, and other organizations from as far away as Brooklyn and New Jersey. Most of the members of the Oratorio Society were joyously present. They would finally get the musical home of which they had dreamed for years.

The festivities began in the late afternoon. "A fanfare of trumpets" sounded the beginning of the ceremonies.[130] Applause greeted Morris Reno, President of the Music Hall Society and an officer of both the Symphony and Oratorio societies. He led the proceedings. Reno spoke briefly, predicting that the hall would be a "magnificent dwelling place for music."[131] While he acknowledged the place of the Oratorio and Symphony societies in the life of the new building, he also firmly stated that this was a place that would welcome all kinds of music—and, further, it was intended "for the use of all."[132]

E. Francis Hyde of the Philharmonic Society also said a few words. Despite the fact that this group was not a major force in the development of the space, it was to become closely allied with it in years to come. It was the city's first major orchestra and, as such, was a critical part of its cultural life and history. Both Hyde and the members of the Philharmonic Society were an important presence on the occasion.

The ceremony to lay the cornerstone on May 13, 1890. Hundreds of members of the Oratorio, Symphony, Philharmonic, and other musical societies, as well as key Music Hall Company members and guests, gathered for this momentous occasion (courtesy Carnegie Hall Archives).

Soon, the castle air from *Das Rheingold* was heard from the band, a fitting selection for the day on which this new "castle" of music was being dedicated. This opera had been a particular favorite of Leopold Damrosch. Now, both the music and the occasion recalled memories of his inspiring role in the lives of his family, friends, and musical groups.

Then, a most dramatic moment arrived as Walter Damrosch brought Mrs. Louise Carnegie forward with respectful dignity and ceremony. At the appropriate time, and using her beautiful silver trowel specially made by Tiffany & Co. for the occasion, she carefully smoothed the mortar to secure the cornerstone for the new building. This trowel became a cherished possession of Mrs. Carnegie's, and she displayed it on her mantelpiece throughout the remainder of her life.[133]

Beneath this cornerstone a copper box had been placed containing material about the Music Hall, its societies, and related musical mat-

The trowel used by Louise Carnegie to secure the cornerstone for the Music Hall. She treasured this item for the remainder of her life (courtesy Carnegie Hall Archives. Trowel on loan to Carnegie Hall courtesy Carnegie Dumfermline Trust).

ters[134]—a time capsule of sorts. Inside the box were histories of the two major groups that were the motivating forces behind the creation of the hall—the Oratorio Society and the Symphony Society.[135] The minutes of the Oratorio Society stated that the items also included the names of its directors and present members, copies of its by-laws and charter, and a photograph of Leopold Damrosch.[136] In addition, *The Sun* reported that copies of various documents from the Philharmonic Society and the Music Hall Association, programs from assorted musical groups, photographs of Andrew Carnegie and Walter Damrosch, and representative contemporary coins and newspapers were also included. Finally, and in honor of Leopold Damrosch whose inspiring dream of a new music hall lived on, was a copy of his cantata, *Sulamith*.[137]

Morris Reno next introduced Andrew Carnegie. There was wild enthusiasm from the surrounding crowd as he came forward. When the applause had subsided, Carnegie spoke movingly of the noble aims of the Hall. The new building, he said, was intended to be a place for music as well as a platform for "all good causes."[138] He was emphatic that this edifice was not being created for gain but for love of music and for the good and higher aims that would affect the world. This would be "no ordinary structure," he predicted; it would most likely be intertwined with the country's history.[139] A great cheer from the crowd punctuated the end of Carnegie's speech—fervently led by Walter Damrosch, who then "tossed up his hat"[140] with visibly joyous enthusiasm. It was a buoyant assembly, and one that took its time to disperse when the ceremonies drew to an end.

Walter Damrosch had much to toss up his hat over that week. Not only was the cornerstone in place for the much anticipated new Music Hall, but he was also about to celebrate a very special event in his life several days later. It was one that had parallels to a similar occasion that had taken place almost three years previously, the evening before the *Fulda* sailed.

On May 17, 1890, in a lovely home overlooking Lafayette Square in Washington, D.C., a sunny parlor was decorated in fragrant roses—Scotch roses, American beauties, Baroness Rothschild roses. They were accompanied by gladioli, peonies, snowballs, and other flowers—offering a beautiful contrast to the seating covered in white dimity. Family and distinguished guests filled the room—among them, President Benjamin Harrison and his wife, Vice President Morton, Andrew and Louise Carnegie, and General W. T. Sherman. At the sound of the piano playing Mendelssohn's *Wedding March*, the bride entered and the simple wedding ceremony began. It was followed by a wedding breakfast with champagne as well as a cake set in a framework of roses. The proceedings were tasteful and elegant but not overly lavish. Both the bride's brother and sister had passed away several months' previously.[141] An event of grand proportions would not have been appropriate. Despite her own intense personal grief, the mother of the bride bravely offered a most gracious welcome to all who attended, determined to ensure her daughter's happiness at her wedding.

Although the bride wore a traditional wedding gown, she left the premises in a "handsome gray traveling dress"[142] and joined her groom in a carriage bound for a brief stay in Baltimore, after which they were scheduled to embark on a sea voyage for Germany on their wedding trip. Mr. Walter Damrosch and Mrs. Margaret Blaine Damrosch were beginning their own married journey. It would thereafter be intertwined with that of Andrew and Louise Carnegie and with one of the most famous concert halls of all time.

• THREE •

The First Notes Performed

The music of Peter Ilyich Tchaikovsky was popular in America, and Leopold Damrosch, who was partial to the composer's works, had not hesitated to include them in his concert programs. At the beginning of 1880, he even wrote to Tchaikovsky to say how much he admired and enjoyed his music, having twice presented the *Suite No. 1*, which he referred to as *Suite Op. 43*, "with great success"[1] and to the obvious delight of audiences. Damrosch vowed to include additional works on future programs and specifically mentioned a new symphony and the Violin Concerto as possibilities in this regard. He hoped to receive orchestra parts for these works in time for upcoming concerts.[2]

Once more, Walter Damrosch followed in his father's footsteps. He, too, was drawn to Tchaikovsky's music and even conducted the American premiere of the composer's *Fourth Symphony* in February of 1890.[3] Tchaikovsky had international stature, and Damrosch knew that his works had wide appeal in the U.S. Now, while in the throes of planning a special inaugural festival to open the Music Hall, he knew something was needed to announce to the world that this was not just another concert space but one of significant and lasting value. Along these lines, including some of Tchaikovsky's compositions in the five-day inaugural Festival programs would be a good decision. Yet, if the great composer himself could be there in person to conduct these works, it would definitely be cause for enthusiasm on an even grander scale. Certainly Damrosch had a keen sense of good music and public tastes as well as a fine grasp of what would help get the new concert hall off to a successful start. The power of having a world-renowned celebrity composer as part of the Festival was matchless. Walter Damrosch moved boldly forward. He requested permission from the Board to invite Tchaikovsky to take part in the event. After receiving approval, Damrosch then contacted the composer's tour manager, Hermann Wolff, to set things in motion. Wolff wrote to Tchaikovsky in September of 1890 to tell him of this most flattering possibility and predicted that when the plan was settled, it would be an "American triumph" for the composer.[4]

Wolff was a Renaissance man and a savvy one, at that. Although he studied music, he had also worked at the Berlin Stock Exchange. In addition to this, he managed to take a job with a music publishing firm and was quite valuable to them because of his knowledge of and fluency in several languages. All of this acumen and experience was to be useful in his future career as a concert manager. Through his various contacts, he eventually met and began managing tours for a number of high-profile musicians, pianist Anton Rubinstein being the first. Others included Sophie Menter and Hans von Bulow. He soon built an impressive roster of clients. In the 1880s he created a successful concert agency, Musicwolff. Its activities ranged from organizing single events to managing international tours. Wolff was also behind the formation of a well-known Berlin concert space, Bechstein Hall. It was inevitable that Wolff would eventually cross paths with Tchaikovsky, and their association, begun in 1888, was an important link in the arrangement of details for the composer's trip to New York—an event that was to be a major coup for Walter Damrosch and the Music Hall's inaugural Festival.[5]

The time was right for Tchaikovsky to make the journey to America. On the musical side, he was in a creatively prolific period and his recognition on the international front was high. Emotionally, the trip promised a welcome diversion, although it would not be without its difficulties. Tchaikovsky was given to fits of depression, and right around the time that the possibility of a journey to New York was up for consideration, this depression was seriously deepening. He had experienced a sudden break in his long-term relationship with Nadezhda Filaretovna von Meck, a most unusual association and one that was defined by correspondence only—over 1,200 letters representing the only contact in their fourteen-year link. Von Meck had offered consistent encouragement, not to mention significant monetary help for the composer. Yet she ended all contact abruptly. No explanations were offered.[6] Tchaikovsky was devastated.

Forgetting his emotional shock, there was a practical side to consider. He was now in need of money, and the concerts in New York would yield him $2,500—a more than handsome fee by the standards of the time.[7] Also, Tchaikovsky had wanted to visit America. Now was his opportunity. He wrote to his friend and publisher Peter Jurgenson that he considered it "mad to lose the chance" of making the trip.[8] Tchaikovsky wanted this engagement badly. To make matters more complicated, he had been suffering from neuralgia in his right arm and had been forced to cancel other conducting appearances.[9] This was different, though. He would see it through. This was America, and it was something that he longed to do.

In January of 1891, Morris Reno—head of the Music Hall Corporation Board—sent off the specific details of the proposed trip.[10] As soon as the composer accepted, there was much excitement in New York. In another letter written by Reno to Tchaikovsky in March of 1891, he spoke of everyone's delight at the composer's forthcoming arrival and how both Leopold and Walter Damrosch had been great supporters of his music. Reno's correspondence was followed by letters from the Steinway Company's Charles Tretbar and music critic Henry T. Finck, both also in praise of the composer's music.[11] Just the presence of Tchaikovsky alone would be a spectacular event in itself.

Tchaikovsky was not scheduled to arrive in New York until late in April. The actual week-long official inaugural Festival in which he would participate—to be held in the Main Auditorium of the complex—would only begin on May 5. Before this time, however, there was one space in the building that was already up and running for use—the Recital Hall.

In a descriptive souvenir booklet, the Recital Hall was referred to as "the second great room" within the complex. This space was set apart, being beneath the Main Auditorium and functioning separately with its own entrance on West 57th Street. With seating for 1,200 people, its main floor was complemented by a balcony and side galleries. The booklet even noted its suitability for "public functions," indicating that it was not only intended for musical events alone; but it had the flexibility to be converted into a ballroom or dining room. Special mention was made of its beauty, lighting, ventilating, and superior acoustics.[12] This attractive and useful venue was already in demand, and the month of April was to be filled with an eclectic array of events there. From musical recitals and lectures to patriotic celebrations and academic functions, much would be packed into this short span of time, giving audiences a taste of the variety of ways in which the new music complex could serve the public well.

Even before this, however, the Recital Hall was in use. Although April would officially mark its public opening, there was another important occasion that took place prior to everything else. As a result, one private meeting and one public concert vied for the honor of being the first to send forth musical notes throughout the entire building complex as a whole. On March 12 of 1891, the regular rehearsal of the Oratorio Society took place in the Recital Hall, and it was stated that all future rehearsals would be held there unless otherwise indicated. The minutes of the Society offer in detail the specifics of this evening: it was even noted that the weather outside was rainy that day. There were 364 singers present: 152 sopranos, 81 altos, 45 tenors, and 86 basses. The works to be rehearsed were Leopold Damrosch's cantata *Sulamith* and Heinrich Schutz's *Seven Last Words of Christ*. The Secretary who recorded the evening's information was William Burnet Tuthill. He succinctly describes the proceedings, as follows.

> This evening the first public occupation of Music Hall occurred. There were a large number of visitors. Mr. Carnegie was present and addressed the audience.
> The selection of "Sulamith" the first work to be sung in the building was made by the Secretary, as in some sort a memorial to Dr. Leopold Damrosch, whose constant wish and desire was that the Oratorio Society should some time have a fitting place in which to sing.
> Wm B. Tuthill
> Sec'y[13]

Although this was a regular rehearsal, it was far more special than just an ordinary meeting, as Tuthill indicated. A review of the evening appeared in *The Sun*, and it revealed that the Recital Hall "was opened last evening"[14]—a beautiful space decorated in white with delicate gold trimmings. The reporter pointed out that Walter Damrosch interrupted the rehearsal frequently with words of gratitude and praise for the superb acoustics in the room. He also made a speech and then invited Andrew Carnegie to do the same. Enthusiastic as always, Carnegie several times stopped his talk to personally bring individuals to the stage and subsequently describe their contributions to the enterprise. Both of the Renos were singled out in this manner, and Carnegie paid lavish tribute to Morris Reno calling him a "great man" and a major catalyst in moving the Music Hall project forward. Then he personally brought Oratorio Society soprano Marie Reno forth, clearly affirming that she was the first to suggest to Leopold Damrosch that he should found this Society.[15] Although this might not have been the first officially public event at the Recital Hall, it was nevertheless a special and celebratory occasion.

April 1 was declared the public opening of the Recital Hall. As fitting as it was that the Oratorio Society first used the building and sang its music there—and particularly the music of Leopold Damrosch—it was equally fitting that the first public event was a piano recital—one given by the prolific Franz Rummel. The piano still held forth in popularity and influence in New York and elsewhere. Audiences loved hearing this instrument, and pianists, pianos and piano manufacturers were always in the news.

That very morning in *The New York Times*, there was a report of a large meeting held the previous day of industry moguls from the Piano Manufacturers Association of New-York and Vicinity. Familiar names within the piano world were present there—from Decker, Estey, and Kimball to Everett, Kranich, and Steck. The site of this gathering was the famed Delmonico's restaurant where there was not only the opportunity to discuss business but also to enjoy an exquisite meal, something for which the establishment was well known. The topic of the day was pitch—not just any pitch but the New-York Philharmonic pitch, as it was so named. The assembled group was in agreement that all pianos in the U.S. should conform to a uniform pitch, and this was the version they had chosen. It was somewhat higher in vibrations than others, such as the French diapason pitch, but they believed that their choice was appropriate and that uniformity within the industry was a positive goal. Before adjoining for their meal, however, it was decided that a committee should be appointed to further assess the issue before the final decree was made. Members of this committee included some household names in the piano world—William Steinway and Ernst Knabe being at the top of the list.[16] This was yet another testament to the power of the piano in nineteenth-century America and also of the power of two highly regarded competing instrument brands. Both Steinway and Knabe would integrally figure in the life of the new Music Hall.

Whether or not Franz Rummel was aware of the pitch issue reported that day in the newspaper is anyone's guess. However, he was certainly aware of the importance of specific brands of pianos and of the influence of the top members of the illustrious "pitch" committee—particularly William Steinway. Rummel was a Steinway artist. His name would be included as such, along with a select group of other distinguished pianists, in an advertisement in the inaugural Festival program in May, even though he was not scheduled to perform at that time. Rummel's role, however, in the Music Hall complex would be a singular one. On that particular April 1, he would arguably attract more notice in the musical world than William Steinway, Ernst Knabe, and the star-studded gathering of piano manufacturers.

Franz Rummel had the honor of being the first performer to give a public recital within the new Music Hall building complex. His matinee concert that day was advertised as the "inauguration of the Recital Hall,"[17] and he gave his audience a performance more than equal to the occasion. One reviewer eloquently praised him for his ability to "play with velvet-tipped fingers"[18] as well as to "evoke the thunders"[19] of the piano. It was a landmark concert for a landmark occasion.

Despite the celebratory nature of this event, Rummel has been virtually forgotten over the ensuing years—whether due to the inevitable
passage of time, his low-key stage persona, a career that preceded the age
of recording, or any of a host of other reasons. However, he was a pianist
of distinction in his own era receiving worldwide acclaim for his impressive talent. Admired for his vigor and ability to closely identify with the
composers whose works he played,[20] Rummel was said to have once "elec-
trified the audience" with his performance of a work by Liszt at a Philharmonic Society concert.[21] In addition, his refined personal style, pleasant
temperament, and appealing manners attracted a large social circle of
friends.[22]

Although born in England, Rummel was of German heritage. His
family was a musically active one. After studying in Brussels, he eventually
taught there at its Conservatoire. The accolades that Rummel received in
Europe were truly impressive. Belgium's King and Queen publicly received
him in the State Box after one of his performances, and the royal Courts
of Stockholm and Copenhagen were always present at his concerts. Liszt
warmly predicted the young man's future musical success after Rummel
played some of that composer's works for him.[23] Encouraged by Rubinstein—who also foresaw that he would rise as a "leading pianist" worldwide[24]—Rummel began a serious concert career, traveling widely in Europe
and eventually coming to America.[25]

When he arrived in the U.S., Rummel continued to be an active touring virtuoso. A dozen years before the Recital Hall inaugural, he received
high praise for his Steinway Hall concert, the first of several. His interpretation of Beethoven, Mendelssohn, Schumann, and Chopin earned him
solid appreciation and marked him as a pianist, according to one reviewer,
of "incomparable ability."[26] He was surely known well by audiences and
highly enough regarded to have received several mentions in newspapers
early in 1880 when he fell and broke his leg in Providence, Rhode Island.
This incident rendered him incapacitated and unable to perform his previously booked concerts. Even more eye-catching than the mishap itself
was the marked personal attention that it elicited from the musical world.
Rummel was so well thought of by his contemporaries that a number of
them joined forces to produce a testimonial concert in his honor and in
sympathy for his unfortunate accident. Among them were piano manufacturing czar William Steinway and famed concert artist Julia Rive-King.[27]

At some point during his tours, Rummel met Cornelia (Leila) Morse
from Poughkeepsie, New York, who became his wife in 1881.[28] The daughter of the late Samuel Morse, known for his work in creating the telegraph

as well as the Morse Code, Leila Rummel was a gifted linguist and exceptionally well-traveled as a result of numerous journeys abroad with her famous father. An accomplished pianist, she often played duets with her husband.[29]

Coincidentally, the Rummels were married in the same year as architect William Tuthill and his wife. Each couple had a son who would become a musician—the former a fine concert pianist, and the latter, a composer and professor of music. Similar to both the Carnegie and Damrosch nuptials that were to take place several years later, Franz and Leila Rummel's wedding was also a modest event because of recent family deaths. Their ceremony, too, was decorated with abundant roses—in their case, the generously budding branch of a Marshal Neil rose tree.[30]

Rummel continued to be a busy performer. He had already been lauded for concerts at Steinway Hall just prior to his wedding, where in addition to works by Liszt, Mendelssohn, and Chopin, he also included compositions by Rubinstein as well as by "Mr. Florsheim of this City."[31] (The latter was an interesting programming choice and one that Rummel would repeat again when he performed at the new Recital Hall ten years later.) However, after marrying, the couple moved to England where Rummel continued to concertize. Two months after his wedding, he was praised for a performance of Grieg's Piano Concerto there at the Crystal Palace.[32] Over the next few years, Rummel continued with a hectic concert schedule. In the months before his inaugural concerts at the Recital Hall alone, he appeared at The Lenox Lyceum with Theodore Thomas[33] and at the Madison Square Theatre,[34] among others. Just a few weeks prior to his April 1 concert, he performed in Milwaukee where he was called "a great artist."[35]

Given his prolific experience on the concert stage and his many favorable reviews, it was certainly not surprising that Rummel was the performer to inaugurate the new Recital Hall. However, the details that led to this are not known. He was a favorite with the public, though, and his concerts were much anticipated. The April 1 event was no exception. Of course, a chance to see the new Recital Hall was much anticipated, too.

Tickets to Rummel's performance were priced at one dollar with $1.50 for reserved seating. According to advertisements, they could be purchased at E. Schuberth & Company's store at 23 Union Square. Schuberth's was a well-respected music publishing firm that had its original roots as a New York branch of a Leipzig business and, as a result, issued much European music. It eventually became established in the musically active 14th Street and Union Square area and was the first company in the United

States to publish Victor Herbert's works—not only his early operettas, but also his well-regarded Second Cello Concerto.[36] And it was Edward Schuberth himself who recommended Leopold Damrosch to the Arion Society as a fine candidate for musical director.[37] Without this connection, there was a chance Damrosch might not have relocated to America when he did.

Franz Rummel was scheduled to appear twice at the Recital Hall, both on the 1st and on the 4th of April. In a small entry, *The Times* said that these were his farewell recitals[38]; however, this was not mentioned in other newspapers or Recital Hall advertisements. He did go on tour during that spring, though, with the Boston Symphony Orchestra,[39] and perhaps this was what the news item was referencing. The highly regarded pianist Vladimir de Pachmann's "Farewell Recital" at Chickering Hall was also being performed that week.[40] Farewell recitals appeared to be a good draw. Farewell recital or not, Schuberth had to have done a brisk business in ticket sales—Rummel's audiences were filled. His reputation preceded him—and so did excitement about the new concert venue.

At 2:30 on Wednesday afternoon of April 1, Rummel walked onstage and played the first public notes to resonate in the Recital Hall. It was a long and demanding program that included works ranging from Couperin and Schubert to Brahms.[41] In addition, he performed Beethoven's *Waldstein Sonata* and Chopin's *B♭ Minor Sonata*. Playing these alone on one program would have been sufficiently impressive, but there were many other works that were featured as well. *The New York Times* critic, however, singled out these two sonatas in particular, highly praising Rummel's artistic rendering of both.[42] Already well recognized for his interpretation of the Waldstein sonata, it was later said by a Liszt pupil that in several ways, Rummel played this work even better than Paderewski.[43] Such was Rummel's distinction in this area of repertoire that even his obituary in 1901 noted his expertise in performing Beethoven.[44]

The April 1 program also included a work by Otto Floersheim, the same composer whose works Rummel had performed ten years previously at Steinway Hall. Floersheim was a part of his repertoire, and, to his credit, Rummel helped support the work of local composers in this way. Otto Floersheim (or Florsheim) was a strong advocate of the importance of American composers. He emigrated to the United States in 1875 and became well known for his role as editor of the popular publication *The Musical Courier*. Yet he also received recognition for his compositions, and his works were presented on programs directed by such contemporary luminaries as Theodore Thomas, Frank Van der Stucken, and Anton Seidl.[45]

NEW MUSIC HALL,

CORNER 57TH STREET AND SEVENTH AVENUE,

RECITAL HALL.

FRANZ RUMMEL'S

TWO MATINEE PIANO RECITALS

will take place in the above named new Hall, on

Wednesday Afternoon, April 1st, '91, at 2.30,

AND

Saturday Afternoon, April 4th, at 2.30.

Reserved Seats . One Dollar Fifty Cents
Admission . . . . One Dollar

Seats can now be secured at ED. SCHUBERTH & Co.'s Music Store,
23 Union Square.

Franz Rummel was the first public performer at the Recital Hall on April 1, 1891 (courtesy Carnegie Hall Archives).

The Musical Courier.

PUBLISHED EVERY WEDNESDAY

—BY THE—

MUSICAL COURIER COMPANY.

(Incorporated under the Laws of the State of New York.)

19 Union Square W., New York.

TELEPHONE : - - - 1253-18th.

Cable Address, " Pegujar," New York.

EDITORS:

MARC A. BLUMENBERG.   OTTO FLOERSHEIM.
JAMES G. HUNEKER.   HARRY O. BROWN.
HUGH CRAIG.

BUSINESS DEPARTMENT :

SPENCER T. DRIGGS.   FRANK M. STEVENS.
EPES W. SARGENT.   C. H. DITTMAN.
J. E. VAN HORNE.

EUROPEAN BRANCH OFFICES :

OTTO FLOERSHEIM, 17 Link Str.,
Berlin W., Germany.

LONDON OFFICE :

15 Argyll St., Oxford Circus, W.
FRANK VINCENT ATWATER, Manager.

Cable Address, " Musical," London.

CHICAGO OFFICE : 226 Wabash Ave.

JOHN HALL, MANAGER.

BOSTON OFFICE : 32 West St.
LEIPSIC, GERMANY : GEBRÜDER HUG, Königstrasse 16.
LONDON : Principal London Publishers.
PARIS : BRENTANO's, 37 Avenue de l'Opera.

Subscription (including postage), invariably in advance :
Yearly, $4.00; Foreign, $5.00; Single Copies, Ten Cents.

The *Musical Courier* was a popular publication featuring a variety of musical articles. Otto Floersheim, one of its editors, was also a composer. Franz Rummel performed one of his works at his inaugural Recital Hall concert.

Despite being born abroad himself, Floersheim criticized the advancement of foreign composers over those in the U.S., and he formally proposed the creation of an American Composers' Society.[46] Eventually, though, Floersheim became as forgotten a figure as Rummel himself. At the April 1 recital, Rummel performed Floersheim's work titled "Elevation."[47]

Although Rummel was trying to create a musical atmosphere that was as elevated in artistic suggestion as the title of Floersheim's composition, there were forces working at cross purposes to his goal. A break in the musical spell was upsetting as audience members were continuously being seated during the works in progress. Although there was a notice in the concert program prohibiting this practice,[48] it went unheeded. The distraction was significant. Worse, however, was the noise from the final construction on the main hall above. It was afternoon, and the workmen still needed to do their jobs. Even the reviewers noted how "the pounding of many hammers"[49] offered audible disruption to the more than generous program that Rummel had prepared. Taken in the bigger picture, it was amazing that the construction of the entire complex had come as far and as quickly as it had. Still, finalizing all of the construction details for the official Festival opening was cutting it close, and the Recital Hall was experiencing the backlash of this rush to the finish line. Rummel's concert proceeded, however, as did all of the remaining events of April—despite the competing noise. If nothing else, it was a reminder to all that the main auditorium would soon be open and presenting concerts. The late seating protocol, however, was another issue that needed to be addressed.

The remainder of Rummel's concert included several pieces that were written by composers who, like Floersheim, represented a departure from the more frequently played works of Beethoven, Liszt, and other such familiar names. Rummel was nothing if not diverse in his programming. Salomon Jadassohn and Joachim Raff were among them and, similar to Floersheim, would fade from public memory over the next century. Their works, however, were well recognized in their own era.

Rummel chose to perform *Scherzo* by Salomon Jadassohn who, according to one historian, was once called the "Krupp of composers."[50] Jadassohn was a German who studied in Breslau where the Damrosch family had lived decades before. A onetime pupil of Liszt at Weimar, he eventually became a professor at the famed Leipzig Conservatory. A consummate scholar, Jadassohn created a number of books and manuals for the proper study and understanding of theory, harmony, counterpoint, and form. As a composer, he wrote everything from symphonies and chamber works to piano music.[51]

Swiss-born Joseph Joachim Raff began composing at a young age and was encouraged to send some of his piano works to Mendelssohn who then put in a good word for the young man with his own publisher. This proved to be quite helpful. Raff's subsequent travels brought him in touch with Liszt for whom he worked for several years. Eventually, Raff went into business as a piano teacher and continued composing until he was appointed director of the conservatory in Frankfort. He ultimately received recognition from many quarters for his compositions, even from Walter Damrosch.[52] Rummel's inclusion of works by Floersheim, Jadassohn, and Raff added an appealingly diverse texture to his program. He concluded his concert with the incomparably popular Franz Liszt—two selections from the *Annees de pelerinage: Venezia e Napoli*—the *Gondoliera* and the brilliant *Tarantella*,[53] an especially thrilling piece.

This first recital was thoroughly comprehensive and well received. The critics and the public had been as anxious to see the new recital hall as it was to hear Rummel's performance—they were not disappointed by either. Rummel's playing was called a "genuine pleasure."[54] And the Recital Hall itself was described as "attractive" and "well ventilated."[55] The latter was a particularly striking observation in a review—a well deserved tribute to heating and ventilating engineer, Alfred R. Wolff.

Several days later, on Saturday, April 4, Rummel returned for yet another afternoon in the very same space. It was once more a massive program, enjoyed by another "large audience."[56] While the concert featured many of the same composers, the individual selections were entirely different as compared to the previous recital. Nothing was repeated—certainly a testament to the breadth of this pianist's repertoire.

Even though the Recital Hall was embraced by Rummel and other musical soloists at the very beginning of its existence, it was immediately evident that events other than musical ones were welcomed there. Andrew Carnegie's dream of a multi-use space for the people was quickly becoming a reality. The Recital Hall foreshadowed in miniature what the Main Hall as well as the entire complex would eventually come to represent. The Monday evening following Rummel's second concert served as a prime example as the Grand Army of the Republic (GAR) held a celebration of their quarter-centennial at the Recital Hall. Similar to Rummel's concert, the public was advised that purchases of tickets could be made through the Edward Schuberth & Company Music Store at 23 Union Square.

The GAR was a Union Veterans organization that had been formed after the Civil War and, over the years, grew to include chapters in numerous states with a combined membership that numbered over 400,000 by the time of this particular evening. Ulysses S. Grant and four other U.S. presidents had been counted as members. The group's goals of honoring fraternity, charity, and loyalty were met through regular meetings, projects to help the needy, and work toward building commemorative monuments and ensuring historic preservation. It was an instrumental force in creating the national observance of Memorial Day.[57]

Since this was the organization's silver anniversary, nationwide chapters of the GAR were to hold similar celebrations in various locations on the same night. This event included participation by the Lafayette, Alexander Hamilton, George Washington, and Hancock posts—all local groups within the organization.[58] As Andrew Carnegie had originally predicted, the building would become woven into the history of the country, and this particular evening served as a good initial example since it underlined the impact of past national events while stressing the importance of maintaining noble values in future times.

The occasion was, of course, patriotic, historical, and commemorative in theme. The evening's proceedings included a speech on the influence of the organization at large. There was a recounting of the events of Shiloh. Speeches and readings focused on such topics as loyalty, charity, and fraternity.[59] However, one of the highlights of the evening was an address by Robert G. Ingersoll.[60]

Attending lectures was a popular pastime in the nineteenth century. In an era before mass media and communication, lectures provided opportunities to be entertained, to gain insight into various issues, and to keep informed of current developments on a variety of subjects. The lecture circuit ran the gamut of high profile speakers as well as those who were familiar names on a more local level only. Robert Ingersoll was one of the former. He was well-known in post–Civil War America as a recognized war veteran, lawyer, supporter of civil reform, and Republican Party ally. Major figures from Andrew Carnegie to Mark Twain thought highly of him. Ingersoll's speech in which he nominated Walter Damrosch's eventual father-in-law James G. Blaine for president (and thereby famously referred to Blaine as the "plumed Knight") went down in history. He was a magnetic and much sought-after public speaker and an individual who never failed to engage his audiences—whether the subject was religion or science.[61] The evening prior to the GAR celebration, Ingersoll gave one of his favorite lectures at the Broadway Theatre. The topic was Shakespeare.[62] On this occasion for the GAR celebration, his subject was "loyalty."[63]

Music figured in the program, too, helping to enhance the patriotic flavor of the event with the inclusion of the "Star-Spangled Banner," "Battle

Hymn of the Republic," and "America." The audience was keenly enthusi-astic about the music and sang along with all of the songs' choruses.[64] An announcement also advertised the use of Steinway Pianos. The musicians who performed were an interesting group—violinist Ollie Torbett, pianist Frank Downey, and soloist Gustav Thalberg.[65] Their careers represented the versatility that was the hallmark of musicians during the era. On one evening, they might be performing Beethoven and, on the next, appearing with a popular ensemble at a beer garden.

Torbett was a prime example of this type of versatility. As early as 1885, she was part of a concert program consisting of multiple artists at the University Club Theatre in New York, where a critic singled out her "spirited playing of DeBeriot's 'Scene de Ballet.'"[66] The same year it was announced that she was to be part of the musical company touring with acclaimed American singer Clara Louise Kellogg.[67] And in 1890, as part of the trio of Torbett, Downey, and Thalberg, she received special mention for being "several times encored" on the bill of a variety program in Cali-fornia that played to a packed audience and whose featured headliner was a humorist.[68] Now Torbett was performing in yet another type of pro-gram—a patriotic presentation for the GAR.

All in all, this celebration did not lack in variety on any level. One of its most striking features took place during the performance of "Marching Through Georgia." Individuals from the Lafayette Camp and youth auxil-iary processed to the platform bearing the colors which had covered Sher-man's coffin en route "from New York to St. Louis."[69]

The following afternoon, the echoes of construction hammers returned to the Recital Hall along with the sounds of classical piano music. Arthur Friedheim, one of the most intriguing pianists on the scene, was scheduled to appear several times at the Recital Hall and also frequently elsewhere during the season. Friedheim had studied with Anton Rubinstein in his native Russia and, subsequently, with Franz Liszt. After a less than har-monious initial association with Liszt, the climate improved vastly as the two became better acquainted. Friedheim subsequently became a com-mitted pupil and favorite of Liszt's and, eventually, assumed a post as his personal secretary. Friedheim even went a step further, though, and began closely emulating Liszt's trademark persona on the concert stage—exhibit-ing a wide range of dramatic facial expressions, theatrically tossing his hair during a bow or other strategic moment, and vehemently attacking the keyboard during various musical passages.[70] Aside from his consid-erable pianist talents, Friedheim possessed a distinct talent for showman-ship along the same lines as his famous teacher and mentor.

NEW MUSIC HALL,
Corner 57th Street and Seventh Avenue.
RECITAL HALL.

TUESDAYS, APRIL 7TH AND 14TH,
AND ALSO
FRIDAYS, APRIL 10TH AND 17TH, } AFTERNS. AT 2.30.

Pianist Arthur Friedheim appeared in four concerts during the April 1891 Recital Hall inaugural weeks. He was known for emulating the dramatic stage mannerisms of Franz Liszt, whose works he frequently performed (courtesy Carnegie Hall Archives).

By the time Friedheim took the stage at the Recital Hall—presenting not one, but four programs between April 7 and 17—he already had a career well worth following. He headlined in frequent concerts in a dizzying number of countries—many with performances offered together with his wife, Madeleine, who was both a concert pianist and a singer.[71]

Long before his performances at the Recital Hall, though, Friedheim had an unusual experience directly connected to the Music Hall project, something he spoke of in his autobiography. While still in Europe, Friedheim was a conductor and pianist as well as a composer of significant note with a reputation that was well defined and far-reaching. Subsequently, the famous concert manager Henry Wolfsohn was exceedingly eager for Friedheim to debut in America and make his mark there. Not only did Wolfsohn urge Friedheim to go on tour but, more importantly, he offered him a commission to compose and perform a piano concerto for a very special occasion—the official festival inaugurating Andrew Carnegie's Music Hall in May of 1891.[72]

Wolfsohn was no ordinary manager. He was recognized for having organized the first musical bureau in the U.S. Although he had studied music with Theodore Thomas and others, his true talents were focused on the successful management of concert artists. When his career got underway, his clients included such names as Josef Hofmann, Mischa Elman, and Fritz Kreisler.[73] Wolfsohn had a fine reputation, and it was logical that he had a reasonable degree of assurance to back up his offer. Friedheim specially journeyed to Weimar to meet with Wolfsohn on the matter, and a preliminary contract was drawn up which also encompassed several appearances at the Music Hall—all as a part of its inaugural Festival. Wolfsohn emphasized that for these events Friedheim would play a Steinway, calling it "the greatest piano on earth"[74]—there was always advertising to consider. Whatever the behind-the-scenes circumstances, however, and despite the renown of both concert manager and performer, the proposed plan never materialized. During the course of writing the concerto, Friedheim was told that plans had been altered, and Tchaikovsky would, instead, be conducting his own famous piano concerto for the event. Wolfsohn had to renege on his concerto commission offer but told Friedheim that he would be scheduled, instead, to perform the Tchaikovsky piano concerto in place of the originally agreed-upon work of his own.[75] Friedheim said no to all of it, responding that the altered situation was "unsuitable to an American debut."[76]

Friedheim's actual American debut was held at the Metropolitan Opera House together with Theodore Thomas and his orchestra.[77] This concert was held on March 31, 1891—one day before Franz Rummel's inaugural concert at the Recital Hall. Franz Rummel attended Friedheim's concert,[78] a nice gesture considering the fact that he had a major event to prepare for the next day himself. An advertisement for the Friedheim event clearly stated that Steinway was the piano of choice for his "first appearance in America."[79] The performance included Beethoven's *Emperor Concerto* and Liszt's *A Major Concerto*.[80] Public reception was enthusiastic, although James Huneker, the *Courier* critic and no fan of Liszt, gave a less than favorable review.[81] This stung.

Despite the fact that Friedheim was not to be a part of the opening festival at the Main Hall, a week after his American debut with Theodore Thomas, he appeared in the first of his series of four concerts at the Recital Hall. An advertisement declared that these concerts were being "respectfully announces[d]" by Charles F. Tretbar, Steinway's famed concert manager at that time.[82] A Steinway theme would run through all of Friedheim's appearances in New York—superb advertising for both performer and piano.

Charles Tretbar was an integral part of life at Steinway and Sons. A trained musician with a keen sense of business and of the inner workings of the artistic world, he became close both professionally and personally with William Steinway. Tretbar was such a valuable and trusted figure that he was appointed a corporate officer of the firm when it moved from a family partnership to formal status as a corporation. Beyond this position, he was essential to the organization as its manager of concerts and artists,[83] a time and energy consuming job in itself. Steinway Hall alone was a popular location for concerts, enough to keep any manager busy. However, the firm's roster of artists was lengthy, and they performed in many other venues as well, adding another responsible component to Tretbar's job. The endorsements provided by these individuals were wonderful advertising for the Steinway brand outside of its own walls and even outside the boundaries of the city.

Charles Tretbar was an ardent supporter of Arthur Friedheim, a pianist who maintained a close association with the firm for years.[84] Tretbar cultivated Friedheim and others as they helped to build an association between Steinway and the new Music Hall complex, and it is indicated that Tretbar acted in a managerial capacity in booking Friedheim's Recital Hall concerts there.

Similar to Rummel, Arthur Friedheim did not lack repertoire at his command for all of his performances at the Recital Hall. They ran the gamut from Chopin to Beethoven to Balakirev. He also included many works composed by his teacher and former employer, Franz Liszt, including transcriptions created by the great master—and by himself—of the compositions of Wagner, Mozart, and Bellini.[85] A review of his first recital commented particularly on the "vigor and dash" of an arrangement by Liszt of Wagner's "Overture to *Tannhauser*."[86] Another reviewer also highlighted this work, defining Friedheim's strength as a "Lisztian virtuoso."[87] Both, however, found technical and interpretive faults in some of the other pieces performed.

It was no secret that Friedheim admired Franz Liszt; therefore, it was no surprise that the third in his series of programs at the Recital Hall was entirely devoted to his works. A performance such as this required stamina, and the taxing undertaking in question included compositions such as the *B Minor Piano Sonata*, several transcendental etudes, and a *Hungarian Rhapsody*, among others—a dozen works in all. One critic, obviously not fond of the composer, compared Friedheim's bombastic approach in playing Liszt to the sounds coming from a blacksmith's shop, complete with "blows of the sledgehammer."[88] Perhaps this critic was influenced by the sounds of construction that were still consistently audible from the main hall—a situation for which the manager included a note of apology in the program.[89]

On April 10, the same day as the second of Friedheim's concerts, the Recital Hall was again the site of an event of an entirely different nature. The "University of the City of New York Women's Law Class"—eventually to become New York University—held its graduation ceremonies there that evening.[90] These women were the first to have completed such a course of study. The accomplishments of these graduates were honored at a time when women's achievements were just beginning to become more visible, though still hard won and with a long road ahead. Interest in law on the part of women was growing as evidenced not only by this graduation event, but also by a new group that was advertised in the evening's program. The Woman's Legal Education Society was a group organized the previous year and one committed to offering a dozen annual lectures on law. Among its directors was Mrs. Abram S. Hewitt, wife of the former mayor.[91] This was another indicator of positive changes to come.

According to one rather patronizing newspaper account, the women graduates of this law class were not intending to actively practice law, only to enhance their understanding of the subject. Therefore, they did not pose a competitive threat to their male counterparts. In keeping with this sentiment, the women did not wear traditional graduation gowns but, instead, were in white dresses, resembling the "sweet girl graduate."[92] In reality, some of these women would break this confining mold, entering into law as a profession and succeeding on an equal level with men. Additional class members would achieve high recognition in other endeavors. This event was a beginning, though, and it foreshadowed other women's groups and causes that were to echo both in the nation and throughout the Music Hall building in subsequent decades.

A number of the speakers for the evening came from the group of graduates themselves. Melle Stanleyetta Titus was one of them. She focused on the "Origins of Our Law."[93] Titus was one of the women who would build a professional career, first becoming a lecturer at the school. Several years later, she became the first woman to practice law in New York State as a part of the Circuit Court of the United States in New York's Southern District.[94] Her example of achievement served as a role model for many others.

Mrs. Theodore Sutro was also among the speakers that evening, her topic being "Why I Study Law." She was the class valedictorian, in itself an inspirational accomplishment, and was also a featured piano performer during the ceremony, playing a Liszt *Hungarian Rhapsody*.[95] A versatile and talented woman, Mrs. Sutro had already graduated from the Grand Conservatory of Music in New York before becoming the first woman law student at the University. Also a writer and a painter, she went on to contribute her considerable talents toward charitable, educational, and musical causes.[96]

In addition to other speeches and the presentation of the certificates, there was more music. At the start of the program, the Eden Musee Hungarian Band-Concert Band performed. This group—the first of its kind in the city—was associated with the famed wax works museum, an institution opened in 1884. The band soon became so popular that it was hired for private functions, often for elegant members of society.[97] For this particular event, the group performed pieces by Erkel and Liszt. Although Liszt was quite popular on all concert programs of the day, Ferenc Erkel was lesser known. However, this Hungarian-born composer's work was well paired with the Eden Musee Band, since Erkel had composed that country's national anthem and founded its national opera as well.[98]

Other musical selections included movements from Beethoven's *Piano Concerto No. 4 in G*, performed by Amy Fay and Josephine Bates. Amy Fay was an American pianist who had studied abroad. Her name became especially well known through her popular book, *Music Study in Germany* which contained lively details of her time as a pupil of Franz Liszt. The book became a classic. During her lifetime, Fay concertized,

lectured, wrote for musical journals, and developed "piano conversations"—recitals that included discussions of the repertoire she performed,
similar in approach to Walter Damrosch's piano/lectures. She also became
active in forming and supporting women's musical groups and related
activities over the years.[99]

Josephine C. Bates was a busy pianist as well. A pupil of German
pianist Theodor Kullak, she first performed for New York audiences in
March of 1879 at Chickering Hall in a program which featured her as
soloist in Beethoven's *Piano Concerto No. 3 in C minor*.[100] Bates and Amy
Fay were to perform together again several years after the Law Class event
at a benefit concert in Hardman Hall.[101]

The school's glee club chorus sang a "New York Medley" and two
works by John Wall Callcott—"She Was But Seven" and "Where Are You
Going My Pretty Maid."[102] This particular group—the New York University
Glee Club—was organized in 1873 and made its debut that same year at
Chickering Hall.[103] Chorus and glee club groups were popular during this
era, especially within colleges, and Callcott was among the top glee composers and favored by choruses such as this one.

Of those who appeared at the Recital that April, Frank Damrosch
was to become the most well known. A quieter public presence than his
younger brother, Walter, his contributions to music were still profound.
On the afternoon of April 21, he offered a lecture on the future of school
music, sponsored by the city's Association of Principals of Primary Depart-
ments and Schools.[104] Education was a lifelong commitment for him.

As a young man, Frank Damrosch traveled to Denver where he initially
entered into business. As time went on, however, he re-entered the musical
field, serving as music supervisor in the Denver school system and founding
a chorus within the city. He returned to New York after his father's death
and subsequently became associated with the Metropolitan Opera as its
chorus master, a position he was to hold for a number of years. Before the
end of the 1890s, he became the public school music supervisor in New
York City. It was obvious that he enjoyed working with singing groups. An
active conductor, he assumed leadership of the Oratorio Society in 1899,
a family tradition by this point, and remained there for ten years. He also
organized People's Singing Classes and a companion People's Choral Union,
helping to educate working-class individuals who enjoyed singing and
wanted to learn more about music. Damrosch was perhaps best remembered for his part in creating the Institute of Musical Art, a school that
would ultimately become the famed Juilliard School of Music.[105]

That evening, after Damrosch's lecture, a mixed orchestral/piano concert was presented. A. Victor Benham was the pianist, and the conductor was Frank Van der Stucken.[106] According to one historian, the "Grand Orchestra"[107] was the group that performed. Benham's concert closely followed two other recitals that he had recently given at Hardman Hall—yet another piano manufacturer's concert space, this one located at Fifth Avenue and 19th Street. The Recital Hall program that evening even carried an advertisement for Hardman pianos.[108]

Beethoven's *Emperor Concerto* was a major work on the program. Mendelssohn's "Scherzo" from *A Midsummer Night's Dream*, as well as selections by Gluck, Chopin, and Saint-Saens were also included.[109] A prior advertisement for the concert promised an intriguing addition to the program, stating that Benham would create an improvised sonata based "on given themes."[110] This turned out to be an amazing feat. Benham took a theme from "Don Juan" and spun an entire sonata from it, finishing with an improvised fugue. One reviewer called it a "stupendous performance,"[111] praising not only the stunningly improvised work but also the whole recital as a unique experience. Benham was a young pianist who had studied with both Rubinstein and Massenet.[112] He continued his concert career in New York for many years.

Although his name is not generally remembered today, he had an active concert career after his Recital Hall program, traveling in subsequent years to cities including Berlin, Vienna, Budapest, and Geneva.[113] He also concertized frequently in London.[114] An active teacher, he later held posts as head of Michigan Conservatory of Music[115] and as piano instructor at the New York College of Music.[116]

Similar to Benham, the name of the conductor for this concert, Frank Van der Stucken, has faded somewhat through the years, although a society was later formed in his honor. Born in Texas and relocated during his early youth to Europe, Van der Stucken studied in Antwerp and Leipzig, worked in Breslau, and met Liszt in Weimar. He came to New York and successfully took over the conductorship of the Arion Chorus after Leopold Damrosch's tenure there. Active as the director of numerous festivals and a champion of American music, Van der Stucken was also a prolific composer[117] drawing the admiration of Liszt, Grieg, and others, and attracting critical acclaim. One of his most unique accomplishments was his role as advocate and conductor of many "novelty concerts." These events gave an all-important opportunity for American composers to have their new symphonic works performed for the first time.[118] His name appeared frequently during this era at musical events, and he was invited by Andrew Carnegie to attend the formal inauguration of the Music Hall.[119]

Perhaps one of the most well-known of the pianists on this April Recital Hall calendar was Leopold Godowsky. Years later referred to as "the pianist's pianist,"[120] he was said to have the ability to produce a remarkable sound, although he did not always thrive to his fullest powers in front of a large audience.[121] During his childhood in Russia, Godowsky's musical studies were sparse at best. However, his amazing affinity for music as well as his ability to duplicate compositions he heard on the piano gained him recognition at a very young age. He later went to the Berlin Hochschule and, subsequently, was either taught, coached, or at least played frequently for Saint-Saens in Paris—it was not abundantly clear which was the case.[122] However, the strength of this important musical association has frequently been acknowledged. Godowsky eventually became known for the technically difficult paraphrases he created of the Chopin Etudes.

Godowsky first came to America on tour in 1884 with a violinist from Belgium.[123] Although he went to Europe once more, he returned to the U.S. in late 1890 after a four-year absence, receiving a warm welcome in the American musical world.[124] On his Recital Hall program, Godowsky performed Beethoven's *Appassionata* Sonata, Schumann's *Fantasy in C*, several Chopin compositions, and two Liszt transcriptions of Wagner's works.[125] This was a taxing line-up. However, there was another significant portion of the concert—"assisted by" soprano Emma Heckle. During this, Godowsky collaborated on Schubert Lieder, works by Brahms, Schumann, and Wagner, and a selection composed by the pianist himself—"Absent, Yet Present."[126]

Emma Heckle was an experienced singer by the time of this concert. She had performed in major American cities and also abroad, receiving excellent press reviews. A program for an 1881 performance of Haydn's *Creation* in which Heckle was featured contained quotes from numerous reviews of previous concerts in various cities. "No applause ... was more fully deserved," exclaimed the *Cincinnati Commercial*. And the *Detroit Free Press* felt that the public should be thankful to the hosting organization "for the privilege of hearing her."[127]

In New York, Heckle's musical activities were eclectic. In the summer of 1887, she was one of a dozen singers to perform with Gilmore's Band at his famous Manhattan Beach concerts. This spectacular event, including a chorus of members of American, German, and Italian opera groups, ended with fireworks befitting a Gilmore presentation.[128] However, she also appeared in more formal settings, including at Steinway Hall the February before the concert with Godowsky.[129]

The final event held at the Recital Hall prior to the building's inau-

gural Festival, took place on Monday evening, April 27. The featured performer was Lillie P. Berg. However, a number of other artists appeared on
this program, too. Berg was a soprano and a teacher of voice culture in
New York. She operated a private music school at 231 West 42nd Street.
This was more than just a single-teacher studio. She had other teachers
on staff for both voice and piano and offered advice on selecting additional
instruction in language, art, speech, and other disciplines. Students from
outside New York who wished to study with Berg could arrange to stay at
her home or at another residence selected by her. These details were
arranged by reaching her through the offices of William A. Pond & Company at 25 Union Square,[130] another venerable music publisher and store
that had firmly established roots in the city.

Berg stated that she had developed a system for voice training that
was quite successful and was grounded in the "scientific principles"[131] that
she described in fair detail in her well-presented teaching brochure. Her
course of study for pupils was in-depth and prepared them for performing
in every situation from opera to drawing room events. Hers was a busi-
nesslike enterprise with a clearly stated fee schedule. Twenty private half-
hour lessons with a teacher supervised by Berg cost $30. The same amount
of time with Miss Berg herself was set at $60.[132]

Lillie Berg's own vocal studies in Germany and Milan not only gave
her a solid grounding as a teacher but also supplied her with excellent
opportunities to work as an organist, choir director, and accompanist.[133]
She was nothing if not versatile. She traveled often to London, not only
to concertize and pursue further studies, but also to meet with various
composers to gain a deeper understanding of their works in order to craft
a better interpretation of them. These individuals included Blumenthal,
Tosti, and others.[134]

Her elaborate brochure from the 1890–91 season contained glowing
testimonials in her honor from professors at the Royal Conservatory of
Milan and from famed opera singer Italo Campanini, who would soon be
a major performer at the Music Hall's inaugural Festival. An exhaustive
list of references was also included—ranging from the wives of General
Daniel Butterfield and former New York City mayor William Russell Grace
to Steinway's Charles F. Tretbar and the President of St. John's College at
Fordham.[135] Excerpts from a bevy of concert reviews from New York to
London followed. Berg was a prolific performer, and she had given recitals
locally at Metropolitan Hall, the Metropolitan Opera House, and at private
concert soirees.[136]

By the time of this recital, women were fast rising in the music world, not just as amateur musicians but as professionals, as well. Prior to this, studying music was often considered a "finishing" type of pastime, something that provided elegance and culture to a young woman's life. However, with the rise in popularity of opera in America, there were more opportunities for women singers on the professional stage. Pianists in this sector were also becoming more common, especially after Amy Fay's book was published—a work that underlined the fact that women could, indeed, study seriously and play on the concert stage. Teaching music was also a highly popular field, so much so that women who pursued careers in this area were given a separate job category by the U.S. Census Bureau—with the number of members in this group increasing eight times the original number between the years of 1870 and 1910.[137] This was a serious enough field to have produced several women who founded conservatories of music—including the innovative Jeannette Meyers Thurber, who began the National Conservatory of Music in New York, an institution that boasted many name performers on its staff of teachers. Lillie Berg was among this rising number of professional performers and teachers of serious students of music.

On her Recital Hall program, Berg sang works by Donizetti and Lassen, both accompanied by none other than Leopold Godowsky. The pianist performed a number of other roles in this concert as well. In addition to accompanying Berg in her solo presentations, he also played solo repertoire, most notably the Liszt transcription of Wagner's Overture to *Tannhaeuser*. He joined Berg and violinist Victor Kuzdo for Gounod's *Serenade* and led off the program in a duo piano rendition of Saint-Saens' *Danse Macabre* with Franklin Sonnekalb. The program also presented various ensembles of singers, with Berg joining them in some of the larger works.[138] It was at this concert that the "Lillie Berg Quartette" was featured. The members of this group included Berg, Florence Meigs, Enrico Arencibia, and Chas. H. Bigelow, Jr. Vocal ensembles performed Costa's *Quartette-a Canone*, Pinsuti's *Spring Song*, and Henry Smart's *King Rene's Daughter*.[139] The latter work—referred to as a "pretty cantata"[140] in the *Times*—was sung by a large ensemble, including women of social prominence. In addition to contralto singers Florence Meigs and Agnes Stuart, the group included some familiar names recognizable from the pages of New York history: Dyckman, Riker, Grace, Stebbins, and Ludlam, among them. This was a time when socially prominent women enjoyed becoming involved in the arts. Berg counted some as pupils, and she was evidently glad to share the spotlight with her students. However, at the close of an article about the concert, there were some condescending words directed at the socially visible performers, declaring that if they appeared on the concert platform, that all were required to "bow their heads in awe."[141] Yet the fact that amateurs and professionals graciously blended together on the stage—no matter what their social standing—was something to be noted and applauded, and Lillie Berg deserved praise for her professionalism in organizing and encouraging such an enterprise.

Events subsequent to this concert illustrate just how well regarded Lillie Berg was within the musical community. Not long after the Recital Hall event, she became quite ill for a long time. Serious financial troubles followed. In February of 1893, a group of performers volunteered their talents at a concert with the proceeds designated for Berg's benefit. There were singers, string players, and, notably, pianist Arthur Friedheim, who performed selections by Chopin and Liszt at this event. Together, they raised $1,500 for the ailing Miss Berg, who was able return to teaching the following year and continue in her career for several more.[142]

Although the events of March and April 1891 at the Recital Hall were to be overshadowed by the inaugural Festival presented in the Main Auditorium the following month, they still held a place of singular importance. Some of the names have been forgotten, and some of the groups have faded or changed. Yet their efforts are worth remembering—with a mix of talent, accomplishment, enthusiasm, and versatility that provided a richly textured and inspirational story. Theirs were the first notes performed. Theirs were the first words spoken. Theirs were the performances and events that were first intertwined with the history of the Music Hall itself.

• Four •

Prelude to the Festival

Isaac Hopper's construction team was making remarkable progress. They were reportedly engaged day and night working at full speed toward the completion of the project.[1] Only one year would separate the May 1890 cornerstone laying ceremony from the five-day inaugural opening Festival beginning on May 5, 1891—an event that everyone was waiting for with eager anticipation.

Walter Damrosch was responsible for an increasingly dizzying array of details in preparation for the Festival—from repertoire to soloists to rehearsal plans and more. His Oratorio and Symphony societies would, of course, play a major part in all of these performances, and the January minutes of the Oratorio Society firmly stated that all subsequent rehearsals from that time on would be devoted to practicing the music for the Festival.[2] Name soloists from the opera were also to be featured in many of the works. However, there was special excitement in the air over the imminent arrival of Tchaikovsky. Arranging for him to be a part of the proceedings was a notable accomplishment on the part of Damrosch. Tchaikovsky's presence alone would help to make the event a truly world class occasion. A guest of such recognized stature who would not only be present at the new Music Hall but who would also conduct several of his own works in the bargain promised to be a highlight of mammoth proportions and had the potential to draw positive attention on both local and global levels. Audiences were certainly familiar with Tchaikovsky's music. His *Fourth Symphony* had seen its American premiere with Walter Damrosch during the previous year.[3] And more recently, Theodore Thomas had conducted the composer's *Hamlet Fantasy Overture*. Critic Henry T. Finck, never at a loss to speak his mind, gave this work lavish praise.[4] The public responded in kind to all of it. Now Tchaikovsky, arguably the most impressive musical figure to visit America, would be participating in the high-profile Festival for the new Music Hall.

84

As if preparations for this event and the arrival of its distinguished guest were not enough to occupy his time in the earlier months of 1891, Walter Damrosch was characteristically busy with other activities. He continued presenting the performance/lectures that would be closely identified with him for the remainder of his life. Wagner was one of his specialties. He gave his premiere talk on the first act of *Parsifal* in early 1891[5]—one of a series of lectures that he offered over the course of six weeks in January and February focusing on both *Parsifal* and *Die Meistersinger*. The announcement for this series further explained that Damrosch would hold to his recognized format of providing commentary on the music while performing the relevant examples of the works on the piano.[6] This structure was drawn from his time in Scotland and the many pleasant evenings as a guest of the Carnegies, and it was one that he adhered to with much success over the decades.

Lectures, however, were far from Damrosch's only pursuits. The breadth and variety of his activities ran a wide cultural and social gamut. In early January of 1891, he led his Symphony in a glittering musicale in the home of Mrs. W. K. Vanderbilt. This was a lavish setting by any standards and an event that received detailed attention from the press. The guests were elegant—the women especially so in their beautiful gowns and "flashing jewels."[7] The orchestra played works by Wagner as well as lighter compositions—all performed in the enormous dining hall aglow with illuminated stained glass windows and chandeliers. Special emphasis was placed on the music, though, and Mrs. Vanderbilt insisted that full attention was to be devoted to the performance. It was thoroughly enjoyed by the fashionable audience.[8]

Mrs. Vanderbilt and her wonderful mansion were the epitome of the Gilded Age lifestyles of the rich. From fashion and jewelry to homes and furnishings, opulence was the key word, and a European influence in these areas was treasured. Searching for Parisienne-style gowns and accessories, women shopped the Ladies' Mile in New York. Pearls and diamonds were the adornments of choice, and homes were no less luxurious. Eye-catching paintings and sculpture were favored items on display. Elaborate cabinets and other furniture, some designed by the incomparable Herter Brothers—who also supplied decorations for the Music Hall—filled each room. All of these trappings clearly defined the wealth and status of such prominent families.[9] A musical event such as the one given by Mrs. Vanderbilt with Walter Damrosch and his Symphony further added to her status by visibly demonstrating that she was not just rich but also a connoisseur of the arts. Damrosch, of course, gained visibility for his groups and made important connections in return that often proved helpful in gaining support for various artistic projects. It was no surprise that many prominent members of this social group were eager to attend the upcoming opening of his new Music Hall.

Walter Damrosch, however, was committed to more than just high level society functions and exclusive musical evenings. He did not neglect those who were far from Mrs. Vanderbilt's social scale. His involvement in a series called People's Free Sunday Concerts illustrated his commitment to providing everyone, particularly those from the working classes, with an opportunity to become acquainted with all types of good musical works in a fine setting—and free of charge. Individuals only needed to show their union or Knights of Labor cards to gain admittance to these events. The first orchestral concert in the series was held at Cooper Union on February 2, 1890. Damrosch chose a program that ranged from the "William Tell Overture" to Gluck's "Dance of the Blessed Spirits," to Mendelssohn's "Wedding March." He very much believed in these concerts as a vehicle for bringing music to many audiences, so much so that he refused any remuneration for his services. The audience came from all types of backgrounds. They sat appreciatively silent during the proceedings but shouted bravo in what was reported to be "a dozen tongues"[10] at the conclusion.

By the time the next season of these concerts began in 1891, a mere two months prior to the opening of the Music Hall, the series was so popular that the hall at Cooper Union was filled an hour before the concert began. Once more, Damrosch and his orchestra offered an eclectic array of works—a Liszt *Hungarian Rhapsody*, Mozart's *Ave Verum*, and Nicolai's *Overture to The Merry Wives of Windsor* among them. The audience was also treated to an appearance by opera singer Marie Ritter-Goetz who sang Mozart's "Cradle Song" and other works. Ritter-Goetz was on the roster of featured performers for the upcoming Festival. According to one reviewer, individuals in the audience forgot about their difficult struggles for a while, all smiling "under [the] magic influence" of the music.[11]

Not all was smooth sailing for Walter Damrosch, though. He had not had an easy time of it as his plans for the Festival moved forward. The press, not always kind to the young conductor, hit with full force while he was organizing this event. His detractors not only took aim at him but also hurled vicious attacks at his father-in-law, James G. Blaine, and at Andrew Carnegie as well.[12]

This situation began escalating when the German opera program at the Met was having some difficulties. Walter Damrosch had been asked to conduct the works sung in that language, and, over time, it became painfully apparent that some of the singers assigned to him were not familiar with German or, for that matter, the most compatibly suited to perform this style of opera. Things deteriorated. Sometimes several languages ended up being sung during a given opera and then related issues erupted. The Met decided that the solution was to insist that all works be sung in either French or Italian—even the Wagnerian ones. German opera in German was abandoned for the time being. Damrosch was not happy, and although he had already been planning to leave the company to devote more time to his own groups, this parting was not without a bitter aftertaste.[13]

When Damrosch left the opera, members of his orchestra departed the Met with him. He had a goal in mind for this group, though, and it was a noble enough one. Damrosch hoped to create a permanent orchestra system similar to the one in place in Boston. Careful planning on financial, practical, and artistic levels was required; but, if successful, his musicians could devote their efforts to the Symphony and not be forced to cobble together a living by continually running from job to job. His detractors, however, only saw this in negative terms.

From the get-go, the *Musical Courier* had nothing good to say about this plan. They predicted its failure, their labeling of Damrosch as a poor conductor as their prime reason.[14] Things went from bad to worse when an editorial in this periodical hurled additional accusations. This editorial's ensuing plotline contained sufficient twists to be worthy of an opera in itself. First, it was asserted that James Blaine wished to wreak havoc on the Met for slighting his son-in-law in the German opera debacle, accusing him of funding the expansion of the symphony toward its proposed goal to allow Damrosch to rise unscathed from the operatic ashes. But the claims did not end there. It was further insinuated that Blaine had urged the navy to award Andrew Carnegie a lucrative contract, prompting Carnegie to then also give substantial funds to the symphony himself. The absurd editorial forged ahead, hinting at cover-ups, questionable politics, behind-the-scenes deal making, and more.[15]

Existing circumstances were taken and reported totally out of context, and the allegations were not factual. Of the three individuals slandered, though, Walter Damrosch was the most affected. Blaine and Carnegie were both long experienced with the antics of the press through their years in highly prominent positions. They paid no attention. Damrosch was young and rising in his career, though, having put his whole heart into his musical projects only to see them attacked. It was not a pleasant situation.

However, like Blaine and Carnegie, Damrosch would not dignify these false statements with a comment. He responded in an admirable manner. Still, the press in general continued to delight in criticizing him at every turn. Summed up, they resented the connections he had through family, marriage, genuine friendship, and hard work—all making him an easy target. Although Damrosch was certainly not the only musical figure whom the press attacked over the course of time, he was clearly among the more visible. And as the driving force behind Andrew Carnegie's new Music Hall, that visibility was heightened even further. Added to this was Damrosch's well-acknowledged personal magnetism and ability to attract financing at high levels as well as his energy and ability to organize plans on a grand scale—all at such a young age. These ingredients mixed in a potent combination, and the press was unrelenting in its take on all of it.[16] Still, Damrosch continued with his projects and with his plans, deserving high marks for dealing with the situation in a dignified manner.

Despite the machinations of the press, the excitement over the opening of the Music Hall was undiminished. Once word was out about its luminous nature—complete with the presence of an internationally renowned musical figure—tickets were in high demand. From honest purchasers to scalpers and, eventually, to ushers with an eye to business, it was a sure bet that no seat would go unoccupied on opening night. Subscriptions went on sale April 6 at the Music Hall itself and ran through the 18th.[17] Prices began at $5 in the balcony and went on up to $10 for the parquet.[18] Single tickets opened up on the 21st after subscription sales closed. The public wanted these singles, complaining that subscriptions were unaffordable.[19] Advertisements for tickets sold at Miller's Theatre Ticket office as well as Tyson's Theatre Ticket Office appeared right through opening day,[20] despite the fact that the house was a reported sellout before then.

Almost immediately, complaints of sales to speculators arose along with accusations that management had turned away from acknowledging such activities. Morris Reno eloquently refuted such claims in *The New York Times,* clearly outlining the policy for sales as well as stating that an appointed person was stationed within the building's lobby to turn away known ticket speculators. He, of course, granted that there was little that the management or anyone else could do to stop unknown associates who were acting on said speculators' behalf.[21]

On another level, *The Sun* ran an intriguing ad stating that box seating for the Music Hall Festival was to be auctioned on the evening of March 31 at the Recital Hall—this to be conducted by Robert Somerville of Ortgies & Co.[22] The location of the sale was said to be in the "lecture hall" in another account of the event.[23] This firm usually advertised auctions of fine paintings, books, and other related items; therefore, these tickets were considered to be in a similarly high quality category. The event did not disappoint. Even Andrew Carnegie was there to observe the activities. Premiums were paid for choice seating, and E. Francis Hyde of the Philharmonic Society offered the highest amount for one of these—$210 for a box opposite the stage. Other luminaries were there to bid, including John D. Rockefeller. The prime lower tier boxes brought in $1,600 in premiums alone.[24] Clearly, the auction was successful. With regular sales and auctions and every means of obtaining tickets, all available seats were spoken for well before the May 5 opening night.[25]

While the public was still in hot pursuit of tickets, the Festival's honored guest, Peter Ilyich Tchaikovsky, was embarking on his journey to New York via the steamship *La Bretagne.* This ship was one of four French vessels that had been built in recent years. It was a comfortable ship with many lovely appointments, including interior decorations provided by Allard of Paris. Allard had been responsible for the interiors of Vanderbilt mansions and other such notable projects.[26]

This voyage was an emotionally draining one for Tchaikovsky. At the start of the trip, there were several distressing events that did little to put the composer in a peaceful frame of mind for his upcoming American adventure. He had hoped to see a familiar face on board—the wife of his old friend and former classmate Hermann Laroche. She would have been someone to talk with and a person with a common frame of reference who could have provided a sense of home while on a long journey to a very new place. The woman, however, did not appear. This turn of events, coupled with his immediate sense of homesickness, was acutely distressing. His gloom was only compounded when a fellow passenger committed suicide by jumping overboard and Tchaikovsky, being one of the few people fluent in German, was asked to translate the suicide note. Added into the mix was a round of bad weather—including a hurricane—a bout of seasickness, encounters with some tiresome passengers, and the theft of his wallet which contained 460 gold francs. All of it was overwhelming for the emotionally sensitive man, and he longed deeply for the trip to end and to be able to return to Russia quickly. One of the few ways he found peace was in contemplating nature, and when the weather cooperated, Tchaikovsky enjoyed watching the vast expanse of the ocean, especially at sunset.[27]

On April 26 Tchaikovsky got his first glimpse of New York when his ship docked. From the moment he stepped foot onto American soil, his social life went into exceptionally high gear—even for someone so used to being in the public eye. An eager greeting committee was already at the dock to meet him. Among them were Morris Reno, President of the Music Hall Company; his daughter, Alice; and her unnamed companion. (The newspapers mistakenly thought that Alice was Tchaikovsky's wife.) They were joined by Ferdinand Mayer of the Knabe Piano Company as well as E. Francis Hyde, President of the New York Philharmonic Society.[28]

Linguistically, this was a diverse group. Reno and Hyde were at a distinct disadvantage—their skills limited to English. Hyde smiled, and Reno deferred to his daughter. The nameless young man with the group, thought to be a friend of Alice's, remained silent. Alice Reno's fluency in French, though, made her a real asset to this meeting since Tchaikovsky's English was lacking but his French was quite good. Ferdinand Mayer's presence was also quite helpful since he spoke German, as did Tchaikovsky.[29] The others did their best to communicate however they could, rendering the conversational scene fairly chaotic.

The group headed for the Hotel Normandie where Tchaikovsky was to stay during his time in the city. Located at Broadway and 38th Street nearby to the Metropolitan Opera House, this hotel had been built by Isaac A. Hopper,[30] whose construction company was still hammering the final touches into place at the new Music Hall. Well recognized in its day, the Normandie had opened in the fall of 1884 and was praised for its restaurants and cutting-

Peter Ilyich Tchaikovsky, the famed Russian composer, was invited to conduct several of his works during the Music Hall's opening Festival. He was warmly welcomed in New York and was considered to be the star of this inaugural event (Benjamin R. Tucker Papers, Manuscripts and Archives Division, The New York Public Library, Astor, Lenox and Tilden Foundations).

edge sanitary facilities.[31] It subsequently attracted many high-profile guests, especially musicians such as Hans von Bulow who stayed there during his concert series in 1889. Its convenience could not be denied since part of this series had been performed at the Metropolitan Opera House,[32] a scant block away. Pianist Xavier Scharwenka preceded Tchaikovsky's visit by only several months and had also been an honored guest at the Normandie.[33] The hotel's rooftop had also been the scene of festivities for the official lighting of the Statue of Liberty in October of 1886, with celebratory gun salutes and other patriotic trappings located there.[34] Ironically, the hotel's proprietor was also the Citizens' Auxiliary Committee Treasurer for the GAR, the same organization that had recently held its anniversary event at the Recital Hall.[35]

Now Tchaikovsky needed to settle in at the hotel to prepare for the upcoming days, ones that promised to be busy. Not only was it his first visit to America, but he was also bombarded with fresh sights and sounds as well as with a number of new and eager-to-please individuals with whom it could be sometimes difficult to communicate language-wise. The composer suffered episodes of melancholy, and the overwhelming nature of his initial experience seeing New York, accentuated by his turbulent sea voyage, only added to his distress. He was tired, sad, and homesick. On that first day, despite an invitation from Morris Reno for dinner, he politely asked to remain alone for the evening.

The welcoming group finally departed, and Tchaikovsky stayed for a while in his in hotel room, alternately reveling in his privacy and bursting into tears. Diversion soon came, though, from his immediate surroundings. The composer became deeply absorbed in the wonders of his room—from its electric lighting to the marvels of the bathroom, with its "hot and cold running water."[36] Thereafter, he took a walk along Broadway. Just observing New York was a revelation—its sights and its people providing another fascinating distraction for a while. During the course of his stay in New York, he continually commented on the uniqueness of the landscape—tall buildings intermingled with the ordinary, the amazing length of Broadway, the various modes of transportation, the diversity of the people on the street. Upon returning to his room that first evening, he shed some tears once more before going to sleep.[37]

It would have been difficult for Tchaikovsky to be continually despondent—he was just not given enough time. The dinners, meetings, rehearsals, tours, interviews, and visits were to occupy a staggering amount of his days and evenings. Everyone in America was determined to show the composer just how proud they were to have him as a guest, and the musical community and the press in particular went out of their way to warmly welcome him. He was a celebrity in every sense of the word. It was flattering—and overwhelming.

The morning of April 27 began with visitors. It was Tchaikovsky's first full day in New York, and it was to be packed with activities as all of his ensuing days would be. First, there was a visit from Ferdinand Mayer, a key member of the Knabe piano firm. Mayer talked cordially with the composer, and although his friendliness was sincere, the upcoming weeks would also reveal that he did want to establish a solid association in the hope that Tchaikovsky would endorse the firm's brand of pianos. No one could blame him for this, particularly since it was the Knabe firm that underwrote much of the cost of Tchaikovsky's trip, and they also supplied one of their instruments for use on the opening night of the Festival.[38] This was not as widely advertised as it could have been. A hoped-for endorsement was business as usual with every piano firm during the time and, to Knabe's credit, they did not approach Tchaikovsky immediately with their request.

Knabe was an old and respected company that was created in the

GRAND, SQUARE AND UPRIGHT

PIANOS.

THESE INSTRUMENTS HAVE BEEN BEFORE THE PUBLIC FOR FIFTY-FIVE YEARS, AND UPON THEIR EXCELLENCE ALONE HAVE ATTAINED AN

UNPURCHASED PRE-EMINENCE,

WHICH ESTABLISH THEM

Unequaled in TONE, TOUCH, WORKMANSHIP and DURABILITY.

Every Piano fully Warranted for Five Years.

BALTIMORE:	WASHINGTON:	NEW YORK:
22 & 24 E. Baltimore St.	817 Pennsylvania Ave.	148 Fifth Avenue.

Representatives from this leading piano manufacturer were exceptionally hospitable to Tchaikovsky during his trip to America.

1830s in Baltimore as Knabe and Gaehle, and their quality instruments held their own in the competitive market. They famously received a commission from Francis Scott Key in 1838 to create a custom square piano for use in his home.[39] When the firm opened a branch in New York, they eventually added a concert hall, as did many of the other major piano companies.

Now, Knabe's own Ferdinand Mayer, who had also been a part of the greeting committee at the dock, stopped by to meet with the composer. However, they did not have long to spend in leisurely conversation since Morris Reno and a reporter soon arrived. Lingering, though, was out of the question; since Reno needed to bring Tchaikovsky to the Music Hall.[40] There was no time to be wasted. Mayer walked with them to their destination. This was to be Tchaikovsky's first encounter with the new Hall, and it did not disappoint. It was, in his words, "magnificent."[41]

When the little group arrived, an orchestra rehearsal of Beethoven's *Fifth Symphony* was in full progress with Walter Damrosch at the podium. This was one of the works that he had so painstakingly studied with von Bulow during his trip to Europe several years before, and one for which he had received such a favorable review for conducting upon his return. Tchaikovsky took in the entire scene, noting that Damrosch's attire was informal by European standards—the composer was astounded to see Damrosch conducting without a frock coat. It was a marked difference in custom. That said, Tchaikovsky liked Walter Damrosch from the start, and it was patently obvious that the feeling was returned by him as well as by the orchestra. Loud applause greeted their famous new visitor, followed with a welcoming speech from Damrosch. Once more, there was another eruption of enthusiastic applause. This type of scene was to be repeated over and over in the upcoming days. Tchaikovsky would be left with no doubt that his arrival in New York was greeted with warmth, enthusiasm, and respect.[42]

After these preliminaries, Tchaikovsky had the opportunity to rehearse with the orchestra. Their time only allowed them to focus on the first two movements of his *Suite No. III*, an intricate work that would be performed in the middle of the five-day Festival. Tchaikovsky called the orchestra "splendid."[43]

The day had been eventful already, but it was far from over. Everyone was eager to show hospitality to the composer. After his portion of the rehearsal was finished, Ferdinand Mayer once again took over, bringing his companion to breakfast, gifting him with cigarettes, and accompanying him to buy a hat. As if this was still not enough, Mayer continued their

tour in the Broadway area, making a stop at the Hoffman Bar, a local institution that Tchaikovsky found quite fascinating.[44] It was a place that he
mentioned in his diary and would return to on several occasions during
his stay in New York.

The Hoffman House Hotel, specifically its famous Hoffman Bar, was
a must-see for visitors to the city. The hotel itself had already been up and
running when Ned Stokes, a privileged and flamboyant young man, was
released from prison where he had spent a remarkably short time for
shooting and killing robber-baron millionaire Jim Fisk. The two had had
long-running conflicts over business issues as well as a beautiful actress.
Stokes purchased an interest in the hotel and proceeded to transform it,
placing particular emphasis on its gentlemen's bar. Here, a number of absorbing artworks and decorations were on display, most notably Bouguereau's
famous painting *Nymphs and Satyr*. After being exhibited at the 1873
Paris Salon, it was purchased by an American collector. Thereafter, it
remained for the enjoyment of all for twenty years at the Hoffman House
Bar, intriguing visitors from the everyday tourist to such well-known
names as Buffalo Bill Cody and Ulysses S. Grant.[45] A wide range of notable
and interesting individuals could always be found at the Hoffman House.
During the time of Tchaikovsky's visit, it was there that John Drew signed
a contract with theatre impresario Charles Frohman, helping to seal his
fate as a star.[46]

The space that housed the bar consisted of a fifty-by-seventy-foot
mahogany paneled interior, Turkish rugs, and a brass footrest that set the
tone for similar establishments, although it was arguably at the head of
its class.[47] Tchaikovsky was suitably impressed by the uniqueness of the
setting and its many impressive trappings and returned on more than one
occasion to Hoffman's for a dinner alone. As his time in New York progressed, he craved solitude, and it was becoming more and more difficult
to find. At Hoffman's, though, he appeared to find some occasional solitude and privacy.

Back at his hotel after his time with Mayer, there was little respite.
Morris Reno arrived and thus touched off another round of whirlwind
events—first for a meeting with his family and then on to a quiet dinner
with Walter and Margaret Damrosch at their home.[48] Then, together with
E. Francis Hyde of the Philharmonic, the men proceeded to visit the
Carnegies. It was the composer's first meeting with the benefactor of the
new Music Hall, and he immediately took to Andrew Carnegie and, also,
to his wife Louise, and he was struck by the resemblance between the
millionaire and Russian playwright Alexander Ostrovsky. Previously,

Tchaikovsky had written incidental music to *The Snow Maiden* and a score for an opera based on *The Voyevoda*, both works by Ostrovsky. Therefore, it was a resemblance that would have quickly come to mind, given his close association with the dramatist's writings. The little group spent a pleasant time together that evening, during which Walter Damrosch played many of Carnegie's favorite Scottish tunes on the "excellent Steinway."[49]

Still eager to show the conductor the city and to continue to demonstrate how pleased they were with his presence, Damrosch, Hyde, and Tchaikovsky next visited the Athletic Club. During the Gilded Age, clubs of all sorts were popular. Centered around a common theme—be it ethnic, theatrical, university/school, political, literary, athletic, or other—these impressive establishments offered places to meet, socialize, do business, and pursue activities of mutual interest. Tchaikovsky was amazed by the Athletic Club with its fine facilities. He particularly mentioned its swimming pool. The evening, however, did not end there. The threesome then went for refreshments at what the composer referred to as a "serious club" before, at long last, Tchaikovsky returned to his hotel, thoroughly exhausted.[50] This first day was only an example of what was to follow on this tiring, although thoroughly hospitable trip.

Tchaikovsky never ceased to express his amazement at the open warmth, friendliness, and amiable customs of Americans. He clearly stated in his diary that only in Russia could such equivalent hospitality be enjoyed.[51] Homesick as he was, his hosts gave him little time to amply reflect on this melancholic yearning for Russia, though. His next full day was to be as close to as active as the previous one.

The composer still craved a bit of solitude and was able to take a stroll and eat breakfast alone. But this quiet time was short-lived. An associate of Ferdinand Mayer's collected him and, after another stop at the popular Hoffman Bar, they went together to Knabe's piano store.

However, it was not pianos that occupied their time. Ferdinand Mayer was eager for the composer to visit the studio of the famous and unusually eccentric photographer, Napoleon Sarony. Here, Sarony spent time capturing the likeness of the composer and, also, entertaining him with amusing antics.[52]

Sarony was a leading portrait photographer of the time, his fame akin to that of Matthew Brady. He was equally unique in his art and his personality and enjoyed photographing actors, writers, and others in cultural professions. His roster of famous subjects included Sarah Bernhardt, Oscar Wilde, Edwin Booth, Walt Whitman, Ellen Terry, and scores of others.[53] Sarony's places of business included a well-known location at 37

Union Square that was equipped with a studio, exhibition gallery, and visitors' lounge in what was best termed as a "salon d'art" setting. In 1885,
when he moved to 256 Fifth Avenue, a number of other professional pho-
tographers followed suit, clustering in this new area. The man was obviously a leader in his field. A unique character in dress, behavior, and speech,
he was greatly instrumental in raising photography into a true art, thus
helping it to gain copyright protection.[54] Tchaikovsky was fascinated with
this highly unusual man and was warmed by his friendliness.[55]

As already seemed to be the case, Tchaikovsky was only beginning
another long day's adventures. After their time at Sarony's studio, Mayer
next collected his wife and daughter, and the foursome went on a carriage
ride in Central Park. It was another wonder that impressed their guest.
He called it "superb."[56] Although the land had been set aside for this beautiful park and the formal design and accompanying work begun in the
1850s, it wasn't until 1876 that Central Park opened officially. Its lovely
green lawns, wandering paths, bridges, and lush trees and vegetation were
certain to have appealed to Tchaikovsky, who many times spoke of the
wonders of nature. Here was a refuge from city life and a well-planned
oasis of which New Yorkers were understandably proud. The carriage ride
through the park with the Meyer family was one of the more peaceful
interludes in Tchaikovsky's frenetic day.

The evening, however, was another story—again filled with activities.
The composer accompanied Damrosch, Hyde, the Renos, and the son of
Theodore Thomas to the performance of an oratorio by Max Vogrich—a
work which Tchaikovsky found boring.[57] Vogrich, whose name has been
forgotten today, was an Austrian composer and pianist who had lived in
New York City for a while. During this time, he was active in the Liederkranz
Society and became friendly with William Steinway, who mentions him
in his diary in relation to this group and to social events. Vogrich also
performed at Steinway Hall. As a composer, he wrote operas, cantatas,
symphonies, and other types of compositions over time. The work performed on that particular evening—"The Captivity"—was composed in
1884.[58] It is likely that Damrosch and some of the other members of the
group knew Vogrich during his time in the city or through William Steinway, with whom everyone was acquainted.

The evening included a meal at Delmonico's restaurant,[59] an activity
which perhaps held slightly more appeal than the concert. A New York
institution from earlier in the century, this world-famous establishment
had moved a number of times over the course of many years, with locations downtown, the once-fashionable 14th Street area, and Fifth Avenue

and 26th Street among them. The latter locale raised the restaurant once more to its true height in popularity in the final decades of the century. It was also not without its celebrity lore. Ned Stokes, of Hoffman Bar fame, reportedly broke newspaper magnate James Gordon Bennett's nose on the premises.[60] Elegant surroundings, the rich and famous, and sumptuous food—from oysters to baked Alaska—were *de rigueur*. Tchaikovsky was once more impressed and understandably exhausted.

The days that followed were no more relaxing, but Tchaikovsky was still warmed by the hospitality and enthusiasm of his hosts and of Americans in general. He made special mention of E. Francis Hyde and his wife and of the unique time that they spent together.[61] Hyde had become president of the New York Philharmonic Society in 1888. His interest both in music and in the organization grew long before this when he began going to their concerts in the early 1870s. An acknowledged music lover, he possessed an impressive library of music and took an active interest in events of the cultural world. However, Hyde's professional career was focused on law and business. Together with his brother Clarence, their law partnership specialized in securities, estates, and corporate work. Later, Hyde moved into the banking world, and he eventually became a vice president of Central Trust Company. In addition to his work with the Philharmonic, he was also active in a number of other organizations including the American Bible Society, Princeton Theological Seminary, and the Bar Association.[62]

The New York musical community was a tightly interwoven one. Even though the Symphony Society and the New York Philharmonic were competitors on some level, this did not preclude interactions of its various board members and personnel and did not necessarily suggest any untoward hostility. It was understandable that the Hydes would want to meet and show hospitality to Tchaikovsky, despite the fact that the New York Philharmonic would not be a part of the inaugural festivities at the new Music Hall. Tchaikovsky spoke fondly of both Hyde and his wife saying how they were "soft and kind to me."[63] He also praised Hyde for his obvious efforts to communicate using his limited resources in French and German—mixing a few words here and there in an earnest effort to get his meaning across.[64]

Morris and Marie Reno were also eager to show their hospitality and hosted a formal welcoming dinner in Tchaikovsky's honor. It was an elaborate and beautiful affair with women in evening gowns, lovely flowers, and food. Little framed portraits of the composer were given as gifts to the ladies, and small slates with excerpts of Tchaikovsky's works accompanied the ice cream boxes set aside for the guests. These held room for autographs by the composer. Andrew Carnegie, Marie Reno, and Margaret Damrosch sat near Tchaikovsky. He enjoyed their company and conversation tremendously, although the length of the evening and the amount of food served eventually became overwhelming.[65]

The days following this event saw reporters drop in to see the composer. One of them who received special mention from Tchaikovsky was William von Sachs. Not only did this music critic for the *Commercial Advertiser* visit the composer at his hotel, but he also invited him to tea at his own apartment on May 1.[66] Von Sachs, a pianist as well as a journalist, was praised by the *Musical Courier* for his "polished ... flexible ... sparkling" writings.[67] Tchaikovsky found him "amiable,"[68] and the *Courier* not only remarked on his handsome look but also on his strong and enthusiastic opinions on music. He was quite an admirer of the works of Vogrich,[69] the composer whose oratorio Tchaikovsky had only recently heard performed.

The composer also met with journalist Ivy Ross who implored him to write a piece for her newspaper—*The New York Morning Journal*—with his thoughts on the music of Wagner. Despite his fatigue and busy schedule, he graciously complied. Ivy Ross had joined the paper the previous year. Writing under the pseudonym of Cholly Knickerbocker, she covered society events and did so with the voice of an insider, rather than as a starstruck spectator of the high social scene. Ross was to hold this position for thirty-two years through the paper's transition into the *New York American*. She not only wrote about the society happenings, but was also friendly with the people involved. She covered high-level weddings and interviewed international figures and celebrities.[70] The meeting with Tchaikovsky came during the early part of her career.

As promised, Tchaikovsky completed the Wagner piece for the *New York Morning Journal*, and it appeared on May 3, 1891. He was quite candid, praising Wagner for his impact on the world of music and for his artistic gifts. In an interesting turn, though, he felt that the man's greatest strengths were in his ability to write symphonic type music as illustrated in the prelude to *Lohengrin* and other similar works. He believed, however, that in writing for the opera Wagner fell short, not able to translate the same musical qualities into works for voice as he could for instruments. Tchaikovsky also decried what he referred to as "Wagnerism"—or a denial of all other major composers in favor of this one man.[71]

There were many other visitors aside from reporters who showed up at Tchaikovsky's door in the ensuing days. One who received special mention in his diary included "Mrs. Wilson." She was the pianist Helen Hopekirk Wilson, who not only visited Tchaikovsky at his hotel, but also played for him at a tea hosted by William von Sachs. A pianist and composer born in Edinburgh, she performed under the name of Helen Hopekirk. After studying in Europe with Salomon Jadassohn and others at the Leipzig Conservatory, she played many concert tours in Europe and the U.S., making her American debut in Boston in 1883. Her repertoire was extensive, and the *Boston Evening Traveler* stated that it was only rivaled by Rubinstein.[72] She was married to her concert manager, William A. Wilson, and the couple eventually moved to Boston in the late 1890s where Hopekirk joined the faculty of the New England Conservatory of Music[73] and became a part of the famous Boston composers' circle of the day, a group which included George Chadwick, Amy Beach, and others.[74] Although Tchaikovsky found her a tiring visitor the first time they met, he enjoyed and admired her performance of Borodin's *Serenade* on the piano on this occasion.

Tchaikovsky had the opportunity to meet with the Oratorio Society chorus several days after his arrival. It was as warm a welcome as the one that he had received from their counterparts in the Symphony. An enthusiastic ovation rang through the Hall upon his arrival at the 8:30 rehearsal. At the end of the session, he praised their singing with sincerity.[75]

On the same evening as the rehearsal, Tchaikovsky made special mention of meeting not only William Tuthill, whom he referred to as the "amiable architect," but also his chief assistant, Waldemar R. Stark (or "Starck")—a man who received high praise from Tuthill for his professional abilities. The composer was to learn that Stark was a Russian-turned-American citizen as well as a socialist and an anarchist. They had an opportunity to converse in Russian after which they promised to meet again.[76] Not much has been recorded about Stark; but aside from his obvious talent in the architectural field, he also supported those who spoke out against tsarism. He was said to have been the patron of *Znemia*, a fairly short-lived publication created by Louis Miller that featured articles composed by Russian exiles. Although the readership of this and other related Russian periodicals consisted mainly of a Jewish population, Stark (or Staleshnikov, as was his original Russian name) was not Jewish, but was certainly sympathetic to their plight in Russia and elsewhere.[77]

During this busy pre–Festival time, Tchaikovsky was also taken on sightseeing visits. These ranged from the cultural—Schirmer's music store—to the financial—the Stock Exchange and the Federal Reserve. At the latter site, the composer was amazed upon seeing the labyrinth of vaults and was permitted to hold a stack of new bills worth a fortune.[78] This special treatment attested to his fame. There were also additional concerts to attend, such as the one at Chickering Hall given by Charles Santley, a once popular English baritone appearing in his only New York concert during this time period.[79] Ferdinand Meyer had insisted they go. In Tchaikovsky's opinion, the performance fell short in depth of expression, but Santley was received with friendly enthusiasm by the audience, obviously long-time fans. Although his voice was no longer at its peak, the crowd thoroughly enjoyed and supported him.[80] While there, they were quickly intercepted by Henry T. Finck and several other critics for additional social conversation.[81] And still, all of this activity was interspersed with an overabundance of dinners, given at every opportunity—including gatherings with the Renos, the Damrosches, and the Schirmers.

With all of the many tours, dinners, visitors, and social engagements, it seemed almost impossible that Tchaikovsky would be able to concentrate on his music. And time was required for the rehearsals needed to prepare for his portions of the Festival. When these rehearsals took place, there were associated stresses to be dealt with, some of which caused marked frustration for Tchaikovsky. First, there was the extraneous noise factor. The pounding of hammers and sounds from the work crews were still audible, just as they had been during the opening concerts at the Recital Hall in earlier weeks. From the point of view of the construction team, there were many last-minute details to attend to and much to get ready in the final days before the first gala concert. They had a job to finish. However, these sounds were disturbing for everyone, especially Tchaikovsky. Then there was the cumulative fatigue of the entire group to be considered, as well. The May 2 session, in particular, caused "a terrible effect on my nerves,"[82] confessed Tchaikovsky. All of these factors combined made the some of the final days of the rehearsals less than successful. Not everything was able to be practiced as it should have been, and the time for the actual performances was drawing perilously near. Stress was becoming accentuated.

However, in the midst of this seeming chaos, the evening prior to the May 5 inaugural day itself was a quiet one. Tchaikovsky had dinner with the Renos—in the "family circle," as he referred to it. He gravitated toward the warm, comforting atmosphere they created. Walter Damrosch visited afterward, and the composer "played four-hand" with Alice Reno.[83] It was an enjoyable evening, one of relaxation, and a pleasant way to pass the time before the big day ahead.

FIVE

Opening Night—Tuesday
May 5, 1891

Lights were blazing everywhere. Their high-wattage energy was matched only by the excitement of the crowd. Carriages choked the streets, impatience growing as the waiting line grew to the quarter-mile mark on West 57th Street. Their passengers were eager to arrive at their destination. "All was bustle"[1] while the police officer on the street was having a tough time of it as the crowd continued to swell in number, their individual faces outlined with distinction in the splash of brilliant illumination. It was May 5, and the new Music Hall was ready for its opening night. The cultural landscape of New York and the world would change forever.

In his diary, Tchaikovsky freely admitted to worries over the gala evening's events.[2] Being given few idle moments to collect himself during the day surely had not helped. It was his first visit to America, and he was scheduled to conduct on the opening night of the widely publicized new Music Hall, all in front of a dazzling array of luminaries included in the "audience of five thousand"[3]—perhaps a somewhat over-estimated figure, although the size still promised to be staggering in number. His socially packed day had been interminable and only served to heighten his stress.

The morning began well enough with a relaxing interlude during which the composer took a few minutes to chat with a servant who brought him tea. Max was Russian and had also once lived in Germany. Tchaikovsky craved some connection to his homeland; but after being abroad for a while, Max's Russian language skills were rusty. No matter, he and Tchaikovsky enjoyed their conversation in whatever Russian the young man could muster.[4] Yet, after this, the day grew more wearisome.

As proved to be the norm by this point, visitors began arriving in rapid succession to see him. Franz Rummel headed the list that day. He

MUSIC FESTIVAL

In Celebration of the Opening of

MUSIC HALL

CORNER 57TH STREET & 7TH AVENUE,

MAY 5, 6, 7, 8, and 9, 1891.

The Symphony Society Orchestra,

The Oratorio Society Chorus,

BOYS' CHOIR OF 100, (Wenzel Raboch, Choirmaster.)

AND THE FOLLOWING ARTISTS:

P. TSCHAIKOWSKY, the eminent Russian composer, who will conduct several of his own works.

FRAU ANTONIA MIELKE, Soprano,
MLLE. CLEMENTINE DE VERE, Soprano,
MRS. GERRIT SMITH, Soprano,
MRS. TH. J. TOEDT, Soprano,
MISS ANNA LUELLA KELLY, Soprano,
MRS. KOERT KRONOLD, Soprano,
FRAU MARIE RITTER-GOETZE, Contralto,
MRS. CARL ALVES, Contralto,
MRS. CLAPPER-MORRIS, Contralto.

SIGNOR ITALO CAMPININI, Tenor,
HERR ANDREAS DIPPEL, Tenor,
MR. THOMAS EBERT, Tenor,
HERR THEODOR REICHMANN, Baritone,
HERR EMIL FISCHER, Bass,
HERR CONRAD BEHRENS, Bass,
MR. ERICSON BUSHNELL, Bass,
FRL. ADELE AUS DER OHE, Pianist.
MR. FRANK L. SEALY, Organist

WALTER DAMROSCH,   -   CONDUCTOR.

THE MUSIC HALL COMPANY OF NEW YORK, Limited.

MORRIS RENO, President.

FREDERICK WILLIAM HOLLS, Secretary.   STEPHEN M. KNEVALS, Treasurer.

DIRECTORS.

John W. Aitkin,	Frederick Wm. Holls,	Sherman W. Knevals,
Andrew Carnegie,	Wm. S. Hawk,	Morris Reno,
Walter Damrosch,	Stephen M. Knevals,	William B. Tuthill.

A summary of the Festival performers as well as of members of the Music Hall Company (courtesy Carnegie Hall Archives).

came with a request that he was to make more than once—namely, to beg Tchaikovsky to conduct at one of his upcoming concerts while the composer was to be on tour in the U.S. Tchaikovsky needed to decline. Close on Rummel's heels was a reporter, a friendly sort, who was still under the impression that Tchaikovsky had a wife with whom he had traveled to New York.[5]

A solitary lunch at the hotel and a walk on Broadway followed, but a subsequent few stolen moments at a café offered the composer no peace. A chance meeting with Anton Seidl disrupted his solitude with another unwanted conversation. A highly praised individual, Seidl had been an assistant to Wagner and a prolific conductor in Europe before joining the Metropolitan Opera as a conductor in 1885. He would soon begin leading the New York Philharmonic in 1891 and, with them, would later receive acclaim for the premiere of Dvorak's *New World Symphony* at the Music Hall in 1893. Despite being a Wagnerian specialist and having presented the American premieres of several of the composer's operas, Seidl performed the music of a wide range of composers.[6] He was, of course, especially eager to chat with Tchaikovsky. Pleasant though this conversation might have been, it allowed for little relaxation.

Even after returning to his rooms, Tchaikovsky could not enjoy a few moments to himself. A fellow traveler from his steamship journey to New York appeared with a request for money, claiming that he had been robbed in Central Park. Elements of the man's story did not exactly ring true, and Tchaikovsky decided to talk with Morris Reno before getting involved any further.[7] Tranquility was obviously in short supply. As the evening approached, Tchaikovsky's mixture of anxiety and anticipation grew to a new high, exacerbated by the busy day and, in part, by his previous visitor. Finally, Morris Reno's son-in-law, Leon Margulies,[8] arrived at the hotel to escort him to the gala opening concert.

Several years previously, Margulies had married Anna, the oldest daughter in the Reno family.[9] Although he was not much in the spotlight during the Music Hall's building project and the gala opening preparations, his connection to its people and organizations was increasing, and by the time of the inaugural Festival, he was acting as Morris Reno's secretary.[10] More responsibilities were to follow in subsequent years.

However, on the evening of May 5, Leon Margulies had been sent to accompany Tchaikovsky to the Music Hall. With little fanfare, they rode an "overcrowded trolley"[11] to their destination. Although perhaps a welcome diversion from the anxieties of the day, it seemed a fairly low-key means of transportation for such an important guest on so momentous an occasion. The scene became more magical, though, at the moment they caught sight of the "brilliantly lighted"[12] new building, now teeming with people. The Music Hall, which Tchaikovsky deemed "unusually impressive and grand,"[13] appeared before them in all of its opening night splendor.

The Music Hall was definitely the place to be that evening. Other top-drawing events could not compare—not even *Work and Wages* at the

Grand Opera House, *Beau Brummell,* with the highly popular Richard Mansfield at the Garden Theatre, or the farewell performances of *Poor Jonathan* playing at the Casino.[14] In addition, *Mr. Wilkinson's Widows* at Proctor's was marking its fiftieth performance, and in celebration of the event, the incomparable producer Charles Frohman had arranged to distribute souvenirs to the ladies in attendance—fine silk opera cases with enclosed powder pouches.[15] Still, there was little comparison. No ticket was more desirable that evening than one for the opening of Andrew Carnegie's new Music Hall—as proven by the size of the crowd gathered outside.

This eager audience had been waiting early on, and when the doors eventually opened, it was fortunate that the staff hired for the evening was comprised of Metropolitan Opera workers—all of them savvy in dealing with crowds. Otherwise, the atmosphere would have been totally chaotic.[16] The seats were totally filled, and although tickets had long been sold out, some individuals bought admission at the door and "cheerfully stood" in any open space.[17] Many did their best to bribe ushers to gain entrance to the Hall. Some were successful.[18] Despite this seeming disorder, when everyone was inside, a certain air of dignity took hold. The crowd was in awe of its new surroundings.

The spectacular electric lighting was a continual topic of conversation on that evening and well beyond, praise going to its "4,000 electric lamps," all well placed throughout.[19] Additional accounts placed the number even higher. The beautiful illumination enhanced the decorations of "white, salmon, and gold,"[20] and its cumulative effect on the total atmosphere was stunning. The lighting helped the audience to appreciate these visual aspects of the hall as they studied them from their comfortable seats—at least those who did manage to have secured seats.

Although the audience was well dressed and many in attendance were among the city's more wealthy and notable, there was not the same emphasis on clothing and accessories alone that had been more traditionally prevalent at the opera. The attendees, however, certainly did cut admirable figures, and one newspaper deemed them "finer"[21] overall than some opera crowds—it was, after all, opening night. However, the audience was particularly focused on the new hall, its music, and its special guest.

The advertisements by upscale establishments in the evening's program booklet, though, indicated that reasonably high-level ticket holders were expected to be attending, especially those in the choice box seats. In one of the booklets, three firms shared the final page ads, obviously appealing to the numerous tastes of an upscale clientele. Among them was the refined Theodore B. Starr establishment at Fifth Avenue near 25th Street, where silverware, jewelry and precious gems, as well as bronze and porcelain items were a part of their appealing stock. Another ad was devoted to Schaus's Art Gallery near Madison Square. It advertised works by Gerome, Meissonier, Daubigny, and others that would nicely adorn the rooms of a fine mansion. Finally, B. Altman & Co., a fixture in the Ladies' Mile shopping district on Sixth Avenue, carried a half-page ad for "imported costumes" as well as for dresses made to order[22]—perfect for women who enjoyed wearing the latest styles that were in vogue on the international scene.

The sought-after box seats were occupied by those who would have read these advertisements with some interest or at least a passing knowledge of the businesses they featured. Notable personalities filled these places in honor of the occasion. Andrew and Louise Carnegie were seated in Box Number 33. This grand hall was his gift to the city's music lovers,[23] and throughout the evening the audience would continually show its appreciation for this gesture. The Carnegies were joined by former mayor Hewitt and his wife; the Reverend Mr. Eaton, who had presided at the Carnegie's wedding ceremony; and Alexander King.[24] King was a long-term friend, also of Scottish heritage, who years before had introduced Andrew Carnegie to Louise and her family.[25] Observers saw Carnegie "dashing around" before the concert with his usual display of energy, quickly visiting several other boxes to greet guests he knew.[26] The evening belonged to him as much as to anyone, and he was clearly enjoying it.

In another box, Margaret Damrosch was seated with her sister and their parents. The press took special note that her father, Secretary of State James G. Blaine, was not only in the audience but was also Walter Damrosch's father-in-law. For the Carnegies and the Blaines, there were attractive arrays of red roses adorning the railings of their boxes,[27] and applause greeted both men as they took their respective seats.[28] Carnegie, however, received a standing ovation.[29]

A glittering array of the well-known filled additional boxes. They included John D. Rockefeller; Mr. & Mrs. William C. Whitney; E. Francis Hyde, President of the Philharmonic Society; and various directors of Carnegie's Music Hall Company—William S. Hawk, Sherman Knevals, and Frederick W. Holls, among them.[30] The impressive list continued: retail businessman William J. Sloane; Columbia University president Seth Low; and Met Opera managing director Edmund C. Stanton.[31] There were also friends of Andrew Carnegie who came from Pittsburgh specifically to hear the performance—among them were H. C. Frick, Pittsburgh Art

School president John W. Beattie, William L. Abbott, and Cornelius N. Bliss.[32]

Of course, William Steinway was also a boxholder.[33] Even though he had been initially skeptical about the new Music Hall when the idea was first announced, he was far from reluctant to occupy prominent seating on opening night or to have his piano associated with the new concert space. In a souvenir program, the first full-page advertisement was for "Steinway Grand and Upright Pianos," with the location of their warerooms and concert hall on 14th Street duly noted, along with both London and Hamburg addresses. Also well featured in this advertisement was a listing of artists who endorsed the Steinway brand. It was impressive. From leading composers Hector Berlioz and Charles Gounod to such concert pianists as Rafael Joseffy and Anton Rubinstein to conductors Theodore Thomas and Anton Seidl—the names alone were enough to elevate the reputation of these pianos. Among them were those who were recently a part of Music Hall news, including Franz Rummel and Arthur Friedheim, who had appeared at the Recital Hall in April. Adele Aus der Ohe was included, as well.[34] She was scheduled to perform on the closing day of the Festival as soloist in one of Tchaikovsky's most anticipated works. William Steinway was perceptive enough to realize by this time that the new Music Hall was not to be lightly dismissed and that many international musicians would fill its stage in the years to come. Obviously, he wanted them to use and endorse his piano. Securing opening week advertising was a step in the right direction. By now, he was convinced of the value of this new space, and in his diary he pronounced it "glorious."[35]

There was a Steinway competitor that was not to be outdone. William Knabe & Co. filled the next page of advertising, listing their locations at Fifth Avenue near 20th Street in New York, as well as in Baltimore and Washington. Similar to Steinway, the firm emphasized their excellent grand and upright pianos and, in addition, their line of square pianos. Although no names of endorsement were included, Knabe stressed its service to the public for over half a century, proudly describing their product "unequalled" in many ways—"tone, touch, workmanship ... durability."[36] It was a modest and tasteful advertisement. Few, though, would have taken issue with something more forthright in nature, particularly since Ferdinand Mayer of the firm had been quite kind to Tchaikovsky during his stay in New York and since the company had also absorbed much of the expense of this trip. In addition, they provided a piano for the Music Hall's opening night.[37]

Tchaikovsky was settled into one of the box seats during the first part of the program. His own role in this performance would not take place until after the intermission. Now he shared the space with the Reno family, individuals of whom he was especially fond.

Damrosch family members were not in the audience. Instead, they were onstage with the Oratorio Society. Helene Damrosch's lovely voice was an important part of the soprano section, just as it had been when her husband had formed the organization almost two decades previously. Joining her were her three daughters—Marie, Clara, and Ellie. Helene's sister, Marie Heimburg was also part of this group. She had been with the Oratorio Society since its inception,[38] and during its early years, she had performed solo parts in its productions of Brahm's *German Requiem* and Mendelssohn's *Elijah*.[39]

All of the concert's participants were assembled onstage long before the necessary time,[40] and the space was an impressive sight filled with chorus and orchestra members. Three hundred women singers,[41] all in "pure white" dress, occupied the five rows of raised seating[42] in a curved formation.[43] Later, Andrew Carnegie referred to them as an "array of beau-

A historic sketch of the opening night audience.

tiful angels.”[44] Behind them were the two hundred members of the men's chorus. The Symphony Society Orchestra occupied half the stage, forming a semi-circle around the conductor's podium.[45] Together, they produced an unforgettable and dramatic sight.

At 8:00 p.m., the signal for the beginning of the festivities was given—a flash of electric lights. The entire hall was illuminated, brilliantly spot-lighting the well-arranged performers in a visually striking fashion. An audience observer later commented on the amazing power of the electric lights to heighten the effect of this total scene so that each chorus member seemed to be etched individually on the stage. Any movement or action—the wave of a hand or the nodding of a head—would have been especially noticeable to the audience and could have detracted from the appreciation of both the visual and aural aspects of the performance. However, the chorus was serene, presenting a professional and aesthetically striking tableaux.[46]

At last, all was ready.

Suddenly, enormous applause broke out as Walter Damrosch entered, taking the stage to conduct the opening piece—"Old Hundred." The grand swell of chorus, orchestra, and organ was an inspiring start to the evening. This was a well-known hymn, and, according to *The Sun*, many in the audience rose and sang with those onstage,[47] joining in the familiar words that praised "God from whom all blessings flow."[48] It was a work that was often performed at special events or concerts, and, on this night, it had a distinct meaning—a musical expression of gratitude. These were the first public notes to resonate in the main Music Hall.[49] Loud applause followed.

Morris Reno was the next to appear. Tchaikovsky had empathetically noted that Reno was especially worried about giving his introductory speech that evening.[50] Now the moment had arrived. His was not a long talk. Reminiscent of his address at the cornerstone laying ceremony the previous year, Reno welcomed everyone and spoke of the high hopes for the new hall, declaring that it would be a place of memorable "artistic triumphs" since it had been created with exceptionally high ideals.[51] He then introduced Bishop Henry Codman Potter, the individual who would officially dedicate the hall.

Unlike Reno, Potter was not reluctant to take his place on the new stage and speak. The Bishop of the Episcopal Diocese of New York, Potter was a highly regarded clergyman and familiar public figure and also one who was quite active on behalf of various social causes. A liberal theologian, he fought to help the poor, the working classes, and the oppressed.[52]

His was a unique position as a leader in the affluent Episcopal denomina-
tion. He had both the ability and the flexibility to associate with those of
wealth, while at the same time advocating with effective results for the
many at the other end of the social and economic scale.[53] No stranger to
other great moments in New York City's history, he had offered the benediction at the Statue of Liberty's dedication five years previously and was
a key figure in planning and fundraising for the eventual building of the
landmark Cathedral of St. John the Divine.[54] He also contributed the opening prayer at the cornerstone laying ceremony for the Washington Square
Arch in May of 1890—joined by Frank Damrosch, who led a chorus as
part of the festivities.[55] Bishop Potter was a busy man. He had even conducted a wedding service earlier that same afternoon for the Rector and
a choir soprano from the Church of St. John the Baptist.[56]

According to many accounts, including Tchaikovsky's, the Bishop's
speech was rather lengthy. In the meantime, a restless audience was impa-
tient to get to the musical heart of the program. Potter continued to wax
eloquent, though, leaving no stone unturned in honoring those who had
paved the way for the Hall to be built and in describing the institution's
lofty mission and potential. He outlined more
than an ample amount of the history of the
major musical groups in New York, going
back to the roots of the Arion and New
York Philharmonic societies, reviewing the days when Carl Bergmann
had served as conductor of both. He
then moved on to praise Leopold
Damrosch and his great achievements in creating the Oratorio and
Symphony societies as well as his
infinite musical and directorial talents. There was applause from the
crowd at each mention of Damrosch's name. Theodore Thomas was
briefly and smoothly included and in
a very positive way. Despite his rivalry
with the elder Damrosch, he had been an
integral part of New York's musical
world and was due recognition for
his role in its history. Potter continued on, happily expounding on

**Bishop Henry Potter gave the mem-
orable dedicatory address to officially
open the Music Hall.**

music's purpose: for recreation, inspiration, and the conveyance of ideals that mere language was incapable of handling.[57] The Bishop was nothing if not thorough.

All was not totally dry, though. While speaking of the city's need for such a high class and appropriate music hall as the one that was opening on that very evening, Potter showed a flair for entertaining humor. It was unfortunate, he noted, that prior to this moment, great music was sometimes heard in less than dignified edifices—where perhaps the previous evening a clown had performed, a prize fight had been staged, or circus-variety performers had "swallowed dinner knives" or "jumped ... through balloons."[58]

He went on to liberally praise Andrew Carnegie for his work toward the completion of this and so many other worthwhile projects—all so significant in ensuring the happiness of so many.[59] At last, Potter dedicated the concert hall to "the noble ends" for which it was intended,[60] formally declaring, "I pronounce this building open."[61] At the conclusion of the speech, everyone stood while a stanza of "America" ("My Country Tis of Thee") was sung by the choruses and the audience.

During this time period, "America" was considered to be the country's national anthem. The words to this beloved song had been penned as a school song by the Reverend Samuel Francis Smith in 1831 at the request of Lowell Mason. Believing it to be a patriotic German tune, Mason was unaware that it also served as the melody for the British anthem "God Save the King." The American version of the song premiered at a Boston Fourth of July celebration for children.[62] Thereafter, it was performed on important occasions such as the one being held that evening and had also been heard at the dedication ceremony for the Statue of Liberty five years previously.[63] It was only in 1931 that the "Star-Spangled Banner" was declared the country's official national anthem.

The dedicatory portion of the evening was now concluded, and the audience would finally be treated to some of the music it had been eagerly anticipating. Walter Damrosch once more raised his baton to much additional applause. It was time for Beethoven's *Leonore Overture No III*.

This piece had a long history and was originally intended as an opening to the opera *Leonore*, later called *Fidelio*. Beethoven created four versions of the overture in the span of a decade. *No. III* eventually stood alone as a composition that could be performed as a complete and independent concert piece. In the context of an opera, though, its length and content did not quite strike the right balance, overshadowing or prematurely foretelling the action onstage. Years later, Mahler and other conductors tried

PROGRAMMES.

TUESDAY EVENING, MAY 5TH, 1891.

"OLD HUNDRED."

ORATION. DEDICATION OF THE HALL

By the RIGHT REVEREND HENRY C. POTTER, D.D.

NATIONAL HYMN, "AMERICA."

OVERTURE, "LEONORE" No. III, ... BEETHOVEN

INTERMISSION.

MARCHE SOLENNELLE . . . . . . TSCHAIKOWSKY

Conducted by the Composer.

TE DEUM, ... BERLIOZ

(First time in New York.) For Tenor Solo, Triple Chorus and Orchestra.

SOLOIST—SIGNOR ITALO CAMPANINI.

WEDNESDAY EVENING, MAY 6TH, 1891.

ELIJAH," Oratorio for Soli, Chorus and Orchestra, . . . MENDELSSOHN

SOLOISTS

FRAU ANTONIA MIELKE, MISS ANNA L. KELLY, FRAU MARIE RITTER-GOETZE, MISS MAC PHERSON,
HERR ANDREAS DIPPEL, MR. THOMAS EBERT, HERR EMIL FISCHER, MR. BUSHNELL.

THURSDAY AFTERNOON, MAY 7TH, 1891.

OVERTURE TO "FIGARO," . . . . MOZART

GRAND FINALE, ACT II, "FIGARO," . . . . . MOZART

FRAU MIELKE, MLLE. DE VERE, FRAU GOETZE, HERR DIPPEL, HERR REICHMANN,
HERR FISCHER, HERR BEHRENS.

SUITE No. III, for Orchestra, ... TSCHAIKOWSKY

Conducted by the Composer.

ARIA FROM L'ESCLARMONDE, ... MASSENET

MLLE. DE VERE.

ARIA FROM "LE ROI DE LAHORE," . . . . MASSENET

HERR THEODOR REICHMANN.

PRELUDE AND FINALE FROM "TRISTAN AND ISOLDE," . . . WAGNER

A page from the program booklet for the Festival, listing the repertoire and performers for the first three concerts (courtesy Carnegie Hall Archives).

inserting it before the final scene. However, this drained power and drama from the conclusion of the opera. Beethoven's first version of the *Overture*, subsequently referred to as *No. II*, was used in the opera's initial performance in 1805. He later re-worked both opera and *Overture*, composing the dramatic *No. III* to be performed in its place. Eventually, he wrote yet another overture that was more suitable for operatic purposes. By this time the title of the opera had been changed to *Fidelio*. Another version of the *Overture* was discovered after Beethoven's death and mistakenly thought to have been an earlier version; hence, it was labeled *No. I*.[64] Beethoven felt that audiences did not understand *Fidelio* as an opera, but he also believed that in time, its merits would be realized. He did state, however, that while he recognized the value of *Fidelio*, he was in his "true element" when working within the symphony form.[65]

The *Overture No. III* is a work that stands on its own. It traces the complete dramatic range of action that takes place over the course of the opera itself—from the wrongful imprisonment of Florestan to the heroic actions of Leonore, his wife, who develops a plan to rescue him before he is killed.[66] The piece proceeds solemnly, reflecting Leonore's descent into the prison where her husband is confined. His lament follows as does a dramatic development in the music. Then, a trumpet call—usually played offstage[67]—signals the arrival of help. What follows is a wonderful combination of themes, culminating in the victorious finale.[68]

That evening at the Music Hall, the singers onstage were spellbound as Beethoven's music unfolded. The same was true of the audience. According to one newspaper account, the prominent socialite Mrs. Whitney stilled her fan, and James Blaine was so totally absorbed that he surely must have forgotten all about the complex international issues that weighed so heavily upon him.[69] Even William Steinway, fresh from a challenging day of meetings in resolving a troublesome situation with transportation workers, could finally immerse himself in the music and divert his attention from business concerns.[70] Any disruption to the music left listeners aghast. A sneeze that erupted from a little girl in the audience drew severe glares.[71] Tchaikovsky, as he sat in nervous anticipation of his own upcoming part in the program, enjoyed the *Overture* and complimented it in his diary as "very well performed."[72] Later, the critics would also heap lavish praise on both conductor and orchestra.[73] At the conclusion of the *Overture*, there was wild applause, and Walter Damrosch acknowledged the audience many times over.

A touching moment then followed. Damrosch turned again—this time directly facing Andrew Carnegie—and bowed once more. It was a heartfelt bow of gratitude to the man who had turned the dream of the Music Hall into a reality.[74]

A brief intermission was next—said to be one of only seven or eight minutes long.[75] At whatever length, though, the audience now had a chance to further admire the Hall's many attractive appointments, to mingle for a few moments with their fellow attendees, and to again study their program booklets.

One of the program's most intriguing advertisements was a page of extensive details about The National Conservatory of Music of America. This school had just been incorporated, and their director was still to be chosen. In the not-too-distant future, Antonin Dvorak would fill this position. The ad listed some familiar faculty names. Bass/baritone Emil Fischer, who would be appearing in the Festival, was responsible for teaching the opera class. The chorus and orchestra classes were led by Frank van der Stucken, who had conducted a Recital Hall concert in April. And two eminent critics/music writers—James G. Huneker and Henry T. Finck—were on the piano and history of music faculties, respectively. Victor Herbert taught cello. It was obvious that the president of the school—Mrs. Jeannette Thurber—had a wonderful eye for marketing. In her extensive ad, she featured both orchestra and chorus classes weekly—thematically in keeping with the featured groups at the Festival—as well as children's solfeggio classes, appealing to families in the audience.[76]

Andrew Carnegie was among the original supporters of this institution. Mrs. Thurber had envisioned creating a conservatory teeming with national pride that could hold its own worldwide. Open to all gifted students—minorities, women, handicapped, and the poor included—it was to offer the highest quality musical education and opportunities possible. This was no idle dream. Mrs. Thurber had been the force behind a number of impressive musical projects in the past—Theodore Thomas's concerts for young people, a Wagner festival, a lecture series, and the American Opera Company. By the time of the Music Hall's opening, her conservatory had become an established presence in New York. Initially formed in 1885, the original list of incorporators included Mr. & Mrs. August Belmont, William K. Vanderbilt, Theodore Thomas, William R. Grace—and Andrew Carnegie.[77] This was an educational institution with noble aims, something that Carnegie believed in whole-heartedly. Just as the Music Hall aimed to establish itself on behalf of the city and the nation as a cultural institution that was equal to any in the world, Mrs. Thurber sought to do the same with her conservatory of music. This was a goal that Andrew Carnegie would respect.

Soon, the audience settled quietly once more in anticipation of a highlight that was scheduled next on the evening's program. Peter Ilyich Tchaikovsky, the Festival's eagerly awaited international guest, walked onstage to triple rounds of applause.[78] He then took the baton to conduct his much awaited *Marche Solennelle.*

Tchaikovsky was not overly fond of this piece when he first composed it in 1883, and he was even less fond of the pressure exerted upon him to write it in the first place. While immersed in creating the instrumentation for his opera *Mazeppa*,[79] and at the same time pre-occupied with family concerns, he was commissioned to write a cantata as well as a march—into which the Russian national anthem was incorporated—in celebration of the coronation of Alexander III as the new czar.[80] This was not the first time he had composed a work for this individual. Seventeen years previously, he created the *Danish Festival Overture* in honor of the czar's marriage. This time, though, Tchaikovsky was compelled to write quickly and called his resulting composition "noisy but bad."[81] He was clearly frustrated that he had to undertake the project and interrupt his work on *Mazeppa*. As necessary, though, he completed both commissioned projects, and the *Coronation March* was premiered in Moscow on May 23, 1883. It later became known as either the *Festival March* or the *Festival Coronation March*.

In a unique coincidence, the Carnegies had visited Kinghorn in Scotland while on their wedding trip in 1887. On this occasion, they attended an unveiling of a statue of the Russian czar, Alexander III, to whom Tchaikovsky had dedicated the *Coronation March*. Both Andrew Carnegie and James Blaine spoke formally at the ceremonies, which also commemorated a new public park.[82] Now, four years later, this *March* occupied a featured place on the program at the inaugural Festival of the new Music Hall, and, of course, both Andrew Carnegie and James Blaine were present at this event, as well.

Although Tchaikovsky might have wished for enough time to compose something specifically for the evening, he decided instead to use the *Coronation March* for his initial turn at the podium on opening night. He changed the title to *Marche Solennelle* in the hope that the public might consider it a new work for the occasion. This backfired. Audiences were so familiar with Tchaikovsky's music—enthralled with it—that they immediately knew the identity of the composition, despite the title change.[83] No one seemed to mind, however.

The audience was enthusiastic about the performance, and "doubled" their applause at its finish.[84] Despite Tchaikovsky's thoughts on the matter, the *Marche* was a crowd pleaser, so much so that, later, *The Sun* referred to Tchaikovsky as the "lion and hero" of the event that evening.[85] However, the composer's demeanor on the podium presented a far more humble and modest image than this statement might have indicated. One account even found him to be "a trifle embarrassed" with the applause, although fully confident and strong upon picking up his baton and doing a superior job of conducting his composition.[86]

Tchaikovsky was not fond of comments such as this that appeared in the American press pertaining to his stage mannerisms and conducting style. He had long struggled with discomfort in front of audiences and often felt markedly unsettled while he was onstage.[87] The newspaper comments further underlined his incipient anxieties on the podium. Yet his work and its performance were enthusiastically received, and these personal observations were just the custom with American reviewers, disconcerting though they might have been for the composer.

Afterward, Tchaikovsky joined the box occupied by the Hydes during the second portion of the concert.[88] He liked them, and, similar to the Renos, their company provided both support and comfort on that particularly stressful evening. Tchaikovsky was not the only individual to change boxes during this latter half of the program. James Blaine joined Andrew Carnegie at this time, as well.[89]

The final musical piece on the program was the *Te Deum* by Hector Berlioz. This was its New York premiere. Not many years before, Berlioz, along with Liszt and Wagner, had been considered to be "avant-garde composers." Through the efforts of Carl Bergmann, Theodore Thomas, and Leopold Damrosch, their music was gradually assimilated into the concert repertoire. Leopold Damrosch, in particular, presented performances of some of the complete works of Berlioz—*La damnation de Faust* in 1880 and the *Requiem* in 1881, to name two[90]—particularly admirable accomplishments at the time. Now, Walter Damrosch was to present the complete *Te Deum* in the Music Hall of which his father had dreamed.

The *Te Deum* was originally performed in Paris in 1855 with Berlioz at the podium. At this premiere, there were between 900 to 950 performers in total, according to varying accounts.

The concert took place at the Church of Saint-Eustache on the evening prior to the opening of the city's World Exposition, and the church's recently installed organ integrally connected the two events. Since it was a new instrument, it was hoped to be defined as a "wonder of engineering," thus drawing interested crowds from the Exposition to hear it performed.[91]

Certainly an expansive composition, Berlioz had planned for it to be performed with the organ at the opposite side of the concert space from the choruses and orchestra. Adhering to the composer's vision, however, was impractical at the Music Hall, given its design and the need for everyone to be onstage together. This fact was carefully critiqued by one reviewer[92] who wondered at Walter Damrosch's choice of it for this program. Another, however, hailed him for conducting this massive work "with rare good judgment."[93]

Although the *Te Deum* is recognized as a hymn and part of Catholic liturgy, its secular uses are linked with festive or celebratory occasions. In Berlioz's interpretation, the approach to this theme is grand, including not only the organ but also two regular choirs, a children's choir, and an orchestra—all strategically located within the performance space. The work itself contains six movements that the composer referred to as hymns or prayers. There are also two orchestral sections and a march. The latter was only to be used in connection with military events, and an instrumental section is often cut as well. *Te Deum* is filled with the multiple textures of voices and instruments and contained many innovative compositional features for its time.[94]

The tenor soloist for the evening was Italo Campanini. It was no surprise that the audience gave an enthusiastic response to his performance. He was well known in New York and had appeared in numerous venues over many years, performing at the opening of the Metropolitan Opera House on October 22, 1883, in their production of *Faust*. He sang the title role to Christine Nilsson's Marguerite. The new millionaires—including the Vanderbilts, Whitneys, and Harrimans—thrilled to the performance. Although this was a unique occasion for them, both singers had already performed the same work at the Academy of Music to an audience of "old" money.[95]

Campanini was always a favorite, but he was even more so now. Audiences were especially delighted that he was a part of this opening night since only less than a year previously, he had made his return to the concert stage after having a tumor surgically removed from in between his vocal chords.[96] Despite his previous medical situation, he resiliently picked up his career and was evidently as busy as ever. Subsequent to his recovery, he appeared in concert at Chickering Hall in

The popular tenor Italo Campanini was soloist in the *Te Deum* by Berlioz on opening night.

June of 1890 and continued to perform thereafter in a wide array of events. Two days previous to the Music Hall Festival, he sang at a concert with Gilmore's Band at the Lenox Lyceum where he was not only featured with other singers but also with famed violinist Maud Powell.[97] Campanini was no stranger to the Gilmore group, having been a famed part of their popular Manhattan Beach concerts in the past.[98] Now, he was warmly welcomed by the audience at the Music Hall. His was the only solo part in the *Te Deum*, and even though one reviewer felt that his voice was still not in top form, his delivery was praised[99] and the crowd was delighted.

The Tribune particularly mentioned the Boys' Choir of 100[100] that participated in the performance. This group and their Choirmaster, Wenzel Raboch, were prominently advertised in the program. Raboch was an active musician in the city. An Austrian by birth, he came to the U.S. at an early age and studied both violin and organ. A versatile organist and choir director, he held positions at a number of institutions over time, including St. Michael's Roman Catholic Church, Temple Shaaray Tafila, and, particularly during the time of the Music Hall Festival, at St. Chrysostom's Chapel of Trinity Church.[101] At this chapel, located at Seventh Avenue and 39th Street, he was both organist and choirmaster, directing a singing group of 35 boys and men.[102] Two days after the opening night at the Music Hall, he played the chancel organ at the high celebration of Ascension services at Trinity Church where the combined voices of 100 singers formally processed for the occasion. Bishop Henry Potter preached.[103]

In contrast to some evenings at the opera, the audience was respectfully quiet during this performance. Many followed the text of the work almost as closely as the members of the choruses[104]—a testament to their interest in the fine performance as well as to their regard for the magnitude of the evening's significance. The evening was an enormous success, receiving cheers and praise from all quarters.

By this time, William Burnet Tuthill should also have been receiving standing ovations as the evening drew to a close. However, the architect did not have the opportunity to enjoy any accolades—or even the concert itself. Tuthill had carefully studied and planned all aspects of the new Music Hall's design. He was a consummate professional in the world of architecture and a passionate devotee in the world of music. He would have attended to every aspect of the Hall to guarantee the safe and solid construction of the building itself and to ensure its superior artistic properties—visual and, certainly, acoustical. After asking for input from the finest consulting architects of the day, he had analyzed every minute portion of the project. Tuthill was thoroughly aware of the smallest of details as well as of the big picture.

Still, Tuthill was human. As such, he succumbed to doubt on opening night. Even before the concert had gotten underway, he looked out over the hall, his eyes focusing on the galleries. There, eager audience members inhabited every available seat. Others stood packed in the aisles. Suddenly, from his vantage point backstage, the columns that supported those galleries, even though made of steel, took on a fragile look. Worry consumed Tuthill. He quietly slipped out of his beautiful new Music Hall and left for home where he spent the night reviewing and re-figuring all of his calculations for those columns. He needed to reassure himself that they were correct and could withstand the weight of such a crowd. Of course, he had been accurate all along, but he did not sleep until there was absolutely no hint of a lingering doubt in his mind.[105]

Those who were fortunate enough to hear the concert and to have been a part of this stellar evening left the Hall to face a dilemma. Since there was no organized place for them to pick up their passengers, carriages jammed the area nearby. According to one account, there were a number of people walking up and down the street in a challenging effort to find their coachmen.[106] This chaos outside didn't matter in the long run, though. The evening had been a success. The concert was praised, and the public was thrilled with its famous special guest. The new Music Hall was awe-inspiring, receiving high marks on all counts for its fabulous acoustics, its visual beauty, and—as one critic especially noted—its cheerfulness.[107] While various audience members were in search of their carriages, reporters were already contemplating superlative words with which to describe the event—and the building—in their forthcoming reviews. The *New York Herald* complimented it as a groundbreaking building for the specific use of orchestras and choruses.[108] Above all, the acoustics were a marvel, deemed "simply perfect" by *The Sun*[109] and "splendid"[110] by the *Herald*. This evening was the just the start of the Music Hall's subsequent historic journey to worldwide fame.

· SIX ·

Second Day—Wednesday
May 6, 1891

New York City woke to a stunning shock on May 6. Early in the morning, the thermometer plummeted to thirty-eight degrees—unheard of in the vicinity during the month of May. Then, despite a six-degree rise in temperature, a half dozen snow squalls soon followed. It all sent the public reeling—and in pursuit of heavy coats already packed away for the season.[1]

While local citizens were shaking their heads in disbelief and hurrying about their business in the turbulent outdoors, Tchaikovsky was inside his hotel room scanning newspaper reviews of the previous evening's opening concert. He received a steady supply of these informative clippings from "Mr. Romeike,"[2] an individual to whom he refers several times in his diary.

Henry Romeike was credited with building the first news clipping service in the world in 1881. Originally operating in London, his business later moved to New York where it thrived. During Tchaikovsky's time in the city, Romeike's establishment was located at 110 Fifth Avenue, just a few short blocks from the Knabe Piano firm.[3] This service was unique for its time. Clients were provided with clips on almost any subject, all drawn from a massive resource of U.S. newspapers. Politicians, musicians, and actors who were anxious to discover the prevailing opinions about their activities and appearances eagerly contracted for the service. Eventually, businesses joined their ranks as customers.[4] It was a fine way for individuals to track the progress of their careers and for organizations to assess attitudes, events, and trends within many sectors of industry, culture, and public life.

Romeike sent numerous clippings to Tchaikovsky during his stay, and

119

A depiction of the Music Hall lobby in *Harper's Weekly*. The new building received high praise from many publications.

the morning of May 6 included an impressive number. The Music Hall had certainly captured some headlines. Reviews of the previous evening's gala opening ranged in length, detail, and tone. Taken as a whole, they covered every possible aspect of the event from music and speeches to acoustics and architecture. Several also included a "who's who" of those onstage as well as off, and Tchaikovsky's name was at the head of the list.

The Sun called the evening "A Rare Musical Event," its full, two-column article on the topic featured on the front page. The piece was adorned with attractive sketches of more than a dozen notables—Andrew Carnegie, Walter Damrosch, top festival soloists and, of course, Tchaikovsky—whom they referred to as "the lion and hero" of the event.[5] *The New York Times* declared that "It Stood the Test Well," praising the Hall and confirming that there was now an institution where a wide variety of music could be presented "with advantage."[6] In addition to its concert review, this article also offered an in-depth description of the building, with many specific details about its architecture, decorative aspects, and significant interior and exterior features. *The Morning Journal*, in "Music's New Home," described the event with glittering adjectives and reverential awe, waxing eloquent on the inspiring conducting of Tchaikovsky. The evening, they stated, was one "long to be remembered."[7] Perhaps the *New-York Herald* summed it up the best: "Music Crowned in Its New Home." Lovely sketches of key individuals as well as of the building itself were interspersed throughout the article, which went to great lengths to relate everything about the evening—from the music and the performers to the notable box-holders and the outside scene prior to the concert. In total, the piece called it a "great event" in the city's "musical history."[8]

Tchaikovsky carefully studied these and other articles. There was little doubt that the critics had received him well. And the audience welcomed him with obvious enthusiasm, expressing their appreciation of his music, his leadership of the orchestra, and his presence.

Several critics, however, gave in to their penchant for commenting not only on the music but also on the composer's stage appearance and style. This distressed Tchaikovsky greatly. "It angers me," he confessed to his diary after reading these occasionally awkward portrayals that accompanied the analyses of the music and the performances.[9] A few reviewers overestimated his age, perhaps taking a cue from his white hair and beard. Others noted in detail his "jerky bows" and seeming embarrassment.[10] Tchaikovsky took all of it to heart, dismayed that these articles had not confined themselves to his music alone. He had always struggled with self-consciousness when appearing onstage. Now the press in their eagerness to report on every minute detail related to their famous visitor only made him feel more ill at ease.

The candid observations that distressed him, however, were only a part of the story. There was also much praise given for his conducting style and general bearing. *The Sun* referred to his movements as "energetic" and further stated that each one had "decision and meaning."[11] *The Press* complimented him on being a "fine-looking man,"[12] and the *Morning Journal* commented on his "wonderful personality."[13] Initially, however, the composer did not focus on these laudatory comments as much as he did on the discomforting ones. In later days, though, he began to more fully realize just how highly regarded he was by the American press and public.

There was to be a reprieve from conducting for Tchaikovsky on the second evening of the Festival, although he still had rehearsal responsibilities during the day in preparation for his additional appearances that week. Therefore, in mid-morning, he walked to the Music Hall. Walking afforded him some solitude, and it also provided additional opportunities to observe the people and the sights in a place so new and unique to his eyes. He was continually amazed at the city's wonders, writing to a friend of his particular surprise to see "buildings with 13 stories."[14] At this point in time, taller edifices were becoming more common. The Pulitzer Building alone rose to an even higher sixteen stories.[15]

Tchaikovsky's focus that morning was a rehearsal of his *Suite No. III*. It went smoothly and, although his official duties for the day were completed, there were still immediate demands on his time. Drenched in sweat from conducting the orchestra, he was thrust into a meeting with Marie Reno, her oldest daughter (presumably Anna Reno Margulies), and several other women to discuss his forthcoming plans in America after his time in New York was complete.[16] After a prospective sightseeing trip to Niagara, he was scheduled to go to Philadelphia, Baltimore, and Washington, D.C.—all of which he had hoped to avoid because of his homesickness.

Following this meeting, Tchaikovsky prepared to see Ferdinand Mayer, only to be intercepted by an anxious Franz Rummel, presenting himself once more with the hopes of playing the composer's Second Piano Concerto for him in person. Rummel had waited long and patiently that day to again implore Tchaikovsky to conduct the concert in which this composition would be featured. It was a prospect that the already over-booked composer found far from compelling, particularly since it did not include a fee. Once more Rummel was disappointed at being turned down. Tchaikovsky's subsequent meal with Ferdinand Mayer[17] offered a respite from this awkward situation as well as from the rigors of the morning.

A happier visit occurred later on. Peter Sergeyevich Botkin surprised Tchaikovsky after having traveled to New York from Washington, D.C., just to attend the concert. It was both a friendly gesture and a diplomatic one. Botkin was the Secretary of the Russian Embassy and an individual whose family had deep Russian roots and pride. His father was a renowned doctor and scientist who had made a number of vibrant contributions to medicine that were known worldwide, far outside of Russia.[18] Tchaikovsky, too, had made contributions beyond his country's boundaries through his music, and his presence in America was a more than favorable one, underlining the significance of this trip for both nations. Botkin was pleased to come to New York to see Tchaikovsky and also looked forward to the composer's forthcoming stop in the nation's capital.

The second evening's event at the Music Hall drew closer. Tchaikovsky was collected by the Hydes to attend the concert event together.[19] This program promised to be of a different character than the one featured on the first night.

Felix Mendelssohn's *Elijah* was known to audiences and had been presented a number of times in New York over the previous few decades. As early as 1858, there is a record of its well-reviewed performance at the Academy of Music given by the New-York Harmonic Society.[20] The group again offered the work at Steinway Hall in 1867 as part of an extensive music festival. On this occasion, it was reported that *Elijah* drew a much larger audience than the ones observed at performances for both the *Messiah* and the *Creation*.[21] Over time, numerous soloists also began including individual selections from *Elijah* on their concert programs.

In 1873, Theodore Thomas presented this oratorio at Steinway Hall as part of a week-long series of programs. The reviews were more than glowing on all fronts—soloists, chorus, and orchestra included. One critic declared the oratorio itself quite appealing when compared with the "ponderous scores" in the same genre written by other composers, including Haydn and Handel[22]—an ironic statement since Mendelssohn had been a great admirer of Handel.

It was obvious that *Elijah* was a favorite of the Oratorio Society under Leopold Damrosch's direction. They performed it five times between the years of 1876 and 1883 alone.[23] It also appeared as if presenting this work was a family tradition. During the time that Frank Damrosch lived in Colorado, he created the Denver Chorus Club, subsequently directing this group in an 1883 performance of *Elijah*. It was their first concert,[24] and it took place in the same year as an Oratorio Society presentation of the same work in New York.

In 1888, *Elijah* was sung once more by the Oratorio Society at the Metropolitan Opera House, led by Walter Damrosch. It was praised in thoughtful depth by a reviewer who observed that the drama underlying the work was the key to its lasting appeal with audiences.[25] This comment definitely reflected Mendelssohn's intentions when creating this oratorio. Conveying the dramatic impact of the story through music had been of primary importance to him.

By the mid-nineteenth century, Felix Mendelssohn had risen to great popularity as a composer and musician in Europe. He was quite gifted and musically well trained. Assured of fame early on as a child piano prodigy and, eventually, as the teenaged composer of an orchestral overture for a production of *A Midsummer Night's Dream*,[26] his name soon became well known. A defining moment in his career, however, was to come at age twenty. Several years earlier, he had received a most unique gift from his grandmother—a manuscript of the *St. Matthew Passion* by Bach. This inspired the young man. After carefully studying the work, he set a goal for himself of conducting it at a public concert. This, of course, did not happen overnight. Three long years were devoted to the manuscript, examining all of its elements in detail and revising and editing the work to make it ready for a performance.[27]

The result was astounding. Conducting from the keyboard, Mendelssohn revived the long neglected *St. Matthew Passion* in an 1829 concert. This event had long-term ripple effects. Even though Bach's instrumental music was consistently popular, his choral music had faded somewhat over time. The concert went a long way toward renewing the public's enthusiasm for this segment of Bach's work.[28] It also marked the further ascendancy of Mendelssohn's career and provided him with a solid grounding in his knowledge of the oratorio form. He soon became determined to write his own oratorio. *St. Paul* (1836) was the result, a work that he subsequently presented and conducted at England's Birmingham Festival.

St. Paul was a success, and almost a decade later, Birmingham commissioned Mendelssohn to write a new oratorio.[29] Yet, years before Birmingham even raised this subject, Mendelssohn had already been in the process of exploring new possibilities for another such work, having become fascinated with the story of Elijah. The subsequent journey to a completed oratorio on this theme, however, was years in the making.

Mendelssohn initially drafted a libretto together with his childhood friend Carl Klingemann and, later, took up the project once more with another friend, Julius Schubring. While Mendelssohn was drawn to the character of Elijah and the multi-fold drama of his story, the difficulties in creatively capturing the essence of it all had become increasingly obvious to him over time. The project was again put on hold. Enter Birmingham.

In England, of course, oratorios were a traditionally important part of musical culture, and *Elijah* may never have come into being if it had not been for Mendelssohn's warm ties with that country. From its monarchs to its musical groups, the composer was a favorite, and he returned there frequently to perform and to conduct. Therefore, it was no surprise when in1845, the Birmingham Festival approached Mendelssohn with the oratorio commission—one that was to be completed by the following year. By the time *Elijah* was eventually performed, a decade would have passed since the premiere of *St. Paul*.

With the commission a reality, Mendelssohn returned to *Elijah* and his collaboration with Schubring. The two men, however, had different philosophies to negotiate regarding the focus of the libretto. Mendelssohn wanted to emphasize the dramatic elements of both character and story, and Schubring—a Lutheran minister—favored the theological. The dramatic elements, even at a quick first glance, were unmistakable—from Elijah's reviving of the widow's dead son to his own ascent to heaven in a fiery chariot, there was much to work with. However, the religious essence of Elijah's faith also needed to be clearly interwoven into the drama of the narrative. Mendelssohn and Schubring spent time together, carefully working it through. When the libretto was finally complete, William Bartholomew, another friend, edited and translated it. Although the original libretto was based on Luther's German biblical translation, the English version adhered to the King James version of the Bible.[30] Therefore, an additional step was necessary. Mendelssohn and Bartholomew needed to finalize the smooth fusion of music and words in the final translation.[31]

Various historians have said that Mendelssohn created the soprano part in *Elijah* specifically for Jenny Lind to sing. He felt that it would be a "whole century" until another soprano would emerge "as gifted as she."[32] The solo "Hear ye, Israel" contains upper register notes—particularly a high F sharp—that were closely matched to her unique voice, one that so captivated him he even suggested to the Birmingham Festival that they should engage her to perform it.[33] This was not to be. However, the year after Mendelssohn's death, Lind sang the work at Exeter Hall, the proceeds going to a scholarship fund in his name. Later, she expressed her great admiration for *Elijah,* confessing that she believed Mendelssohn "never wrote anything finer."[34]

Certain elements of Mendelssohn's background had similarities to that of Leopold Damrosch. Both were from Germany, both were of Jewish heritage, and both converted to Lutheranism. In the case of Damrosch, the latter occurred upon his marriage. For Mendelssohn, it was a family decision made when he was a boy.

Mendelssohn's family—especially his grandfather, the eminent Enlightenment philosopher Moses Mendelssohn—honored their religious faith but also embraced the concepts of Humanism, a tradition that had grown popular in Europe at the time. Mendelssohn's father, Abraham adhered to these teachings and eventually converted his family to Lutheranism when the composer was a young boy, a faith into which all of the Mendelssohn children were subsequently baptized.[35] This religion also reflected the literature and music prevalent in the country at the time—notably, the writings of Goethe and the instrumental music of Bach. The young Felix Mendelssohn was influenced by all of it. He was, of course, interested in Bach, as seen in his devoted efforts to present the *St. Matthew Passion*. And he also knew Goethe and performed for him in person. Goethe enjoyed hearing the music manuscripts in his collection come to life via Mendelssohn's prodigious keyboard talents.[36]

In addition, both Mendelssohn and Damrosch were superb musicians and held the oratorio form in high esteem. Their respect for the music, the genre, and its subject matter was evident—each equally interested in works that reflected the texts of both the Old and New Testaments. Mendelssohn's *St. Paul* Oratorio, based on the New Testament, told the story of a conversion—in itself apropos to his own family's background.[37] Bach was a strong musical inspiration for this work. The Old Testament source for *Elijah* offered Mendelssohn an appealingly dramatic character and story, one that was also a challenge to convey musically. Handel was a strong influence in this case—a composer whose work Mendelssohn also greatly admired.[38] *Elijah* was first performed at the Birmingham Festival in August of 1846, under Mendelssohn's leadership. Despite its success, he chose to revise the score soon afterward,[39] and this new version was presented the following spring. Years later, the Oratorio Society performed *Elijah* and *St. Paul* as well as Bach's *St. Matthew Passion* and Handel's *Messiah, Samson,* and other works.[40] Leopold Damrosch, similar to Felix Mendelssohn, placed great emphasis on the value of the masterpieces within this musical form.

There existed yet another parallel between Mendelssohn and Damrosch. Both were consummate musicians and tireless workers to the point of exhaustion. Mendelssohn's intense pace—similar to that of Damrosch years later—also contributed to his ill health and death at a young age. He passed away late in 1847 at the age of 38.[41]

Featuring *Elijah* during the Music Hall's inaugural week was a thoughtful choice for the Festival program. The work was not only a favorite piece in the standard oratorio repertoire but it also had exceptional dramatic appeal for audiences, something that was well suited for this occasion. It showed off the accomplishments of the Oratorio Society as well as the abilities of the Symphony Society to good advantage. In their new acoustically perfect home, the audience could now enjoy the music to the fullest. Since these groups had performed *Elijah* together in the past, they were comfortable with the work and could produce a more nuanced and in-depth interpretation. Additionally, the evening served as an appropriate tribute to Leopold Damrosch who had also led them in singing this oratorio in the past and whose inspiration for the creation of the new hall was especially palpable on this opening week. Damrosch believed music, such as that presented in an oratorio, had the power to lift the spirit.[42] In the case of *Elijah*, this was especially true in its moving musical illustration of faith. Damrosch's sentiments on the subject were later reflected in Bishop Henry Potter's opening night dedicatory address during which he stated that music should have the ability to inspire as well as to transmit higher ideals.

The four major soloists for the evening's performance of *Elijah* were from the Metropolitan Opera. Their names were well known, and they possessed excellent voices. On the other hand, they leaned toward a specialty in Wagnerian repertoire, an area of music that demanded a different vocal style than did the oratorio form. A more lyrical quality was needed to express the underlying emotions in an oratorio as opposed to the stronger dramatic expressions required for the German opera style. Also, precise language skills that could clearly convey the English text were of utmost importance in the performance of *Elijah*. The language did not come easily to several of the soloists, a situation quickly pointed out in several subsequent reviews. There were two sides to this particular issue, however. The *New-York Daily Tribune* wryly commented on the subject, saying that audiences had become used to such language problems[43] and were perhaps less troubled by them than the critics.

The star of the evening was, hands down, bass-baritone Emil Fischer. He sang the title role of Elijah. In the past, other singers presented this character with great emotional anguish. Fischer, however, chose to portray him as an individual whose unshaken faith shone through with great dignity in the face of many challenges.[44] It was a masterful performance.

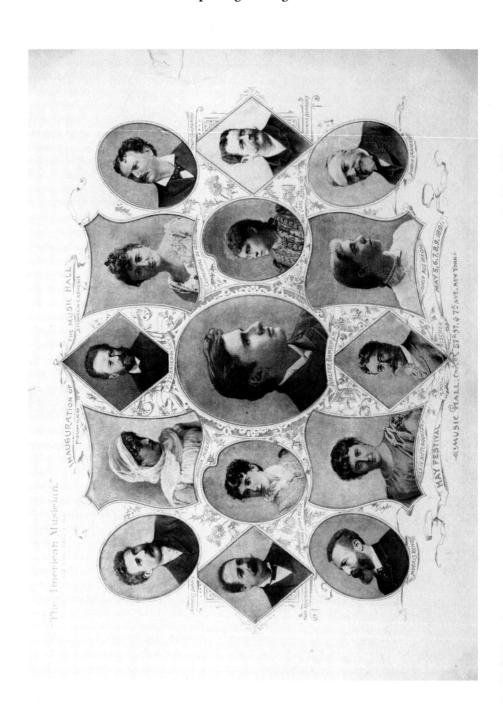

In 1885, Walter Damrosch had been sent to Europe to contract new opera singers "to give glamour" to the Met's cast of stars.[45] Emil Fischer was among those he hired. At that time, Fischer was appearing in Dresden's Royal Opera House. Leaving was a huge step for him and one that permitted no turning back. Since he would be breaking his contract there, he was never to be allowed to sing on the stage of a German opera house again. Fortunately, his move to the U.S. to sing at the Met proved to be a highly successful one.[46]

Fischer came from a musical family. Both of his parents were performers at the Brunswick Court Theatre and encouraged their son to study music, an unusual situation for a large majority of musicians of that era. In an interesting twist, though, Fischer had wanted to become a farmer. However, music eventually held a stronger magnetic appeal for the young man, and he continued to study, eventually appearing in Graz, Hamburg, Rotterdam, Vienna and elsewhere.[47]

Similar to the other soloists at the Music Hall that evening, Fischer was also a Wagnerian. He sang in the United States premieres of *Siegfried* and *Das Rheingold* under the baton of Anton Seidl,[48] and set an early record in his role as Hans Sachs in *Die Meistersinger*, having performed it thirty-four times at the Met.[49] His vocal range and tone were superb, and Walter Damrosch called him the "greatest Hans Sachs."[50]

Damrosch had worked often with Fischer and held fond memories of the man. He considered his first experience as "a full-fledged opera conductor" to have occurred in a performance in which Fischer starred. A work by Peter Cornelius—an old friend of Leopold Damrosch—was being produced, and the regular conductor, Anton Seidl, had become ill. Walter Damrosch stepped in. It was an unforgettable experience for him, and Emil Fischer was an important part of it.[51] Damrosch also recalled a story of the singer in his later years. Fischer's personality was as large as his voice—a man who enjoyed flamboyant attire and generous social entertaining. As a result, he did not save his money. When he grew older, the Met sponsored a benefit to buy him an annuity in order to assure his future comfort and security. Fischer was thrilled at this gesture and new-found financial status—and soon afterward, he married a young member of the chorus.[52]

The critics were almost unanimous in their praise of Fischer's May 6 performance as Elijah—even those from out of town. *The Pittsburgh*

Opposite: A poster featuring cameo portraits of Festival performers and other key individuals connected to the Music Hall (courtesy Carnegie Hall Archives).

Dispatch commended his voice for its "power" and "sweetness." Audiences there had a strong interest in reading about this particular New York performance, not only because of Andrew Carnegie's connection to their city, but also because several of the soloists in *Elijah* were scheduled to appear in Pittsburgh's upcoming May Festival, a large and popular musical event. In this "special telegram" critique, the *Dispatch* was in complete agreement with the other newspapers about Emil Fischer. The reviewer cast some aspersions, though, on the remaining three singers with featured roles—the language and stylistic issues being at the forefront.[53]

Singing the role of the widow was soprano soloist Frau Antonia Mielke. She performed the famous "Hear Ye, Israel," the aria said to have been composed for Jenny Lind. Originally from Berlin, Mielke studied at the Cologne Conservatory.[54] Earlier in her career, she sang as a coloratura but as time went on, she cultivated roles that employed her obvious dramatic aptitude. Her first role was at the Court Theatre of Dessau where she sang in *The Huguenots* in 1878. After performing in many European cities, including the Vienna Opera House and the Cologne Theatre, her abilities were recognized by the Metropolitan Opera, and she was hired for the 1890–1891 German opera season.[55] Later, she appeared at numerous American music festivals, toured Europe, and sang with the Boston Symphony Orchestra in a series of Wagnerian concerts at the invitation of Artur Nikisch.[56]

Mielke was obviously a seasoned performer, but her experience did not completely lend itself to the oratorio style. One review commented that she was less comfortable in singing in this genre than some of the other performers.[57] Having followed Lilli Lehmann at the Met, Mielke had sung such high dramatic roles as Isolde and Brunnhilde,[58] strong Wagnerian characters. The oratorio style required a different approach, and although Mielke's technical skills were certainly in keeping with the requirements of her part in *Elijah*, the combination of her language difficulties and struggle to present a less operatic type of character provided a significant challenge, drawing criticism on the part of the press.

Marie Ritter-Goetze performed the contralto role for the evening. *The New York Times* especially praised her for the solo "Woe Unto Them."[59] Like Mielke, she came from Berlin and when her studies were completed, she sang many Wagnerian roles at the Hamburg Stadt Theater—returning to Germany to sing at the Berlin Opera House after touring. As a result of her success abroad she, too, was contracted for the 1890–1891 Metropolitan Opera season. However, Ritter-Goetze had also had the opportunity to perform operas aside from those by Wagner. Hans von Bulow was once quoted as calling her "the finest living Carmen."[60] Her career also ventured beyond opera, and she appeared in festivals singing in such works as Bach's *Christmas Oratorio* and Dvorak's *Requiem Mass.*[61]

Andreas Dippel took the role of tenor soloist. At the time of the Music Hall's inaugural, he was on a leave from the Stadt Theater of Bremen and visiting New York to appear in the Met's production of Franchetti's *Asraelas* as well as in various concerts.[62] Unlike the family of his fellow soloist Emil Fischer, Dippel's family did not encourage a career in music. Rather, they insisted that he work in banking. Even while holding a job in this field, he continued to pursue his musical studies and activities in the ever-popular singing societies, including the one in his native town of Cassel, Germany. Music was his first love, similar to Leopold Damrosch, and he followed this with a passion, eventually making it his full-time career. In addition to singing in the Bremen Stadt Theatre, he participated in summer performances in Bayreuth, Hamburg, and elsewhere. He was not unknown to oratorio and choral work and had taken the role as the Evangelist in the *St. Matthew Passion.* Hans von Bulow highly praised Dippel and asked him to be a part of a performance of Beethoven's *Ninth Symphony.* Like several of his fellow soloists at the Music Hall, Dippel was hired for the 1890–1891 season at the Met where he appeared in performances of *Siegfried* and *Lohengrin* as well as in non-Wagnerian roles.[63] He had a stellar career in music both onstage and off—becoming a leading tenor at the Metropolitan Opera, rising to co-director of the organization, and going on to organize the Chicago Grand Opera Company. Andreas Dippel eventually left singing, though, and went to Hollywood to work in the technical area of the film industry. Unfortunately, he died there in poor financial circumstances.[64]

The smaller solo parts in *Elijah* were performed by singers who have been somewhat forgotten over time. Anna Luella Kelly and Alice J. MacPherson were among them. The reviewer from *The Sun* especially praised Kelly's "pure, sweet voice"[65] that evening, despite the fact that she did not have a main solo part. Kelly had appeared as a soloist with the Oratorio Society in the 1888 presentation of *Elijah* as well as in the American premiere of B. Edward Grell's *Missa Solemnis* in 1889 at the Metropolitan Opera House.[66] One particularly notable story emerged about her prior to the Festival. A pupil of Mme. Charlotte Varian, she and her teacher were scheduled to do a benefit performance at Chickering Hall in 1884. Kelly bravely went ahead with this event, even though Varian had passed away days before the concert.[67] Alice J. MacPherson also sang in the *Elijah* and *Missa Solemnis* concerts with Kelly. Both women appeared in the

repeat performance of the latter work the following year.[68] MacPherson
favored the oratorio style repertoire, and two years after her appearance
in *Elijah* at the Music Hall, she was again featured in this work with the
Choral Society in Nyack, New York.[69]

Another of the smaller solo parts went to tenor Thomas Ebert. His
vocal skills were considered excellent, and several months after singing in
Elijah, he was one of only eleven out of 233 auditionees chosen to perform
in the choir and special festivals at Temple Beth-El in New York.[70] A versatile individual, he appeared in a wide variety of venues and events during
his career, and a sampling of these indicates that he gave his time and
talent on behalf of many benefits. Several months prior to the opening of
the Music Hall, he sang at an annual benefit for Catholic orphan asylums
held at the Metropolitan Opera House. It included a mixture of theatrical
numbers delivered by members of the Daly and Hoyt companies, a performer of character songs, and "Mr. Thomas Ebert, the popular tenor,"
among others.[71] Around the same time, he was part of the evening's entertainment at the Star Theatre for a function sponsored by the Five A's—
the Actors' Amateur Athletic Association of America.[72]

Ericsson Bushnell sang a bass role in *Elijah*. He had also participated
in the 1888 performance of the work with Kelly, MacPherson, and Fischer.
Active in choirs, his name appeared in many news accounts of similar
performances during the years after the Festival. In particular, he joined
other singers in special recitals presented at Marble Church[73] and also
performed in the noted quartet at the West Presbyterian Church on 42nd
Street.

Newspaper critics expressed some divergent views on the concert.
The Sun praised the quality of all of the solo artists and commented that
the performance with its 600 chorus members was presented on a "high
plane." The review also noted that the public was thoroughly familiar with
Elijah—a decided benefit. Mention was made of some of the language
difficulties, but it was concluded that the superior vocal talents and sensitive performances were paramount in declaring this a successful evening.
This critic also observed that the audience enjoyed a longer intermission,
allowing individuals to mingle and visit, helping to provide a particularly
cheerful atmosphere within the new Music Hall.[74]

The Times gave some space to discussing the oratorio itself; but when
it came to assessing the performances, the reviewer wrote it off as nothing
more spectacular than business as usual at a regular Oratorio Society concert. Emil Fischer, however, was singled out once more and highly praised
for his dignified and moving portrayal of Elijah, as opposed to the more

dramatically explosive renditions that had been offered by other singers in the past. Although the evening's other soloists were mentioned in passing, the only one individual discussed, aside from Fischer, was Marie Ritter-Goetze, whose excellence of "tone, phrasing, and feeling" was commended.[75]

Comments about language ran consistently through the reviews. The *New-York Tribune's* was no exception. It was concluded that there had been "considerable abuse" of the words, while again conceding that local audiences were accustomed to this circumstance and that the soloists had their hearts in doing the best along these lines as they could. However, the reviewers agreed that the soloists were of a high level musically, despite the fact that some parts were not delivered in keeping with the usual stylistic techniques of the oratorio form.[76]

Aside from the language issues and the numerous viewpoints of the press, this concert represented a major accomplishment on the part of soloists, the Oratorio and Symphony societies, and Walter Damrosch. Defined by Damrosch as "the most dramatic oratorio ever written,"[77] the audience itself was "enthusiastically appreciative"[78] of this performance of *Elijah.* The work had now been successfully presented in a proper setting for the enjoyment of both performers and listeners, and on this second night of the Festival, the Music Hall was once again highly applauded for appearing as "brilliant as on the opening evening."[79]

Tchaikovsky's reaction to the concert was short and to the point. He said nothing about the singers individually. The man was naturally tired from his long day and also from being brought to numerous boxes during the intermissions to talk with many prominent people connected to the Music Hall. He confessed in his diary that he found Mendelssohn's music lovely but the work as a whole overly lengthy. He longed to break free, and as soon as possible after the concert, he walked back to the Normandie. There, he ate at the hotel's restaurant and planned to study some letters from home.[80] He then needed to ready himself for the next day.

• SEVEN •

Third Day—Thursday
May 7, 1891

A stunning array of flowers greeted Tchaikovsky on May 7, the third morning of the Festival. It was a special gift, and a particularly thoughtful one, on the part of Marie Reno. This was the composer's 51st birthday.[1] He was also scheduled to conduct his *Suite No. III* that afternoon at the Music Hall. It was a momentous day on all counts.

Aging weighed increasingly on Tchaikovsky's mind. Over a span of several days, he noted in his diary that some individuals—Andrew Carnegie included—believed him to be older than his actual years.[2] On the day prior to his birthday, a few newspapers commented on the subject when reviewing the opening night concert. *The Evening Post* suggested that he looked more advanced in age because of his white hair.[3] *The Press* placed him at around 55,[4] and *The New York Herald* thought him to be "well on the sixty."[5] These remarks caused him concern.

If his appearance was the result of the stresses of recent years and if it was accompanied by the uneasy awareness of an increasing absent-mindedness, the composer could not say.[6] Yet, whether his birthday and its random concerns factored into his frame of mind or not that morning, one thing was certain: Tchaikovsky's anxiety over the afternoon's concert was at an all-time high, age notwithstanding. Even he was clueless as to why and confessed that he was "suffering unbearably."[7]

The composer's *Suite No. III* was to be featured in the middle of the program that day. It was a work Tchaikovsky had conducted many times previously and one that had been well-rehearsed for the afternoon's concert. There should have been no reason for unusual concern. Perhaps Tchaikovsky's intense anxiety was just the cumulative result of the continual attention he was receiving—an overwhelming cascade of people,

134

events, press, and even hospitality that had filled almost every waking moment since arriving in New York. Gracious and flattering as all of this was, it was tiring and frequently unsettling to a man who relished some solitude.

While Tchaikovsky was dealing with his personal anxieties that morning, tensions of another kind had developed elsewhere in town. In this case, it was Secretary of State James G. Blaine and his family who were experiencing worries for an entirely different reason. Blaine and his wife had come to New York to attend the opening of the Music Hall. It was a welcome change from the intense political world of Washington, D.C., especially in light of a continuing number of high-profile issues in play during this time. Something was always brewing for an individual in Blaine's position. Aside from seeking respite from the rigors of public life, though, the Blaines were delighted to be in the audience at the Music Hall's opening Festival to support their son-in-law, Walter Damrosch, on what was a stellar moment in his career.

On that particular Thursday morning, however, Blaine experienced an attack of severe indigestion, causing him more than a fair amount of distress. At first, he attributed this to an extreme change in the weather pattern—a sudden rise in temperature that morning after the previous day's unusual cold snap with snow in the air. Now, the weather was approaching more normal seasonal conditions. Although the Blaines had been scheduled to return to Washington on Friday, these new developments changed their plans. Worried about her father's health, Margaret Damrosch insisted that her parents remain in New York and that Blaine be checked by a physician.[8]

Margaret called for her own family doctor, Frederic S. Dennis, an individual with close ties to the Carnegie-Damrosch circle. Dr. Dennis had treated Andrew Carnegie during his serious illness prior to his marriage[9] and, later, was also among the intimate group who attended the Carnegie couple's wedding in 1887.[10] He was in the audience for the May 5 opening night at the Music Hall, as well.[11]

After seeing Blaine, Dr. Dennis, in turn, brought in Dr. E. G. Janeway as a consultant to review the situation. The men were colleagues and as recently as in March had been among the eminent guests along with Andrew Carnegie at the Bellevue Medical College commencement.[12] Janeway was a well-known, distinguished physician and diagnostician who had served in the Civil War, was author of numerous respected medical works, and acted as consultant to several major hospitals in New York.[13] Whenever Janeway was called in to review a case, the situation was usually of a more serious nature. Three months previously, he acted as a consulting physician for General William Tecumseh Sherman, who had caught a debilitating cold after attending a special performance of *Poor Jonathan* for military guests at the Casino Theatre.[14] In Sherman's case, complications arose and quickly escalated, ultimately proving fatal. There had been nothing that Janeway could do.

Blaine, however, was more fortunate. Doctors Janeway and Dennis together suggested several days of rest for him at the Damrosch home at 72 West 70th Street. General Sherman—who attended the Damrosch's wedding the previous year—had lived just one block away at 75 West 71st Street. Ironically, a memorial event was being held for him that very evening at the Brooklyn Academy of Music with commemorative speeches to be delivered by a number of dignitaries[15] and "Sherman's March" to be read by its poet Fred Emerson Brooks. Among the musical selections would be "America."[16] Only one month previously—almost to the day—Sherman had been posthumously honored at the Grand Army of the Republic's event at the new Recital Hall, where Brooks had also been featured.

Blaine's situation was kept quiet; but as is frequently the case with someone of his stature, word somehow leaked to the press. When questioned several days later, both Walter Damrosch and his mother-in-law, Mrs. Blaine, cheerfully insisted that all was well. In the meantime, though, details were kept private, with only the immediate family and associates being informed.[17] By the time of Thursday afternoon's performance, both Tchaikovsky and Walter Damrosch each had enough to preoccupy their thoughts.

Given Tchaikovsky's anxiety, it was fortunate that the wait for the start of this concert would not be a long one. Although the Festival's two prior events had 8:00 p.m. curtain times, this one was to begin at 2:00 p.m. Afternoon concerts as well as theater and popular performances were quite common at the time and were offered on most given days in addition to or in place of evening events. Advertisements in *The Sun* on that particular Thursday alone reflected this trend. One could plan on attending an afternoon performance of the popular *Carmencita* at Koster & Bial's on a Monday, Wednesday, or Saturday. Tony Pastor's Theatre presented matinees of *Gus Hill's Big Company* on Tuesdays and Fridays. And in the classical world that week, Arthur Friedheim and his wife were scheduled for an afternoon concert that Friday at the Lyceum. The Music Hall offered two afternoon performances during its Festival, including the one on this particular Thursday as well as another two days later on Saturday.[18]

This afternoon's program was one of the more diverse offered during the Festival. It ranged in tone from the comic to the dramatic and included selections from both orchestral and operatic repertoire. There would also be one surprise substitution. The works represented varying international origins, musical styles, and temperaments. In a marked change of mood from the *Te Deum* and *Elijah*, this concert began with two selections from Mozart's opera *The Marriage of Figaro*—its *Overture* and the *Grand Finale from Act II*. These offered a sharp contrast to the religious material of the previous two days—the *Figaro* excerpts crystallizing the comic and satiric elements of the opera from which they were drawn.

Any performance of Mozart would have pleased Tchaikovsky a great deal since he was an enthusiastic admirer of this composer's music from childhood on. As a young man, he attended as many productions of his operas as possible. Later, he wove some of Mozart's themes into his own fourth suite, composed in 1887 and referred to as "Mozartiana"—one of several influences of the composer on his work. More pertinent to this particular afternoon, though, was that he had admired *The Marriage of Figaro* enough to have translated its libretto into Russian in 1875.[19]

Although the librettist of *The Marriage of Figaro*—Lorenzo Da Ponte— had passed away decades before, he left a stamp on New York's cultural scene worth noting, particularly in conjunction with the Festival week. He had done his best to bring to light Mozart's Italian operas in America and, also, to ensure that opera—particularly Italian opera—was more generally appreciated there. Along these lines, Da Ponte spearheaded the building of a concert space that was devoted to this specific genre. If all of his plans were not completely successful, his enthusiasm and ingenuity helped pave the way for cultural innovations that were to follow.

Da Ponte engaged in a vast number of pursuits over his eighty-nine-year lifetime, being an individual whose career and personal history ran the gamut from the commendable to the bizarre. Before arriving in America, though, among the most famous of his accomplishments was his collaboration with Mozart on three operas—*The Marriage of Figaro, Don Giovanni*, and *Cosi Fan Tutte*. *Figaro* (1786) was the first in this group to be written.

Figaro was definitely spirited in music and comically convoluted in plot. The story was derived from a play by the same name written by Pierre-Augustin Caron de Beaumarchais, a character almost as eccentric as Da Ponte himself. From this play, Da Ponte created a libretto that was tightly crafted and full of momentum. While slyly taking aim at matters of class culture, it did not cross any boundaries that would have offended those in power as did the original work.[20] This was a witty comedy with fine music and had potential appeal for a wide range of audiences. It was premiered in Vienna in 1786, the year of its completion.

Da Ponte came to the U.S. in 1805 after a colorful and somewhat checkered career in Europe, both personal and professional. Immigration seemed the wisest choice for him at the time. In America, he barely made a living by running a bookstore, a boarding school, and a grocery store in turn. However, he was a learned man who was immersed in Italian literature and culture and was knowledgeable about music—after all, he had collaborated with Mozart himself. Above all, he was resilient. As had been the case many times in the past, Da Ponte's life would go through a number of changes before some of his more culturally minded attributes would come to the surface. And in Da Ponte's case, public recognition always seemed inevitable.

In a fortuitous coincidence, Clement Clarke Moore—a scholar probably best known for his enduring poem "'Twas the night before Christmas"— dropped into Da Ponte's store one day. The men began chatting, and through this chance meeting, Da Ponte's life changed once again. Moore introduced Da Ponte to Columbia College, where he subsequently became an Italian professor– the first to hold this position at the school as well as the first to be awarded such a distinction in the U.S.[21] Although the post was not a long-lasting one, it was enough to elevate his profile in the community at large. Ever resourceful, he once more combined his work on behalf of Italian literature and culture with that of music—specifically, opera.

Da Ponte was, if nothing else, an enthusiast and one who was quite adept in keeping up with all significant cultural happenings. In 1825, he warmly greeted the visiting opera group of Manuel Garcia and was soon thereafter responsible for urging Garcia to perform *Don Giovanni.* It was an early performance in America of one of Da Ponte's collaborative works with Mozart. At the time of this event, Da Ponte was seventy-seven years old, and he proudly acknowledged the audience's applause at the performance in honor of his accomplishments as the librettist.[22] But his efforts within the operatic arena were far from over. Heartened by the toe-hold that Italian opera had gained in New York through the Garcia troupe, he embarked on a plan to build a permanent home for opera in the city— Italian opera in particular. On the surface, it seemed a noble enterprise, although perhaps somewhat impractical in the New York of the day, a time when Italian opera needed more overall recognition to ensure the long-range success of such a move.

However, Da Ponte was committed enough to see his Italian Opera

House become a reality—and it did. Previously, there had been only one other such venue in operation, but the edifice had not been built expressly for this purpose, and it was lacking in sophistication. A former mansion that had been used in many ways over time, its Italian opera productions did not even last a whole season before the space became dedicated to entirely different uses—ultimately finishing off the performance year with equestrian presentations.[23]

On the other hand, Da Ponte's opera house was conceived with a singular purpose. He succeeded in persuading a number of wealthy citizens, all eager to be a vital part of the cultural elite, to lend their financial support. They paid a total of $175,000 in advance for boxes in the new house that, in turn, underwrote the costs of construction. Located at Church and Leonard streets, it was by all accounts a beautiful structure with a luxurious interior—and the house was totally committed to presenting Italian opera.[24]

It was an exquisite place—the first to have a complete tier of boxes, enhanced with upholstered mahogany sofas and fitted with blue silk curtains. A fine chandelier, one-of-a-kind paintings on the ceiling, and carpeted floors made this a first-class operation. Da Ponte, acting as co-manager, even imported an Italian opera group to launch the first season at the new house. It opened with a production of Rossini's *La Gazza ladra*.[25] Philip Hone, former mayor of the city, was in a box on opening night, and while he had high admiration for the beautiful opera house, he found the opera itself—as did the audience in general, according to him—too long to be appreciated in a language he did not understand. He had deep misgivings that such a "splendid and refined amusement" would last.[26] Regrettably, he was correct.

The plan was certainly a success from artistic and goal-oriented perspectives. Da Ponte's driving force brought New York its own Italian opera house, opera company, and opera season. It was all a notable cultural achievement. From a financial point of view, though, it was an unparalleled disaster, a situation not unknown to Da Ponte throughout his lifetime. American audiences—as much as they wanted to emulate the high culture and art of Europe—were not quite ready for such an extensive immersion in Italian opera. As Philip Hone had commented, they did not understand the language, particularly when it was sung, and they needed more time to become accustomed to all aspects of this unique musical form. Perhaps with a little patience and additional exposure to opera presentations of this type, audiences might have been drawn in larger numbers to the performances.

On a more immediate level, however, the major backers were stung by the financial shortfall of the enterprise. This did not bode well. Within three years, the theater had to be sold.[27] General speculation offered another reason for its failure –its less than desirable neighborhood. However, when the National Theatre took over the premises, it became a success, casting aspersions on the poor location theory.[28] The time and circumstances had just not been right for this particular project.

Da Ponte's imprint on the musical world, however, remained. He helped to highlight a specific segment of music—the Italian operas of Mozart as well as Italian opera in general. While it lasted, his was the first real Italian opera house of true quality, and it illustrated the potential results when an individual or individuals actively garnered support for superior performance venues with specific cultural purposes in mind. During this particular week at the Music Hall, such a history was worth contemplating.

Gradually, selections of Mozart's operatic music began to be included in recitals in New York. A certain Madam Sontag presented an air from *Figaro* along with others by Bellini and Mercadante in one of her series of six concerts in 1852.[29] Others followed suit. Eventually, full productions began entering the repertoire, as well. The Academy of Music presented the opera in Italian a few years later. In November of 1858, George Templeton Strong, the eminent nineteenth-century diarist, wrote enthusiastically about the production. He attended the second of two performances, sitting in the midst of a packed audience, and praised Mozart for his fine exuberance.[30] *The Times* commented on the work, commending it for embodying the "spirit ... of comic opera."[31] Later, the Parepa English Opera Troupe offered *The Marriage of Figaro* at the Academy during the 1870 season.[32] By the time that selections from *Figaro* were performed at the Music Hall Festival, the opera, or at least portions of it, had become more familiar to audiences. As one critic suggested, however, it was still not heard too often, so it retained some of its fresh spirit of novelty.[33]

The *Overture* from *Figaro* opened the Festival concert on the afternoon of May 7. A composition charged with quick, sparkling lines, it reflects the comic tone and frenetic pace of the plot. In a full production, these elements set the stage for the opera before the action even begins. However, the *Overture* easily stands alone as a concert piece and has evolved as such over time. The *Grand Finale* from the opera's Act II— next on the program—is a stunning work for an ensemble. Similar to the *Overture*, its sprightly pace reflects the fun of a convoluted plot and its antics—intrigue, mistaken identity, romantic pursuit, and related complications—later referred to by Richard Strauss as the "heavenly frivolities"[34] inherent in the work. Through his sensitively created score, Mozart defines each of the characters, musically presenting them as three-dimensional human beings, not just stock-in-trade prototypes. A combination of well-constructed melodic lines, rhythmic patterns, and harmonic structures, as well as carefully drawn instrumentation all blend to convey the individual personalities and actions of the seven characters—from the servants to the Count and Countess.[35] This work allows each soloist an opportunity to display his or her singular vocal talents while, at the same time, demonstrating their combined ability to interact closely together as a unit. Like the *Overture*, the *Grand Finale* can stand apart from a full production of the opera itself. This is a masterpiece of ensemble work and in its deft performance, the strands of the action are smoothly woven together. It is then that these characters truly come to life.[36]

Antonia Mielke, Marie Ritter-Goetze, Andreas Dippel, and Emil Fischer—among the lead singers from the previous night's performance of *Elijah*—appeared in this work. They were joined by three other well-known figures—Clementine De Vere, Conrad Behrens, and Theodor Reichmann.

Already an acclaimed singer in the U.S. by the time of her appearance at the Festival, Clementine De Vere was originally from Paris. Musically educated in Florence, Italy, she made her debut in *The Huguenots* in that city's Pagliano Theatre and, thereafter, performed in Milan, Naples, Rome, Spain, and South America. She also studied with Gounod and sang for Verdi. In New York, De Vere's church position was of an especially high level and, as the soprano for the West Presbyterian church under the leadership of Rev. Dr. Paxton, she was said to have been the most well paid church singer of the time.[37] Other Festival participants—Ericsson Bushnell and Mrs. Carl Alves—performed at the church during her tenure there, as well.[38] De Vere was a popular and busy musician. Later, some members of the church congregation noted how she was especially anxious to complete her solo at Sunday night services in order to immediately leave for an appearance in a concert or an opera.[39] She eventually married Romualdo Sapio, an eminent conductor and also a faculty member at the National Conservatory of Music. De Vere later devoted time to teaching.

Performing in the Mozart work that afternoon with De Vere and the rest of the ensemble were two German soloists, each with somewhat different backgrounds. Conrad Behrens had left his native Germany for Stockholm where he was noticed for his fine voice by the King of Sweden who subsequently sent him to Paris to study. When he returned, Behrens made his debut at the King's Theatre where he remained for years. He joined the Metropolitan Opera in 1890; but by this time, he had already appeared in such cities as Berlin, London, Paris, and Rotterdam.[40]

Theodor Reichmann was interested early on in drama and music, although his parents wanted him to become a businessman. After pursuing his musical studies, he met Richard Wagner who admired his vocal talents, providing Reichmann with the opportunity to sing at Bayreuth for years. He also appeared in Vienna and performed a wide variety of roles before joining the Metropolitan Opera. Reichmann did not confine himself to opera but was also known for his expertise in oratorio and recital repertoire—in the latter category concentrating on the works of Schubert, Brahms, and others.[41]

This star-studded Mozart ensemble was highly commended by the press. One review called it "delightful ... music" which came to "an effective ending"[42] through fine performances. Years before, Georges Bizet said that whenever he heard the music from this opera, he was "altogether

In April of 1891, Tchaikovsky signed this small notation from his *Suite No. III*, a work he conducted to great acclaim during the Festival (courtesy Carnegie Hall Archives).

happy."[43] Both the critics and the audience at the Festival that day had the same reaction.

As engaging as the Mozart selections were, though, the next work on the program—Tchaikovsky's *Suite No. III*—was the highlight of the concert, and once more the composer was received with unsurpassed joy and enthusiasm. The audience now had another chance to hear his work and to see him conduct in person. Later, *The New York Times* referred to Tchaikovsky as "the star of the afternoon."[44] The *Suite* itself was a popular work that possessed a full range of musical styles and contrasts, and *The Sun* stated that hearing this work alone was worth attendance at the concert.[45]

The *Suite No. III* was composed in 1884 while Tchaikovsky was on a long visit to his sister's home. He had hoped to create a new symphony, but this did not materialize at that time. Always inspired by nature, the thought of composing a suite came to him while taking an evening walk in the garden. This began the journey to his new composition.[46]

The *Suite*'s four movements are separately titled, each embodying its own unique sound. *Elegie* stands alone in structure and mood. The lyrical qualities of its two major themes are reflective and almost ballet-like in character.[47] *Valse melancolique*, with its unique "offbeat accents,"[48] emphasizes some of the sadness indicated in its title. The lively *Scherzo* is in direct contrast to the preceding waltz, highlighting the virtuosic skills of the orchestra in a totally engaging manner.[49] Finally, the *Tema con Variazioni*, with a Russian character at its heart, provides an appealing finale for the *Suite*. These variations embrace a full range of stylistic contrasts— with a fugue, chorale, and polonaise included[50]—allowing this final movement the ability to stand on its own as a separate concert piece. The work embodies a prime example of Tchaikovsky's exceptional ability to score for each individual instrument that, when combined, produces a masterpiece of total sound.[51]

The work was premiered in 1855 in St. Petersburg with Hans von Bulow conducting. Tchaikovsky subsequently wrote to Nadezhda Filaretovna von Meck, saying that he had "never ... had such a triumph."[52] The performance at the Music Hall that afternoon was no less brilliant. Reviewers heaped praise on the *Suite*, noting its wonderful contrapuntal and rhythmic elements and intrinsic beauty. The *Evening Post* called it among Tchaikovsky's "most inspired ... works,"[53] with Dannreuther's violin part being particularly singled out as exceptional.[54] Tchaikovsky need not have worried about descriptions of his stage demeanor in this portion of the program. He was recalled several times with cheers, and *The New York*

Times reviewer called his work and conducting "masterly."[55] *The Sun* felt that the orchestra performed its best under the skilled control of his baton, out of respect for both the composition and the composer. It was obvious that the group was honored to work with this man.[56] Once more, the Festival's guest and his music were an unparalleled success, reflected in the thunderous response from the audience.

When the sound of appreciative applause had faded, Clementine De Vere and Theodor Reichmann took the stage respectively to perform their solos—another change of pace within this most eclectic of programs. First, De Vere sang the Aria from the third act of Massenet's opera *Esclarmonde*. This work—with a storyline that drew on an old legend and added hints of the supernatural into its dramatic, motif-filled score—showed a definite Wagnerian influence.[57] It was a role that Massenet had composed with the American soprano Sybil Sanderson in mind. Sanderson had an impressive three-octave vocal range and a capacity to sing high notes well, and this aria was intended to feature these vocal capabilities to the fullest.[58] It was a demanding role that she would ultimately perform a hundred times, and one that not many singers who followed were willing to attempt.[59] *Esclarmonde* received international recognition when it premiered at the Opera-Comique in 1889—and so did Sanderson. The event was well timed—it occurred shortly after the opening of the Paris Exposition Universelle, featuring the new Eiffel Tower. Paris was then a focus for the world. New York was now experiencing its own spotlight with opening of the Music Hall, and DeVere's performance of the same "exacting aria" premiered by Sanderson, was deemed "excellent" by *The Times*.[60] In addition, *The Sun* praised her "phenomenal high tones"[61] that were sung beautifully.

Following De Vere's exquisite performance was to be a solo sung by Theodor Reichmann. The program announced that he would sing another aria by Massenet—this from the composer's grand opera *Le roi de Lahore* of 1877. During its first two seasons, this most popular work saw sixty performances and gave Massenet enough visibility to secure a position at the Paris Conservatory.[62] It certainly would have been appropriate at this particular afternoon's concert. Reichmann, however, made a last-minute substitution. In place of the Massenet, he performed an aria from Heinrich Marschner's opera *Hans Heiling,* called "Ich liebe Dich" by one newspaper, referring to lyrics within the piece.[63] The aria was "An jenem Tag," a work that Reichmann had performed the previous year in February with Theodore Thomas and the New York Philharmonic at the Metropolitan Opera House and, again, at the same venue in November with Walter Damrosch and the Symphony Society.[64]

CLEMENTINE

DeVere-Sapio

IN AMERICA.

SEASON 1895-96.

Concerts, Oratorio, &c.

FOR TERMS, DATES, ETC., ADDRESS

WOLFSOHN'S MUSICAL BUREAU,

131 East 17th Street,   NEW YORK.

Clementine De Vere was a famous soprano who performed in both solo and ensemble works during the opening week. She continued in her concert career and, also, became the highest-paid church soloist of the time.

Heinrich Marschner was a prolific German composer in the early to mid-nineteenth century. Encouraged by Beethoven, Marschner pursued a musical and compositional career, eventually acting as Kapellmeister for both the Leipzig City Theatre as well as the Hanover Court.[65] He was particularly known for his operas, numbering almost two dozen. In style and approach, Marschner bridged an era—his work having been inspired by Weber's *Der Freischutz* while also serving as an influence upon Wagner's *Flying Dutchman*.[66] Years later, Ralph Vaughan Williams even commented that Marschner, along with Weber and Liszt, gave rise to Wagner.[67] Marschner's most popular opera, *Hans Heiling*, was a stellar example of the German Romantic form with elements of the supernatural and the dramatic closely woven together. The aria was a striking one with great audience appeal. Although it provided a certain contrast to De Vere's rendition of the Massenet aria, no explanation was offered for the program change. *The New York Times* said that Reichmann "sang finely."[68]

Next was the arresting finale for the program—an afternoon that had begun with the lighthearted work of Mozart would now end with the serious themes of Wagner—the Prelude and Finale (*Liebestod*) from *Tristan and Isolde.* This was among the composer's most dramatic of operas, and the story behind its creation was no less compelling than the work itself.

It took Richard Wagner several years to complete *Tristan and Isolde*, and it was written during a time of personal turbulence. Wagner needed to begin work on some new music and was hurting financially. He and his wife, Minna, were eventually invited to stay at an estate in Zurich owned by Otto and Mathilde Wesendonck, great admirers of the composer. Wesendonck was an affluent member of the German business community and part of a New York-based silk company.[69] His wife was a poetess. Subsequently, Wagner set five of her poems to music—called the "Wesendonck Lieder"—and these turned out to be the basis for sketches of *Tristan*.[70]

The Wagners were housed in a cottage on the Wesendonck estate, and their stay was designed to afford Wagner the time and quiet to work on *Tristan.* Not only did they have peaceful surroundings where he could compose, but the Wesendoncks were also in a position to offer financial support as the need arose. While this was a very desirable situation for Wagner and quite generous of the Wesendoncks, it also led to some serious complications. The total experience turned out to be more than anyone had bargained for.

Mathilde Wesendonck and Wagner fell in love, and it has been acknowledged that she was the muse for his opera-in-the-works. Things began to fall apart rapidly, though, when Minna Wagner became aware of the situation. In addition, there had already been some bitterness on Otto Wesendonck's part because of Wagner's wanton spending of his funds.[71] It soon became painfully evident that there was trouble in Zurich and that little beyond Act I of *Tristan*'s music would be completed there. The Wagners went their separate ways—he to Venice to write Act II of the opera. Thereafter, Act III was completed in Lucerne. Along the way, Wagner attracted another patron—Ludwig II of Bavaria—who had assumed the throne in 1864. He offered the composer a commission to complete his *Ring* cycle and also enabled the premiere of *Tristan* the following year.[72] Wagner was, indeed, a fortunate man.

Before Ludwig entered the picture and while the intrigue on personal and financial fronts was heading toward an uncomfortable high, Wagner did have the opportunity to present his *Tristan Prelude* to the public, long before the opera's actual premiere. In 1859, Han Von Bulow conducted a performance of the *Prelude* in Prague, and, in 1860, Wagner himself conducted it along with selections from his other works. This concert took place in Paris before an eminent audience that included the poet Baudelaire, who loved the music, and the composer Berlioz, who did not. Berlioz's antipathy to the chromaticism and often unresolved dissonance in the work might have seemed surprising, since his own compositions had been considered to be groundbreaking not so many years prior to this.[73] However, Wagner's works opened up a new spectrum of sound, and even his musical contemporaries needed to assimilate its unique approach and context.

After the German premiere of *Tristan and Isolde* in 1865, it was not long before some of its music made its way to New York. Theodore Thomas conducted the *Prelude* at Irving Hall on February 10, 1866. However, the critic for *The Times* found it "without significance."[74] The atmosphere was not quite right yet for "new music." In March of the same year, the Philharmonic Society played the *Prelude* at the Academy of Music. The actual orchestral performance was highly praised in comparison to the other works on the program, although the reviewer felt that this was due to the amount of time that had been necessary to devote to it. Clearly, it had gotten the lion's share of the rehearsal. Still, as to the music itself, it did not seem to be a favorite of the reviewer who felt that the harmonic changes were "too numerous."[75] Even several years later when Theodore Thomas presented both the *Prelude* and the *Finale* from *Tristan* on January 8, 1872, at Steinway Hall, the reviews were fairly lukewarm.[76]

The music itself represented Wagner's best realized demonstration of infinite or "endless melody," an approach not confined by more traditional rhythmic structures. Instead, it uniquely weaves fragments of the various motives into a unified whole, musically expressing this ancient tale of love and death intertwined.[77] It would take a while for this new sound to settle in with the critics and some of the audiences. But the end result was eventually assured. *Tristan* eventually became part of the standard repertoire. By the time that the Music Hall Festival took place, *Tristan and Isolde* had been performed in its entirety as an opera. Wagner was popular, and the *Prelude* and *Finale* were familiar to audiences and welcomed on concert programs.

In this performance, the quality of the orchestra became a focus for the critics. *The Sun* stressed that the group excelled in this work, perhaps because they had recently played it in an opera production and were therefore better rehearsed and comfortable with the music. Walter Damrosch, though, did not fare quite so well with the same reviewer who said that he set the pace far too rapidly, and thus detracted from the beauty of the work.[78] However, the *Times* praised the young conductor for leading a "well directed" and "vigorous performance"[79]—illustrating that reviewers' tastes and perspectives were often of an individually singular nature.

The entire concert itself was a success, and it was obvious to all that Tchaikovsky was the star of the afternoon. Reporters quickly flocked to Morris Reno's office to interview the composer there, and the gathering crowds looked upon Tchaikovsky with awe.

Audiences with energy to spare at the conclusion of the afternoon's event were free to head to the Casino where a new and much-anticipated operetta was opening that evening. "Appollo; or the Oracle of Delphi" was the featured work and was certain to be a crowd-pleaser since Lillian Russell was appearing in the performance.[80] *The Pittsburgh Dispatch* even noted the opening of this production with enthusiasm, referring to it as "a genuine first night."[81] The Casino was right near the Hotel Normandie, and it would have been a festive change of pace if Tchaikovsky had chosen to attend the show or any other event—theatrical or social—on this evening that marked his 51st year. Yet, when the applause and interviews and general adulation of the afternoon had subsided, all the composer wanted was to be left alone for a while. He turned down dinner invitations from the Renos and Botkin and went off to wander alone, eating dinner and going to some cafes in search of much needed "silence and solitude."[82] This was what he longed for most on his birthday.

• EIGHT •

Fourth Day—Friday
May 8, 1891

The new Music Hall was already a success—from its handsome design and striking interior décor of salmon, gold and white to its superlative acoustics, sending the clear quality sounds of each performance to every corner of the auditorium. Andrew Carnegie was well pleased. "For the first time," he wrote in a letter several days later, "our Oratorio Society was heard under conditions which did it justice."[1] He was also particularly captivated with Tchaikovsky, continually expressing his admiration for the man, and the composer commented on how "awfully kind" the millionaire had been toward him. Carnegie was already talking of a return engagement for Tchaikovsky the following year.[2]

Considering his active part in the Music Hall project and his attendance at the concerts and related events, it would have been logical if a large focus of attention on Andrew Carnegie that week—at least on the part of the press—would have been related to musical subjects. Certainly there was no lack of coverage in this area. However, Andrew Carnegie was a busy man on many fronts, and newspapers throughout the country, not just in New York, took notice of all aspects of his life—even during this busy Festival week. Although his had been a prominent name in the headlines in recognition of his generosity in gifting the city with a wondrous new concert space, news of the man appeared in other articles focusing on a variety of newsworthy subjects. They reflected the multi-faceted sides of this famous benefactor.

During the Festival week alone, one account revealed that Carnegie had been offered an invitation to join the British Economic Association. It was an honor to be asked to be a part of the eighty or so highly regarded European economists who comprised this group but it was doubly so in

Carnegie's case. He was the first American to ever have been asked.[3] In other news, his firm—Carnegie, Phipps & Co.—attracted notice for one of their products. The organization was complimented on the quality of their Harvey nickel plates. Reports indicated that these plates had been tested at the naval proving grounds at Annapolis along with several other samples of plates made by their company. The durability and strength of the Harvey plates were greatly praised.[4] This subject was not without its controversy, however. Another article that week pointed out that the Secretary of the Navy had awarded a contract of several million dollars to Carnegie, Phipps & Co. for the plates—all without any competition. No samples were ostensibly sought from other firms for testing. Plus, the machinery required to create these items came from Scotland and not America, a fact carefully noted and analyzed in the piece.[5] Two additional newspapers also divulged that cast-iron manufacturers in New York were about to wage a war against Andrew Carnegie over the preferential awarding of contracts.[6]

However, while reporters were eagerly commenting on such business news pertaining to the man, notices of his gifts for worthwhile projects were always apparent—and not just the larger ones such as in the many headlines related to the Music Hall. Even tucked away under "noteworthy" or "miscellaneous" in the daily papers, there was regular mention of his generosity. Again, during the same week as the Festival, a news item appeared about his most welcome gift to a town on Orkney Island—a $2,500 library.[7] This was, indeed, a busy man on many fronts.

Walter Damrosch was also busy, although his time was focused on music and all that was related to it. He had, of course, been consumed with rehearsals, social obligations, and the myriad details pertaining to the Festival. However, there were numerous other pending projects for the near future that he needed to contemplate—plans for the Oratorio and Symphony societies for the following season, additional musical lectures, contracts to be negotiated with new talent, and scores waiting to be reviewed, among them.

That week, it was also reported that Andrew and Louise Carnegie along with Walter and Margaret Damrosch were scheduled to sail for Europe on the *Columbia* on May 14,[8] just a few short days after the final concert at the Music Hall. To be sure, the Damrosches would welcome the opportunity to unwind on board the ship after what had been a hectic time between the Festival and James Blaine's indisposition. Years later, Walter Damrosch's daughter commented that such trips at sea were the occasions when her father "really relaxed."[9] Andrew Carnegie and his wife,

Louise, could also look forward to the ocean voyage as well as to their proposed vacation time at Cluny Castle, a more relaxed pace than at home, especially for the perpetually active business magnate and philanthropist.

In the meantime, Tchaikovsky had been a busy individual, as well. The promise of relaxation, however, was out of the question for him at the moment. He would have to wait a bit longer than the others for his own sea voyage—one that would mark his journey home to Russia. By now, the fourth day of the Festival, time was in small supply as it would be for the remainder of that week and, also, in the weeks ahead when he would be on a tour of several other American cities. Tchaikovsky admitted in his diary to even having "difficulty finding time for writing."[10] Yet, in the midst of both programmed and unexpected events, he felt that he must take what little free time was currently at his disposal to express gratitude.

On the previous day, Tchaikovsky had received a unique gift—perhaps as a birthday remembrance or as a token of thanks for his part in the celebratory Festival week, or both. It was a fine replica of the Statue of Liberty.[11] One account states that it was in the form of an ink-well.[12] Whatever the design of the piece, though, the composer was extremely pleased with it. Therefore, he wanted to take the time to say thank you for this "splendid present"[13] and memento of his visit to America.

Dedicated in New York Harbor five years before Tchaikovsky set foot in America, the Statue of Liberty became more famous worldwide with each passing year, eventually becoming a special symbol for immigrants as well as visitors coming to America. Tchaikovsky would have seen it from his ship upon arriving in New York. Years in the making, from its conception in the 1870s to its realization in the 1880s, it was a gift to the American people from the French people—an emblem of the liberty and friendship that each country held dear.

While the project was underway, the famous arm holding the torch arrived in Philadelphia and was placed on display at the Centennial Exposition there in 1876. The following year, it made the journey to New York's Madison Square Park where over the next several years, visitors flocked eagerly to see the famous piece. During the time that the citizens of New York were enjoying this novelty, funds were being raised for the design and construction of a pedestal upon which to rest the entire statue in its new home in the harbor. Fundraising efforts were dismal, though, and the initial amount fell far short of the mark. It appeared as if the project might grind to a halt. If there was no pedestal, there would be no way to properly secure Lady Liberty in the harbor.

Enterprising newspaper magnate Joseph Pulitzer of the *New York World* stepped forward to save the day with a plan to mobilize public enthusiasm. (His newspaper was to later report on the Music Hall's inaugural week and on Tchaikovsky's visit, as well.) Pulitzer was not only a good businessman but he also had an amazing knack for connecting with the public, making the most of this talent with innovative approaches to reporting the news. He was "for the people" and knew how to reach his readers—and he was not above indulging in a bit of sensationalism in the bargain. However, he knew enough to keep all of this within reasonable bounds of respectability while still attracting eager consumer interest. His winning combination bolstered newspaper sales and, also, helped to save the Statue project. This was an issue that was tailor-made for Pulitzer. He urged the everyday man and woman to step forward and not to "wait for the millionaires" to endow the pedestal. This plea resonated with his audience in a big way. Readers began sending in small contributions,[14] seeing their names in print for their efforts. The subsequent $100,000 collected from this campaign was combined with funds garnered by the American Committee of the Statue. The project moved forward,[15] its new pedestal now assured.

Genuine Statue of Liberty fever took hold, and it continued to increase proportionately. The actual dedication and unveiling of the completed statue with the much-awaited pedestal took place on October 28, 1886. Massive crowds jammed the streets to take part in the special day. Liberty souvenirs were in high demand, and shouts from street vendors punctuated the air. It was said that the sculptor himself patented small bronze models of the Statue, hoping to earn some money from souvenir proceeds.[16] Statue of Liberty mementos of all sorts held the spotlight in popularity and continued to do so through the time of Tchaikovsky's visit and well beyond. Therefore, it was not surprising that the composer would go back to Russia with a small replica in his possession, nor was it surprising that it pleased him so well to have received it. It was by that time a famous icon.

Just as Tchaikovsky was an honored international musical guest in 1891, Lady Liberty's sculptor Frederic-Auguste Bartholdi was also received with great enthusiasm in 1886. When he came to New York for the dedication of the Statue, he sailed from Le Havre on *La Bretagne*—the same ship on which Tchaikovsky would journey to America several years later. In Bartholdi's case, his trip was a mere two months after the ship's maiden voyage across the Atlantic.[17] It was a luxurious vessel, as Tchaikovsky was also to discover, with an interior exquisitely created by the Parisien, Mr.

Allard, who had decorated the Vanderbilt Fifth Avenue home.[18] Tchaikovsky later referred to the vessel as "sumptuous ... a floating palace."[19]

Bartholdi arrived in New York to great fanfare, and even his wife received a celebratory bouquet of roses with tricolor ribbons. He was now a hero to the citizens of the city. Richard Morris Hunt—mentor to William Burnet Tuthill and a future consulting architect for the Music Hall—was among the first to have the opportunity to talk with Bartholdi in person. This was no coincidence. Hunt was the architect who finally designed the pedestal for the Statue.[20]

Bartholdi was continually feted. First, he was whisked off to the famed Hoffman House—the same restaurant that Tchaikovsky enjoyably visited several times during his stay five years later. A concert was offered in honor of the entire French delegation, with an orchestra of fifty-four men performing under the baton of Frank Van der Stucken,[21] the same conductor who would participate in one of the Recital Hall's April 1891 concerts. The day of the Statue's dedication and unveiling was one of excitement, and the Grand Army of the Republic proudly marched in the celebratory parade,[22] the first event that gave rise to the ticker-tape custom.[23] Like Van der Stucken, the GAR was also later to be a part of the Recital Hall's opening events. Additional coincidences existed between the Liberty celebrations and the opening of the Music Hall. At the official unveiling ceremony—and after a rendition of "the long meter doxology"—a benediction was pronounced by then Assistant Bishop Henry Potter, who would a few short years later offer his famous dedicatory address on May 5, 1891.[24] And the rooftop of the comfortable Hotel Normandie, where Tchaikovsky would eventually stay, was the site of a hundred gattling guns—a "feu de joie"—that sounded in tribute at the lighting of Lady Liberty.[25]

The Statue of Liberty—and Barthholdi—would further help put New York and, therefore, America on the map as a worldwide representative of freedom and liberty. Later, the New Music Hall—and Tchaikovsky— would do the same for the city and the country in the musical and cultural arena.

Whether or not the composer was aware of the many curious links between his visit and the Statue of Liberty events, it was certain that the gift of the little Statue of Liberty replica pleased him greatly. He expressed only one concern—he wondered if he would be permitted to bring it back to Russia. This he ultimately did,[26] and it became a fond memento of his trip. The gift itself was from the Knabe piano firm with which Tchaikovsky had developed such a friendly association during his stay in America. Therefore, he wanted to take the time to personally offer his thanks for their thoughtfulness.[27] It was a pleasant errand and one that could perhaps ease his frustration after that morning's rehearsal.

Although there had been no major difficulties, the flow of events had disturbed Tchaikovsky. This was the fourth day of the Festival, and the one on which his piano concerto was to be rehearsed in preparation for the next, final day of the week's events. The concerto would be one of the major works—if not *the* major one—to be performed the following afternoon, a composition eagerly anticipated by the audience. As such, Tchaikovsky wanted to ensure that all went well during rehearsal. He commented, however, that Walter Damrosch took too long with his own portion of that day's time allotment and left little to the composer. Despite the fact that everything turned out well, he was vexed over this incident, and his walk to acknowledge the gift was a good change of pace. He found his friend Ferdinand Mayer and others enjoying some champagne at Martelli's,[28] and there he had the opportunity to offer his thanks. Afterward, the lack of time still plagued him and, as usual, his day was filled with another round of visitors.

The number and variety of callers during Tchaikovsky's stay in New York continually amazed him. Today was no different. There was a heart-wrenching visit from an older man, grief-stricken over his son's death. He had written an opera libretto—*Vlast*—for which he wanted Tchaikovsky to compose music. This touched Tchaikovsky deeply but he later needed to refuse the man's request.[29]

Then there was the arrival of journalist Barbara MacGahan. Born Varvara Elagina, she had been married to the late, famous American war correspondent, Januarius MacGahan. Coming to New York in 1880, she gained notice writing for the Russian publication *Severnyi Vestnik* as well as for penning articles on Russia for American publications.[30] While this was a welcome and pleasant visit, the conversation had an unexpected effect. Tchaikovsky was so moved by this opportunity to talk with someone from his homeland that he was overcome with emotion and could not stop his tears. He needed to seclude himself in another room for a while, and this incident caused him a great deal of embarrassment.[31]

By now, the emotionally drained man still had to politely meet with Mrs. Neftel, a charitably active woman and the wife of a noted Russian-American doctor.[32] Following her was flutist Eugene Weiner[33] who had played with Theodore Thomas' orchestra and also organized the New York Philharmonic Club—one of many popular quintettes of the time.[34] The previous year, German composer Wilhelm Popp drew some attention to Weiner by writing a piece for him titled *Bagatelle*—requiring the performer to simultaneously play the flute with one hand and the piano with the other.[35]

Such visitors and their often unusual stories were not the only drain on Tchaikovsky's time and energy. There were also copious numbers of letters to be read and answered. These came from all over the country and a large majority of the correspondents wanted the composer's autograph. Being the polite individual that he was, he did his best to write back to everyone and comply.[36] Attending to correspondence was enough to occupy the composer until it was time for the fourth event of the Festival that evening.

This music to be presented was entirely different in tone and mood than that performed on the previous afternoon, this time focusing on religious themes. It was also to feature several American premieres. The first work was among these—*The Seven Words of Our Saviour*, written by Heinrich Schutz (or Schuetz) in 1645. An intricate composition that required chorus, soloists, a string orchestra, and organ, it had not been heard in America before, although composed more than two hundred years previously. Preceding Bach by a century, Schutz was sometimes referred to as the "Father of German music."[37] It can certainly be said that he had a significant impact on the music of that culture.

Schutz was the son of innkeepers. A guest at the family establishment— Moritz, the Landgrave of Hesse-Cassel—provided a turning point in the young man's future. In addition to his governing duties, Moritz was a composer and greatly interested in music. Impressed by Schutz's abilities, he invited the boy to his court where he provided opportunities for continued musical training and development. This experience paved the way for Schutz to eventually continue his studies in Italy, in particular with Giovanni Gabrieli, whose influence would have a significant impact on him. Later, Schutz served in various musical capacities—from organist to *Kapellmeister*—in several courts in Germany and Denmark.[38] It was the education that he received with Gabrieli, however, that strongly honed his abilities to the point that he could bridge both German and Italian styles in his composing, especially in works designed for performance by large choral and instrumental groups. In doing so, he blended the Italian madrigal styles with sacred words in German, creating something unique that was to have a marked affect on later composers.[39] Although Schutz wrote many types of works, he was especially recognized for his sacred compositions and is commemorated for music in the Lutheran Calendar of Saints along with Bach and Handel.[40]

The Seven Words of Our Saviour was a precursor to the later oratorio

PROGRAMMES.

Friday Evening, May 8th, 1891.

THE SEVEN WORDS OF OUR SAVIOUR, ... HEINRICH SCHUETZ
(Seventeenth century.) (First time in America.)

For Soli, Chorus, String Orchestra and Organ.

SOLOISTS, { FRAU ANTONIA MIELKE, FRAU MARIE RITTER-GOETZE, HERR ANDREAS DIPPEL, HERR THEODOR REICHMANN, MR. ERICSON BUSHNELL.

TWO A CAPELLA CHORUSES : }
a. PATER NOSTER,   } (New. First time in America.)   TSCHAIKOWSKY
b. LEGEND. }

Conducted by the Composer.

SULAMITH, ... LEOPOLD DAMROSCH
For Soli, Chorus and Orchestra.
Soloists, FRAU ANTONIA MIELKE, HERR ANDREAS DIPPEL.

Saturday Afternoon, May 9th, 1891,

FIFTH SYMPHONY, C MINOR, ... BEETHOVEN

SONGS, { "TO SLEEP," . . . . . . WALTER DAMROSCH
{ "SO SCHMERZLICH," . . . . . TSCHAIKOWSKY

CONCERTO for Piano with Orchestra, B Flat Minor, Op. 23, . . . TSCHAIKOWSKY
    I.   *Andante non troppo e molto maestoso. Allegro con spirito.*
    II. *Andantino Simplice.*
    III. *Allegro con fuoco.*

Piano, MISS ADELE AUS DER OHE.

Conducted by the Composer.

PRELUDE, }
    FLOWER MAIDEN SCENE, ACT II, } FROM PARSIFAL,   .   WAGNER
For six Solo Voices and Female Chorus.

MRS. GERRIT SMITH,   MRS. TOEDT.   MISS KELLY,   MRS. KOERT KRONOLD,
MRS. ALVES,   MRS. MORRIS.

Steinway & Sons' Piano used at this Concert.

Saturday Evening, May 9th.

"ISRAEL IN EGYPT" Oratorio, ... HANDEL
For Soli, Double Chorus and Orchestra.

SOLOISTS:

MISS KELLY,   MRS. TOEDT,   MRS. ALVES,   HERR DIPPEL,

HERR FISCHER,   MR. BUSHNELL.

A page from the program booklet for the Festival, listing repertoire and performers for the last two days of concerts (courtesy Carnegie Hall Archives).

style and, as such, greatly influential. According to the program notes for the evening's concert, the work of Schutz is a mid-marker between the music of the mystery and miracle plays that preceded it as far back as the thirteenth century and the well-recognized oratorio form of Handel's time.[41] When the early passion plays began to stray from their religious purpose, they were replaced by more sacred musical dramas created by Italian clergy and composers. Subsequently, the Reformation in Germany led to music that focused on the passion of Christ. Schutz bridged the gap between these traditions and composed passion music within a "genuine oratorio form."[42]

Although written in the mid–1600s, the existence of *The Seven Words of Our Saviour* was only discovered two centuries later in 1855 when a manuscript was found in the library in Cassel, Germany. Thereafter, it was edited and published for performance in a more modern setting several decades later in Europe.[43] The editor of the work's German edition stated that it was worthy of study for its historical value, beauty of form, and example of the honest "German expression of feeling."[44] Along these same lines, *The New York Times* review of the Festival performance pointed out the tenderness of the music, praising Schutz for his multi-faceted achievements, including introducing opera to Germany as well as contributing greatly to the development of the early oratorio form. The work of Schutz, they emphasized more than once, had a significant influence on Bach.[45] *The New-York Tribune* echoed these thoughts, going a step further to express disappointment that no works by Bach were included in the Festival—a performance of which would have perfectly illustrated the links between these two composers. This particular reviewer went into great depth about the structural and musical elements that contributed to the whole of *The Seven Words* and briefly, but meaningfully, traced the development of each of these factors over subsequent years.[46] From a historical standpoint, it was especially significant that the Schutz work was performed by the Oratorio Society, since it represented the early days of the oratorio form itself, a musical genre to which the group was dedicated.

The soloists for *The Seven Words* had already appeared in the Festival—Mielke, Ritter-Goetze, Dippel, Reichmann, and Bushnell. The reviews were not kind to Reichmann, though, suggesting that he was not in his best vocal form that evening and, also, did not make the most of his part. The others, however, were praised for their performances.

The organist was Frank L. Sealy—an individual who played in this work as well as in several other major choral pieces in the Festival. He was a vital, although less spotlighted individual. Sealy was integral to both the Oratorio and Symphony societies, having become the official organist for both in 1885, posts in which he remained for a number of years. In addition, he became a director of the Oratorio Society. A composer as well as a performer, he completed studies with Dudley Buck and others.[47] His *Magnificat* and *Nunc Dimittis*, published by G. Schirmer, received high praise.[48] Sealy eventually went on to be organist at the prestigious Fifth Avenue Presbyterian Church and held administrative posts with both the New York Manuscript Society and the American Guild of Organists. Membership in the Guild more than doubled during his tenure there.[49]

The organ that Sealy played was specially made for the Music Hall by the Roosevelt Pipe Organ Company. Frank Roosevelt had been in partnership with his late brother Hilborne in this firm. Hilborne Roosevelt had not only been fascinated with the organ as an instrument, but he was also quite interested in electricity. After winning a gold medal for his work at New York's Industrial Fair in 1869, he studied with master organ builders in Europe and opened his own organ firm upon his return. He was thought to have been responsible for the first American instrument to possess electric action. After his untimely death, his brother Frank continued in the business,[50] building instruments for many prestigious churches. Certainly Frank Roosevelt was acquainted with the Music Hall enterprise—he had been best man to Walter Damrosch at his wedding in 1890,[51] and it was obvious that they shared an interest in music. The first organ to be placed in the Music Hall in 1891 was built by Frank Roosevelt and his company. According to the American Guild of Organists' archive, this Opus 486 mechanical action instrument had two manuals, 32 stops, and 34 ranks.[52] It also possessed a "classic Roosevelt hallmark"[53]—a doppelflute, which had a distinctively rich sound. A full set of pedals and a sensitive swell box offered the performer additional control and expressive options, and the wind chests were of the company's patent construction. The power source was electric. This instrument was designed to fit the needs of the space and although not intended to be played as a solo concert instrument, it was perfect for use in accompanying choral and orchestral groups[54] in the performance of works such as those featured in the Festival.

This was an evening of premieres. Following *The Seven Last Words* were two choruses, both composed and conducted by Tchaikovsky. These, too, were being presented for the first time in America. Both of them— *Pater Noster* and *Legend*—were scored for unaccompanied voices. Although some reviews suggested that the first of this pair was more similar in tone to the Schutz composition that preceded it, the second—*Legend*—was especially praised for the richness of its music with what was described as obvious roots in Russian and Eastern church themes.[55] This work presented a mystery. According to later research into the text, one that tells the story of the boy Jesus and his garden, it was discovered that the words were originally derived from a poem by Richard Henry Stoddard. It saw translations into Russian by Pleshcheyev and then into German by Hans Schmidt. There was even a type of variation on the text in Yiddish that had been referred to at one point. However, it appears that "Roses and Thorns," the poem by Stoddard, was the original source of all the different versions. Tchaikovsky first wrote the music for this song for solo voice, but he later transcribed it for a mixed choir to be sung *a cappella*. This was the version that was received with such great enthusiasm at the Music Hall that evening.[56] These works were so popular with the audience that Tchaikovsky had to return to the stage to acknowledge their applause once more and provide an encore of one chorus.[57]

The final work of the evening was the cantata *Sulamith* by Leopold Damrosch. This was not a premiere as were the previous works on the program. However, it had only been performed once previously in its entirety on April 21, 1882, at Steinway Hall by the Oratorio Society, the group to which it was dedicated. On that occasion, it was paired with a Bach Cantata.[58] Several years later during a concert presented by the Symphony Society, an air from this cantata was performed by Marianne Brandt.[59] It was also the first work rehearsed in the building complex's new Recital Hall on March 12.

The performance of *Sulamith* at the Festival accomplished several goals. Most obviously, it was a fitting tribute to its late composer, Leopold Damrosch, who had served as the initial inspiration for the creation of the Music Hall. The program notes for the cantata likened

A sketch of Leopold Damrosch whose cantata *Sulamith* was featured during the Festival. He was the founder of both the Oratorio and Symphony Societies.

the reaction of Wotan to Walhalla—fully realized as it had been in his dreams—to what Leopold Damrosch might have felt upon seeing the Music Hall upon its completion.[60] The cantata was also a fine showcase that evening for the Oratorio and Symphony societies, the two groups that Damrosch created and which continued to thrive after his untimely death under his son's able direction. In addition, it illustrated the more contemporary end of the scale in choral music, demonstrating the versatility of the singers and their ability to perform different styles within the repertoire—from the early work of Schutz to the more modern *Sulamith*.[61]

Leopold Damrosch's cantata was set to a text selected from the *Song of Solomon* and was composed in the style of the modern romanticists. The final chorus was quite elaborate and more in keeping with the oratorio tradition or perhaps, as has been suggested, closer to a "symphonic cantata," such as favored by Berlioz.[62] Of course, both Leopold and Walter Damrosch were champions of the works of Berlioz.

The architect's sketch of the Music Hall, an edifice inspired by Leopold Damrosch. Although he did not live to see it, his son and others helped realize his dream of this new concert hall for his performing groups (courtesy Carnegie Hall Archives).

Despite the full and varied range of conducting and performing responsibilities that consumed much of Leopold Damrosch's time over the course of his entire career, he still left a body of compositions that was fairly impressive. They included solo instrumental and vocal pieces, concertos, and orchestral, operatic, and choral works. Some were written while he was still in Europe and others while in America. His *Symphony in A Major* was composed during the year he founded the Symphony Society. However, he did not wish the group to be used just as a vehicle for performing his compositions, so it remained in the background. He also edited a number of scores as well as collections for voice.

Given Damrosch's efforts in working with the Arion group and in building and leading the Oratorio Society in particular, it seemed natural that one of his compositional focuses was on choral music. His major works within this area consisted of *Ruth and Naomi* and *Sulamith*, the latter written specifically for the Oratorio Society. It includes parts for both soprano and tenor solo—on this evening sung by Antonia Mielke and Andreas Dippel. Despite its biblical source, it has some of the expressive qualities of the secular in its movements[63]—much of it a love song or duet with choral narrative. "Sulamith," a variation on the Hebrew "Shulamith," means "peace." It is believed to be the female character in *Song of Solomon*.

The soprano solo in the middle of the work was reportedly written several years prior to the rest of the cantata, composed specifically for the voice of Eugenie Pappenheim,[64] a German opera singer who made headlines with her colorful personal life. She performed in New York and appeared as a soloist with the Oratorio Society on at least one occasion.[65] One critic felt that this solo disrupted the unity of the whole and should be cut in the future. Nevertheless, at the Festival concert, Antonia Mielke sang this piece with great emotion, and the audience showed an enthusiastic appreciation for the entire work. There was an encore of one chorus—"Arise, my love"—which was said to be among the loveliest parts of the cantata as a whole.[66] Tchaikovsky was able to sit with Morris Reno and E. Francis Hyde and enjoy *Sulamith*. He called it a "beautiful oratorio."[67]

This was one of the more understated evenings in the festival. In particular, critics mentioned that perhaps the audiences did not appreciate the "antiquated style"[68] of the Schutz.

However, more praise was heaped upon Tchaikovsky by newspaper reviewers and the audience. The evening was another phenomenal success for the composer, and the premiere of his two choruses was a highlight.

Legend was called "a hit" by *The New York Times*.[69] Once more, it was obvious that New York and America loved Tchaikovsky—his music, his conducting, and his presence.

After the concert, Tchaikovsky joined Morris Reno and Andrew Carnegie. The trio walked to the Damrosch apartment on West 70th Street, a fair enough distance from the Music Hall. They had been invited for a post-concert supper there, an event that the composer referred to as "original" since the men occupied a table separate from the women— something Tchaikovsky found unusual. The cuisine was American, a style that was not to the composer's liking. However, the champagne and conversation made up for the culinary shortcomings.[70]

Tchaikovsky was seated between Walter Damrosch and the concert-master from the orchestra. Soon, he became involved in a conversation with the latter—Gustav Dannreuther, who had played so beautifully in the *Suite No. III* during the previous afternoon's concert. This violinist had solid experience as a member of the Boston Symphony Orchestra as well as with the Symphony Society, but he especially enjoyed chamber music and had formed the Dannreuther Quartet in 1884, a group that was active through 1917 and influenced many other groups including the well-known Kneisel Quartet. Eventually, he taught at Vassar College.[71] His brother, Edward—a pianist and a close friend of Wagner—was on the faculty of London's Royal College of Music and wrote a treatise on musical ornamentation that was famous.[72]

Although Tchaikovsky enjoyed his conversation with the violinist, he confused the man's brother, Edward Dannreuther, with Frits Hartvigson, a Danish pianist who also lived and taught in London and had performed the composer's piano concerto there in 1877 for the first time after its revision.[73] Tchaikovsky was upset over his mistake and concerned if this was another testament to his aging.[74] The experience plagued him afterward—he was worried that Gustav Dannreuther would think ill of him. He later wrote in his diary of his concerns over this type of absent-mindedness.[75] Given the number of people that he interacted with on a daily basis during this trip, it would certainly have been understandable to Dannreuther and to others that some confusion would occur. Still, it was troubling to Tchaikovsky and sadly so, since this was the same man who was said to have been the "chief source of brilliancy" during the entire Festival.[76]

• NINE •

Grand Finale—Saturday
May 9, 1891

Saturday morning, 7:00 a.m. Something was definitely wrong. Smoke curled in the air on West 57th Street. A burst of flames came next. The Annex of the new Music Hall was on fire.[1]

Despite the addition of an increasing number of building safety codes over recent years, massive fires still erupted in public buildings with those in places of entertainment all too common. Several months earlier, both the Fifth Avenue Theatre and Herrmann's Theatre were destroyed in a dramatic blaze that first consumed scenery, costumes, and interior fixtures before taking nearby stores and homes with them. It engulfed one solid block of Broadway.[2] Onlookers watched in horror.

Warnings now sounded for the Music Hall after an alert policeman sent up a two-alarm signal. Three fire companies raced to the call with a half dozen vehicles in total. The Annex—with its offices, meeting rooms, and studios still under construction—was at the heart of the blaze. Materials from unfinished plastering and carpentry projects—all highly flammable items—had been stored in its basement. This was the fire's source. What was worse: the Annex was connected to the main building where the beautiful new concert hall was located.[3]

As swiftly as the fire companies arrived, though, the building's superintendent, J. M. Chesebro,[4] was even faster. He would be the hero of the hour. Chesebro reached the scene with a fire extinguisher moments before the fire companies arrived and succeeded in dousing the flames.[5] All in all, the situation turned out most fortunately with no injuries or devastating destruction resulting. As to the cause of the fire, there were really no answers. One newspaper conjectured that a cigar butt, perhaps still smoldering, might have been accidentally pitched into the basement sometime at the end of the previous day.[6] It was never known for sure. Whatever the cause, though, the blaze was luckily short-lived. There was damage to some of the newer items stored there, particularly doors and woodwork pieces. The total amount of these losses, however, was not more than $1,000.[7] What was especially fortunate was that the fire did not spread, since a two-foot-thick brick firewall separated the building's sections—a fine deterrent to the blaze potentially traveling from one portion of the complex to the other.[8]

That same morning, Tchaikovsky was relaxing in his hotel room, unaware of the excitement that had unfolded on West 57th Street. He spent a while admiring Max's careful arrangements of all the items in his room, especially the growing number of flowers that he had been continually receiving. He was particularly moved by the lovely bouquets from Mrs. White—Gustav Schirmer's married daughter. The two had met at her father's apartment several days previously at a dinner there. Tchaikovsky commented on her friendliness and how comfortable she made him feel. Her gift of flowers was so generous that the composer gave some of the blooms to Max to bring home to his wife.[9]

Once more, there were social obligations, visitors chiefly among them. The American violinist J. Rietzel was first, happy to reveal how much the orchestra members liked their visiting composer.[10] Rietzel was a seasoned musician, experienced in gauging performer's responses to conductors in general. He also knew many of those who were appearing onstage during the Festival week. His information, though, was not a revelation. Time and again, the press had already spoken of the obviously positive reactions of the orchestra toward their guest, one even commenting that there had not previously been another who had led them in such a compelling manner.[11]

Rietzel was followed by Frank Howson[12] and Gerrit Smith from the Composers' Club. Howson was a musician and composer who, after conducting some operas at the Academy of Music, began to specialize in the theater realm, eventually becoming a musical director for Daniel Frohman. The incidental music that he composed was included in shows such as *Prisoner of Zenda* and *If I Were a King*.[13] Howson was also part of the Manuscript Society as was Walter Damrosch and the other half of the visiting duo that morning, Gerrit Smith, one of the group's creators and, also, its onetime president.[14] An organist, choirmaster, and professor of Sacred Music at Union Theological Seminary,[15] he was married to Caroline B. Smith, a soprano who was to perform in that afternoon's Festival concert. The men wanted to discuss an upcoming recital of Tchaikovsky's music to be presented in his honor by the Composers' Club.[16] After this, there was not much time for additional visitors that day. Two concerts were scheduled to bring the Festival to a close in style, the first to begin at 2:00 that afternoon—and Tchaikovsky was once more an integral part of it.

The audience was especially large. Not only was it the final day of the Festival, but it was also the last opportunity to see Tchaikovsky conduct, this time leading the orchestra and soloist in a performance of his *Piano Concerto No. 1.* Despite a reported sellout for the week, individuals were still doing their best to secure some coveted tickets at the last minute by whatever means possible. Although speculators had been supposedly doing their business in and around the Music Hall for quite a while, ticket mania had now grown to a fever pitch. On that particular afternoon, it was rumored that the ushers were running a brisk side business in shady ticket sales. Word had it that if seats were empty for whatever reason early on during the concert, they were brokered out for $1.50 apiece with some bargaining down to a minimum of $1 taking place. Further conjecture suggested that the ushering staff had united in setting up this arrangement and "huckstered spots openly."[17] At the same time, they busily seated latecomers at every conceivably inopportune moment in the program causing those already settled and listening to the music to be clearly vexed. Comparisons were drawn with the orderly quiet at Theodore Thomas, New York Philharmonic, or regular Symphony Society concerts—perhaps with the slightest hint of disappointment at the absence onstage that week of all but the last group mentioned.[18]

Amidst the obvious noise and jostling of the infamous latecomers, the first work on the program—Beethoven's *Fifth Symphony*—was fully underway. This symphony was an audience favorite, and, according to the program notes, the work that was "most strongly associated"[19] with Beethoven in general. It was certainly special to conductor Walter Damrosch, as well, as were all of Beethoven's symphonies.

Beethoven had become an important part of Damrosch's musical life early on. As a child, he remembered his father's farewell concert in Breslau prior to coming to the U.S. during which Beethoven's *Ninth Symphony* was performed to great audience accolades. It was an event that the young Damrosch remembered vividly.[20] Later, Leopold Damrosch presented it once more in New York at the famous "monster" music festival of 1881. For this event, Walter Damrosch had the pleasure of helping his father prepare for the festival by leading rehearsals for some of the many participating groups.[21] But it was not just the majestic *Ninth* that captivated his attention. He was drawn to all of Beethoven's symphonies. At the time he met Andrew and Louise Carnegie on the voyage to Europe, Damrosch was headed to Germany to analyze in depth all of Beethoven's symphonies with Hans von Bulow. Several months after returning from this expedition, the *Times* commented on the fruitfulness of this study as demonstrated in Damrosch's "excellent reading" of the *Fifth Symphony* at an early concert during that season.[22] However, even a few months before that event, Damrosch wrote to his brother Frank, describing one of the informal talks he presented for the Carnegies and their guests in Scotland. The group had so enjoyed his presentation on Beethoven's *Fifth* that he wondered if more formal lecture-recitals, given in conjunction with the New York Symphony and focusing on this and other works, would be popular with larger audiences. Louise Carnegie was extremely supportive of the idea.[23] These talks later became the basis for a very important lifelong segment of his career. Over subsequent years, Damrosch conducted the *Fifth* and additional symphonies by the composer numerous times, later commenting that his Beethoven scores, as well as those of others, were "old and worn" as well as "pasted together" through years of use.[24]

Beethoven's *Fifth Symphony* was originally premiered by the composer in Vienna in 1808. Above all, it is a dramatic work. Beethoven himself stated that it had greater narrative unification than any of his previous symphonies—or, for that matter, of those by any other composer. Beethoven was nothing if not emphatic in his proclamations. He referred to the unforgettable opening as a "motif" and not a "theme," something that would be quintessential to the development of the work.[25] The captivating passion expressed in its music made it the source of much commentary after its initial performance and eventually led to its popularity over time. Two years after the European premiere, E. T. A. Hoffmann wrote an essay in which he thoughtfully commented on the *Fifth Symphony*, praising the work as "profound" and suggesting that it opened a "spirit-realm" that reflected an "unknown language."[26]

In 1841, more than thirty years after the Vienna premiere of this symphony, a group of musicians gathered to perform a benefit concert at the Broadway Tabernacle in New York. George Templeton Strong was present and commented liberally in his diary on both the concert and the attending audience. There was some anti–German sentiment prevalent at that time, and Strong was not reticent to express some of his own feelings along these lines. His acerbic comments on the subject spilled into his remarks on Beethoven's *Fifth Symphony*, too, which he called "unintelligible," except for the Andante. Others in attendance must have been of a like mind, since some audience members did not wait to hear the conclusion of the work. They were the poorer for that decision. On the other hand, the musicians themselves were excited about the *Symphony* and believed that the more frequently the public heard it performed, the more they would be drawn to it. They were proven correct, and their strong faith in the work and others like it had an immediate impact of historic proportions. Beethoven's *Fifth Symphony* was the catalyst for the formation of a new orchestra in 1842, only one short year after the concert so scathingly appraised by Strong and his fellow audience members. Those same musicians from the Tabernacle event met and formed the New York Philharmonic Society. On December 7, 1842, this group opened their inaugural concert at the Apollo Rooms with a performance of Beethoven's *Fifth Symphony*.[27] Thereafter, this orchestra dedicated itself to playing quality symphonies such as this and, of course, performed the Beethoven work many times over its long history.

The famous opening notes of the first movement are straightforward, dramatic, and memorable—leaving a lasting impression on the listener. Goethe once commented on their "grand, wildly mad"[28] effect. And Berlioz said that the whole first movement reflected emotions that "agitate[d] great souls."[29] Later, Walter Damrosch echoed one prevailing theory that these notes were the sound of fate knocking.[30] The second movement—the Andante, which was the portion that George Templeton Strong found to be the most attractive part of the *Symphony*—is more mellow. The Scherzo and Finale are performed without interruption and build to the work's triumphal conclusion.[31]

As performed at the Festival concert, Beethoven's *Fifth Symphony* attracted some glowing reviews. Walter Damrosch received praise for his conducting as did the orchestra for the vitality of the performance. The woodwinds were specially mentioned for the superior execution of their parts in the Andante. At the conclusion, the audience offered generous applause,[32] proving that the work had become a favorite in the decades that had passed since the Broadway Tabernacle concert.

The next compositions on the program offered a change of pace from the Beethoven Symphony as well as an intriguing interlude before the larger works that were to follow. Two distinctly different songs were performed—one composed by Walter Damrosch and the other by Tchaikovsky. Both were sung by Mrs. Carl (Katie) Alves.

Alves was a New York native of German heritage with a fine contralto voice. Her talent was recognized early on and upon hearing her perform at the age of sixteen, Leopold Damrosch predicted her rise to the status of a "great artist." She studied voice with Carl Alves, whom she later married. Her debut recital, a program consisting of German lieder, was presented at the Metropolitan Opera House with Walter Damrosch as accompanist. Known for her work in both concert and oratorio genres, Alves appeared with Boston's Handel and Haydn Society on numerous occasions and performed widely at festivals, including many with Theodore Thomas. She became a soloist at the West Presbyterian Church on 42nd Street, as were several other performers featured in the Festival. Alves eventually left the stage to teach after the death of her husband, coming out of retirement once at the special invitation of the Oratorio Society to participate in a performance of Beethoven's *Ninth Symphony*.[33] Tchaikovsky had the opportunity to meet Alves in the Artists' room and later, in his diary, praised her singing and, also, referred to her a as a "lovely woman."[34]

The first of the two songs—"To Sleep"—was composed by Walter Damrosch. His music provided a setting for a poem by Tennyson. The words in a surviving manuscript copy, however, were not taken from the more well-known poem of the same name that was part of Tennyson's larger work *In Memorium*. They were, instead, verses drawn from *The Foresters*, a play that Tennyson based on the Robin Hood legend. In this work, the words were spoken by Robin Hood during a conversation with Little John concerning the seasons of life[35]—the joys and griefs that pass with the day until "all life will sleep at last."[36] The character of Robin Hood was a popular one with nineteenth-century audiences.[37] Damrosch's score indicates that he composed the song for an alto or baritone voice, although a designation for "mezzo soprano" was crossed out on the first page. The piece begins in the key of Gb with an "Andante grave" indication but picks up in tempo in the middle as it moves into the key of Eb.[38]

"To Sleep" was originally performed by Mrs. Alves on April 15 of that year at a concert sponsored by the New York Manuscript Society.[39] This group was created in 1889 for the purpose of furthering the music of American composers. Works were performed from the actual manuscripts before an audience of fellow members only. These events were such a success that the organization soon opened them to the public.[40] The first of these public occasions took place at Chickering Hall in December of 1890, and *The New York Times* enthusiastically praised both the group and its mission.[41]

Next, Mrs. Alves sang "So Schmerzlich"—or "It's painful, it's sweet"— by Tchaikovsky. The subject is love. Tchaikovsky composed approximately a hundred songs during his career, and an introduction to one of the modern collections states that these works reflect some of his most "striking ideas."[42] He based many of the songs on Russian poetic texts, but also used those that were translated from both German and French. Many of these works are melancholy in tone, and all have beautiful melody lines. In addition, the accompaniments are independent gems, unique in their distinct melodic components, frequent use of chromatic phrases, and employment of imaginative harmonic resources. They add a rich texture to the vocal part while creating a superb "mood-picture" all their own.[43] "So Schmerzlich," though, particularly stands out—for in this song Tchaikovsky captured some of the essence of his favorite composer—Mozart. He was extremely fond of *The Marriage of Figaro,* a work that was also popular in his home country. Drawn to Cherubino's aria *Non so piu,* a song of romance both comic and sweet, he found inspiration for "So Schmerzlich." The lyrics came from a poem by Countess Yevdokiya Rostopchina.[44]

The critics did not spend much time discussing the songs, however. *The Times* felt that they did not belong on this particular program, somewhat out of place in comparison to the other works of larger magnitude that were scheduled for that afternoon.[45] Yet the songs did serve as an arresting interlude, and the lack of attention to them might very well have been the partial result of the high anticipation surrounding the work that was to follow.

Tchaikovsky's *Piano Concerto in B Flat Minor* was not only a highlight of the day but also of the entire Festival. Since the composer was going to be conducting and by now had achieved a hero's status, the public was extremely eager to see him in person once more. The work itself was also popular and had a compelling history. Composed in 1874, years before the Music Hall Festival, the early days of this concerto were tumultuous ones for the composer. By this time, Tchaikovsky had already emerged from the St. Petersburg Conservatory as a student, identified for his superior talent by its director, the legendary pianist-composer Anton Rubinstein, who had taken an interest in and mentored the young man. Just prior to graduation, Rubinstein's brother Nicholas, also a highly renowned pianist, offered Tchaikovsky a job teaching at the Moscow Conservatory— a position of honor and one that would help enhance his career. Two of the most famed musicians in Russia had now ratified Tchaikovsky's talent and promise as a composer.

Both as a student and now as a professor, Tchaikovsky continued composing and had the opportunity to hear some of his works performed. He had invested a great deal of effort in his piano concerto and was ready to put it to the test. Not being a pianist himself, Tchaikovsky wanted feedback from an individual who could objectively comment on any issues that might act as impediments to performing soloists, although he was securely confident in the artistic merits of his work. Nicholas Rubinstein seemed a logical choice to approach for such input. Not only was he director of the Moscow Conservatory as well as a top-notch musician and leading Moscow pianist, but he had also invited Tchaikovsky to be on the conservatory faculty. Beyond this, Tchaikovsky planned on dedicating the new concerto to him. Tchaikovsky's intuition, however, nagged at him. Deep down, he had an inkling that Rubinstein might not be the best person of whom to ask an opinion. This intuition turned out to be sadly prophetic. On Christmas Eve of 1874, Tchaikovsky met with Rubinstein and Nickolai Hubert, another professor at the Conservatory—and an individual who was said to always agree with Rubinstein's opinions. Along these lines, Tchaikovsky later wrote of the "servile attitude" of the faculty in general toward Rubinstein.[46] Tchaikovsky played the concerto for the two men. An uncomfortable silence preceded the impending storm. With few preliminaries, Rubinstein decimated the work with mounting antagonism in words and tone. Stunned at this outburst, Tchaikovsky left the room. Rubinstein followed and demanded that Tchaikovsky completely revise the work to his specifications before he would ever consider performing it. Tchaikovsky refused, vowing to publish it as it stood without changing a note—a vow that he kept.[47]

After this incident, there was obviously going to be no dedication to Rubinstein as originally intended. Instead, the honor went to Hans von Bulow who in October of 1875, less than a year after this devastating blow to the composer, performed the world premiere of the work in Boston. Von Bulow thought highly of the concerto, referring to it as "original, noble, mature, powerful, and distinguished."[48] Although some of the Boston reviews were mixed, suggesting that the work was too "elaborate" for the audience, word did get back to Russia via von Bulow himself that the concerto was quite well received in America. This served as the catalyst for two concerts featuring the work, performed respectively in St. Petersburg and Moscow by Russian pianists Gustave Kross and Sergei Teneyev. The most intriguing fact about these events, however, was that the conductor for both was none other than Nicholas Rubinstein, the very individual who had so vociferously attacked the work during the previous year. Obviously, he had changed his mind.[49] Von Bulow also played the New York premiere of the concerto on November 22, 1875, at Chickering Hall with the New York Philharmonic. Leopold Damrosch conducted, filling in for the seriously ailing Carl Bergmann.[50] The concerto's popularity soared, becoming a time-honored and solid addition to the standard repertoire. Rubinstein's scathing comments faded into dust. It appeared that he quickly found value in the work after learning of its success in performance.

Now, on the final day of the Festival, the concerto was being featured as one of its highlights. Pianist Adele Aus der Ohe had the honor of working with the composer during his last onstage appearance in New York. She had already made a name for herself in the concert world, and this afternoon's appearance would add to her reputation as well as ensure her place in musical history. A native of Germany, the young woman's talent was recognized early on during her studies with Theodore Kullak. Amy Fay—the author of *Music-Study in Germany in the Nineteenth Century* and a pianist who had also appeared at the Recital Hall in April—had heard Aus der Ohe perform as a child in Europe. She referred to this experience as "most astonishing."[51] Similar to Fay, Aus der Ohe went on to study with Franz Liszt who praised her playing above that of many others.[52] Intensely dedicated, she stated that music was "holy to me," and she was grateful for her talent as a gift from God.[53] Even in later life when her health and financial circumstances declined, she maintained this positive faith.[54] A serious artist, she performed frequently in Europe, and when invited to come to New York, she was overjoyed. Within a short time of her arrival in 1886, she performed Liszt's *Concerto in E-flat* under the baton of Anton Seidl at Steinway Hall.[55] With this, her fame and fortune in America were assured.

Several weeks after her debut with Seidl, Aus der Ohe performed Chopin's *E minor Concerto* with Walter Damrosch's Symphony Society at the Metropolitan Opera House. She returned there once more to offer her interpretation of the Liszt Concerto, again with Damrosch. A solo piano debut at Steinway Hall soon followed. The reviews as well as the audience reception were spectacular, recalling Liszt's

Adele Aus der Ohe was the soloist for Tchaikovsky's *Piano Concerto No. 1*, a work conducted by the composer. The audience rewarded the performance with "tumultuous cheerings" (Music Division, The New York Public Library for the Performing Arts, Astor, Lenox and Tilden Foundations).

comment on the "fearless certainty"[56] of her style. An exhaustive tour with the Boston Symphony Orchestra was next,[57] and in the months prior to the Festival, Aus der Ohe presented fourteen concerts in San Francisco alone before returning to New York to appear in yet another round of events.[58] It was obvious that this pianist was making a definite impression on the U.S. concert-going public, achieving much artistic and financial success. Tchaikovsky was fascinated to learn that Aus der Ohe had arrived in America virtually penniless and through extensive and successful concertizing over a four-year span had earned "half a million marks."[59] Not long before the Music Hall Festival, she had just turned thirty years old.

Now, on the final afternoon concert before a full audience, Tchaikovsky took the baton once more—this time to conduct his most famous piano

An advertisement for Steinway Pianos, the instrument used for Aus der Ohe's performance of Tchaikovsky's concerto. Many famous concert artists also favored this brand of piano.

concerto. Adele Aus der Ohe, seated at a Steinway piano, followed the descending horns of the orchestral introduction with the "iconic crashing chords"[60] of her piano entrance. This work demanded much of the soloist—sensitive musicianship to bring out its melodic essence, superior skill to accomplish the challenging technical passages, and an "architectural sense" of the work as the whole.[61] In the words of the *New-York Tribune*, Aus der Ohe performed all of it with "elegance and devotion."[62]

As for Tchaikovsky, the *New York World* stated that he had a "rare magnetism" in conducting the work, and from the first notes to the thrilling finale, the "conductor and pianist [were] in rapport."[63]

Tchaikovsky was again the favorite—as conductor and composer—and the crowd was thrilled with Aus der Ohe's rendition of the concerto. The audience "waved their handkerchiefs"[64] and called again and again for the two with "tumultuous cheerings."[65] Aus der Ohe did not want any of the accolades for herself, but deferred respectfully to Tchaikovsky[66] who later said that it was "perfectly performed"[67] by her. The public was totally enamored with all of it. Since this was Tchaikovsky's last appearance at the Festival, *The New York World* made special mention, too, that audiences owed deep thanks to Walter Damrosch for making it possible for them to have an opportunity to experience the presence of the composer in person.[68]

This concerto was a difficult work to follow. However, once more, there was Wagner—both the *Prelude* and the *Flower Maiden Scene* from *Parsifal*'s Act II, an opera long associated with the Damrosch name. Leopold Damrosch had included music from the work on many of his orchestral programs, and his son not only used the opera as a basis for some of his musical lectures, but had also presented it in concert form during which Music Hall architect William Burnet Tuthill played his famous chimes.

In the *Prelude*, the orchestra conjures a mystic realm that sets the scene for this story of a quest for the Holy Grail, a subject that fascinated Wagner. Its evocative sound combines themes from the opera and fuses them into a dramatic whole. This mystical atmosphere continues in the *Flower Maiden Scene* which takes place in a sumptuous magic garden—a part of Klingsor's castle. Here, Parsifal is tested—tempted by the maidens and the evil magic of Kundry.[69]

A group of six soloists and a female chorus performed the *Flower Maiden Scene*. Along with Anna Luella Kelly and Mrs. Carl Alves were several new soloists: each one distinctive in background and style, and each with something special to contribute to the work. Selma Koert-

Kronold took the featured role of Kundry. She had already performed a number of dramatic soprano parts with the American Opera Company under the direction of Gustave Hinrichs. A versatile performer over time, she appeared in productions of *Il Trovatore, William Tell, Faust,* and *La Gioconda.*[70] A few years after the Festival, she returned to the Music Hall once more with Walter Damrosch for a production of *Die Walkure* to benefit the Workingman's School.[71] However, Koert-Kronold ultimately abandoned her operatic career, finding stage life incompatible with her religious convictions. She divorced and moved close to a religious community, joining an oratorio society that presented sacred works aiming to provide "spiritual elevation" for performers and listeners.[72]

The other members of the Flower Maiden Scene had concertized and, also, performed within oratorio and church settings. Mrs. Gerrit (Caroline B.) Smith previously appeared at Chickering Hall and other venues.[73] Well recognized as a member of the quartet that sang at the prestigious Church of the Incarnation,[74] she remained as a soloist for thirty years at the Dutch Reformed Church in New York. Later, after retiring from singing, she became a successful real estate broker and the first woman to be admitted as a member of both the New York and Connecticut Real Estate Boards.[75] Mrs. Theodore (Ella A.) Toedt was trained in Germany and appeared as a soloist with symphony orchestras in Cincinnati, Chicago, Boston, and New York. Like Mrs. Smith, she concertized and appeared in oratorio works, often performing with her husband, a tenor soloist. She later taught at the Juilliard School where she eventually became Dean of Faculty.[76] Finally, there was Mrs. Hattie Clapper-Morris, a contralto, who appeared in a variety of benefit, religious, special interest, and orchestral performances. A long-time soloist in the choir of St. Bartholomew's Church, she also performed with the Theodore Thomas Orchestra on its final country-wide tour. Clapper-Morris was reported to have been the first person to sing "The Lost Chord" within a concert setting.[77]

Similar to the songs performed earlier in the program and despite the popularity of all things Wagnerian in New York, there was little time devoted in the reviews to the *Parsifal* segment of the afternoon. Tchaikovsky and Aus der Ohe definitely captured the press and the public that day. The *New-York Tribune* summed it up well, calling the concerto the afternoon's "most brilliant feature."[78]

This was the closing day of the Festival, and there was more music to be heard that evening. Little time was available after the final notes of the Wagner selections to eat and relax. The final concert soon arrived and brought with it a return to the oratorio—Handel's *Israel in Egypt.*

This was a massive work that included a double chorus with orchestra as well as soloists, all of whom had appeared in other Festival concerts— Anna Kelly, Ella Toedt, Katie Alves, Andreas Dippel, Emil Fischer, and Ericsson Bushnell. However, these soloists had little to do in this work as compared to many other oratorios. There were few arias. One reviewer went so far as to call their parts "uninteresting."[79]

The structure of *Israel in Egypt* was distinctive in that it did not focus on the conflicts and actions of one or more particular individuals. Instead, it told the story of a group of people as they were delivered from trials to triumph, with the chorus itself having the majority of the featured parts. Both musically and dramatically, the talents and achievements of the Oratorio Society were able to be displayed to best advantage, and given the Society's key role as a catalyst in the creation of the Music Hall, it was a well-chosen work with which to close the Festival. The Society, too, had its own story to tell during its years-long quest for a musical home. Here, now, was an excellent opportunity for audiences to hear the music in the new and superior acoustical hall, the type of setting in which an oratorio was meant to be performed.

Israel in Egypt was composed in 1738, pre-dating the composer's famous *Messiah.* It was premiered in London in 1739. At that time, though, audience reception of the work was mixed. Opera-goers were disappointed because they were hoping for significant arias to be delivered with full dramatic fervor by the featured soloists. This had not been Handel's intent. Then there was the issue of the libretto. It was based completely upon scriptural sources, unlike a traditional libretto—a move that raised questions within some conservative sectors. After the initial performance, Handel made some changes to the score, including increasing the use of soloists. Nevertheless, the end result was still not received with enthusiasm.[80]

Handel did not live to see the ultimate success of his work. It only gained in popularity during later years as audiences became better accustomed to the oratorio form and its potential for variation. However, at an event that commemorated his birth centennial in 1784 (although 1783 would have been the accurate date), Haydn was in attendance. He was moved to tears by a performance of *Israel in Egypt*, proclaiming Handel "the Master of us all!"[81]

Despite the fact that Handel altered the score occasionally over time, borrowing themes from chorales, fugues, chamber and other related works by various composers—this oratorio is still one of the most unified in structure, idea, and flow with its many diverse components incorporated into a superbly comprehensive whole. However, in 1844, Mendelssohn carefully edited a score of *Israel in Egypt* for a performance by London's Handel Society, an edition that clearly showed respect for Handel's original intent.[82]

Israel in Egypt draws from Exodus and the Psalms, following the story of the Israelites' bondage in Egypt, exposure to the plagues, and their eventual release and subsequent pursuit by the Egyptians to the Red Sea. It culminates in the group's final victory over oppression and hardship. Over time, this became a popular work, so much so that a performance was preserved on one of the earliest wax cylinder recordings still in existence made in June of 1888 at the Handel Festival in London's Crystal Palace. Four thousand singers were in the chorus on this occasion.[83]

This massive composition allowed both the Oratorio and Symphony societies to assume major roles in telling various parts of the story. There was a particularly fine interplay between the chorus and orchestra in the section that successfully described, through music, the various aspects of the plagues. This "pictorial music" illustrated the story well.[84] Not only was this superbly performed, but also the fine acoustical properties of the space enhanced the vivid sounds of this intricate vocal and instrumental interaction.

The oratorio was thrilling—summed up best in one review for its energy and for a performance that showed "as much finish" as had ever been previously heard in the city.[85]

Tchaikovsky thoroughly enjoyed the performance, calling it "excellent." He also specially mentioned that at some time in the evening's proceedings—presumably during the intermission—that there was an ovation for William Burnet Tuthill.[86]

The architect noted this in the Oratorio Society minutes, documenting that an acknowledgement was offered to both Walter Damrosch and himself for their accomplishments. In his concise and understated style, Tuthill described the events of May 9, as follows.

Last concert of Festival
"Israel in Egypt"

Attendance		
Soprano—135	Tenor—45	
Alto—78	Bass—79	
	Total 337	

During the evening testimonials were given to the conductor Mr. Damrosch, and to the Secretary in his function as Architect of the Music Hall.
Wm B. Tuthill
Sec'y[87]

The new Music Hall and its inaugural Festival were triumphs. However, all of the news accounts made it explicitly clear that the presence of Tchaikovsky added the crowning luster to the magnificent new hall and its splendid concert events. Fittingly, celebrations were to follow.

Walter Damrosch and Tchaikovsky attended a wonderful supper that evening hosted by Willy von Sachs at the Manhattan Club, a place that Tchaikovsky described as "luxurious," although he was not fond of the food. The menu, though, was exquisitely created with a small excerpt from a Tchaikovsky composition prepared for each person,[88] once more, honoring the composer with special recognition. Among the guests at this event were Frank Van der Stucken; Hungarian musician and composer Francis Alexander Korbay, who like Frank Damrosch was a godson to Liszt[89]; and Rudolph Schirmer of the music publishing family—a lawyer and founder of the *Musical Quarterly*, who rose to become president of the firm. Schirmer was connected with both the Oratorio and Symphony societies.[90]

However, the individual who especially intrigued Tchaikovsky on this final Festival evening celebration was Carl Schurz. The composer especially enjoyed talking with him. German by birth, Schurz had emigrated to the U.S., becoming a general in the Civil War, a journalist, a U.S. senator and, eventually, Secretary of the Interior. He was a close friend of William Steinway and worked in many ways to support the German-American community trying to preserve old traditions and customs while, at the same time, embracing the new ones of his adopted country. A New York park was subsequently renamed in his honor, its grounds the location of a historic home that would eventually become the Mayor's residence. Years later, a memorial service for Schurz was held at the Music Hall, which by then was known as Carnegie Hall.[91] Tchaikovsky found the man's company and conversation fascinating, and the two talked at length about Russian writers. The event, which ended at 2:00 a.m,[92] was a congenial and pleasant conclusion to the final day of a spectacular Festival.

• Ten •

Postlude

The cheers and applause of the inaugural week echoed long after the final notes of the last concert ended. All were in agreement that the new Music Hall was exquisite—in the words of Andrew Carnegie, it was "the theme of universal praise."[1] According to *Harper's Weekly*, this was a concert space "capable of meeting any demands."[2] The perfection of its acoustics was unquestioned. It was also a delight to the eye. In sum, the new Music Hall was a total success.

In the remaining portion of 1891, though, the Hall's schedule would initially be a quiet one, with graduation ceremonies for Packard's Business College and Columbia College, a German choral festival, and the New York Scottish Society Halloween Festival, among the events that were held there. Sir Edwin Arnold—the author of *The Light of Asia*, a favorite book of the Carnegies –presented a lecture to benefit St. Mark's Hospital. In mid–November, though, the vibrant pianist Ignace Paderewski added real glamour to the season with a dramatic performance of his *Piano Concerto in A Minor,* accompanied by Walter Damrosch and the New York Symphony Orchestra.[3] To his credit, it was William Steinway—once skeptical about the viability of the Music Hall—who suggested that Paderewski's debut be held there. Steinway called the concert a "grand success."[4] The Music Hall was on its way to a glorious new life, and the individuals who together made it happen now embarked on their own separate paths.

On May 10, 1891—the day following the final concert of the Festival—Andrew and Louise Carnegie hosted a dinner in their home. It was a small and friendly affair, attended by Tchaikovsky, Walter and Margaret Damrosch, Morris and Marie Reno, and William and Henrietta Tuthill, with one or two other friends included. This was a time to celebrate a successful Festival and the public's warm reception of this fine new Music Hall. Thanks to the efforts of the individuals present on that evening, what had seemed improbable just a few short years previously had become a stunning and remarkable reality.

Tchaikovsky was an especially honored guest at the gathering, well appreciated for his key role in the triumphant opening concerts. It was no secret that his presence had been a major part in their success. As the

Louise and Andrew Carnegie hosted a dinner in their home to celebrate the successful opening of the new Music Hall. The small group in attendance included Tchaikovsky, the Damrosches, the Tuthills, and the Renos (courtesy Carnegie Library of Pittsburgh).

Musical Courier went so far as to say, this had not been just a Festival, but "emphatically a Tchaikovsky one."[5] Never had a figure quite so unique captivated New York. The composer would forever be associated with the new Music Hall that had placed the city on a larger cultural map and helped assure its place as a leading venue on an international level. As much as New York would never forget him, Tchaikovsky would always remember the enormous hospitality and enthusiasm of the Americans. There was already talk of a return trip the following season, an idea especially encouraged by Andrew Carnegie, who was by now one of the composer's greatest admirers.

Tchaikovsky, in turn, continued to be fascinated by the likeable Andrew Carnegie whom he found to be a "striking personality"[6] as well as quite modest, despite his great wealth—an individual who did "not put on airs."[7] This feeling of esteem and respect was mutual. During that evening, Carnegie enthusiastically declared Tchaikovsky the "uncrowned ... king of music,"[8] and the millionaire delighted both the composer and guests with an animated and earnestly accurate demonstration of Tchaikovsky's conducting—all with good-natured enthusiasm and admiration. The Carnegies heaped lavish praise and attention on the composer, who was grateful but also a bit shy about all of it.[9] It was everyone's fond hope that he would, indeed, return.

Tchaikovsky did not leave America right away after this celebratory evening. He was treated to a trip to Niagara Falls and, afterward, visited Baltimore, Philadelphia, and Washington, D.C., for another round of concerts, sightseeing, and social events. Again, he was welcomed warmly. Exhausted, he returned to New York once more where there was additional visiting to be done and a tribute in his honor to attend, sponsored by the Composer's Club at the Metropolitan Opera House. There were, of course, many farewells to be said at that time. Both the Damrosch and Carnegie couples had already said goodbye. By the time of Tchaikovsky's final departure, they were already on their own trip abroad. Among the more memorable last farewells came from the Renos, who invited the composer to lunch. Among several parting gifts, the oldest daughter of the family, Anna Reno Margulies, gave him a lovely cigarette case, and her two sisters presented him with cookies to enjoy during his voyage.[10]

Then, the time for the journey finally arrived. Tchaikovsky was going home to Russia. On the day of his departure, he was understandably overcome with fatigue. After saying goodbye to his "dear American friends,"[11] he boarded the *Furst Bismarck* and settled into his cabin. It was time to catch up on some much-needed sleep. Even this was not totally restful, though, and later he was eventually awakened by some movement. The voyage was beginning. He walked outside. It was at this moment that the Statue of Liberty came into view as the vessel sailed out of the harbor toward the open waters. It was his last sight of New York and of America before heading home to Russia.[12] Tchaikovsky would never have the opportunity to return; he passed away two years later.

The other guests who were present at the May 10th dinner given by the Carnegies had also played major parts in the Music Hall project. Although some eventually took separate paths, they would always share a common bond in history that was forged through their singular contributions.

Morris Reno had been a part of everything from the beginning. A friend to Leopold Damrosch, he worked with the Oratorio and Symphony societies before there was even the glimmer of a dream about a new concert hall. He was there for all of the planning, the meetings, the special events—a key figure in the administrative side of things. Along with Walter Damrosch, *Harper's Weekly* equally applauded Reno—both men having assumed "commanding parts" in the creation of the Music Hall.[13] After the Festival, Reno continued in his multi-faceted array of activities—becoming an officer for the New-York College of Music's new building project[14]; incorporating, along with his son-in-law and others, the Musical News Company[15]; and advertising his services in *The Musical Courier* as a "representative of first-class concert artists."[16] All the while, Reno served as president of the Music Hall Company as well as an officer and director of both the Oratorio and Symphony societies. However, he left all three of these positions in 1896.[17] Curiously, his name later appeared as the president and director of a firm called United Incandescent Light Company.[18] Reno died in 1917,[19] his parting from his previous musical sphere somewhat of a mystery. His wife Marie, a soprano in the Oratorio Society, had passed away two years earlier.[20] Almost a quarter of a century before her death, Andrew Carnegie had publicly credited her as being the one to suggest the creation of the Oratorio Society to Leopold Damrosch.[21]

An interesting side note to the Reno family pertains to Leon Margulies, Reno's son-in-law. Margulies, the young man who brought Tchaikovsky to the Music Hall on the opening night of the Festival, was also active in the administrative side of music. During the five or so years following the Festival, he handled business arrangements for several events presented by Walter Damrosch, including high-profile opera benefits,[22] as well as the first production of Damrosch's opera *The Scarlet Letter*.[23] He also served as New York manager for Lillian Nordica[24] as well as a business manager at the Metropolitan Opera for a time.[25] However, his name was mentioned less frequently, as was that of his father-in-law, after an article appeared in *The New York Times* stating that Margulies was suing Walter Damrosch for commissions he believed were due him for arranging singers' contracts.[26] However, his wife Anna—who had gifted Tchaikovsky with the lovely cigarette case—grew more widely recognized over the coming decades. A prominent and respected educator, she opened a Montessori school in New York and successfully operated a school for deaf children. The Margulies' son was deaf.[27] Anna's sister Alice Reno, the young woman who had conversed so charmingly with Tchaikovsky when he arrived in New York, married and moved abroad.

William Burnet Tuthill was also an important guest of the celebratory group on May 10. As time progressed, he was to continue in his work as an architect, writing a number of books on various facets of the subject over the years. Among them were *The City Residence: Its Design and Construction*; *Environment in Architecture*; and *Practical Lessons in Architectural Drawing*. He became considered an expert on the subject of acoustics. Such was his recognition in this area that he frequently lectured on the subject at Columbia University and at various other institutions. His posthumously published work, *Practical Acoustics*, set forth his well-thought-out principles on the subject for future students in the field. Continuing for many years as Secretary of the Oratorio Society and, also, as a member of his Wiederholen Quartet, Tuthill maintained an active interest in music. He became associated with numerous arts organizations over his lifetime and enjoyed his large personal library of music.[28] However, William Burnet Tuthill was never to design another concert hall. The Music Hall was his masterpiece.

The generous host of the evening, Andrew Carnegie, continued to be involved in his many business, philanthropical, and literary pursuits. Not long after the Festival, there was a notice about a piece he had written for an upcoming issue of the *North American Review*. It was titled "The ABC of Money." One of a number of diverse authors to appear in that issue, he was in the company of Robert G. Ingersoll—who had spoken at the Recital Hall's GAR celebration in April—with "Is Avarice Triumphant?"—and P. T. Barnum with "A Trip Abroad."[29] The week following the Festival, Carnegie and his wife set sail for Europe, traveling to Cluny Castle and a summer in one of their favorite places.[30] It was to be a tradition of theirs for years to come. In 1894, in an appropriately fitting move, the Music Hall was renamed in his honor—officially to be known as Carnegie Hall—a name that would come to be known and respected worldwide. In 1901, Carnegie

sold his steel corporation, making him by far one of the wealthiest indus-
trialists in America. Over the ensuing years, he was still unwavering in
his financial support of many worthwhile causes, donating millions to his
favorite projects for the common good. A great advocate for peace, Andrew
Carnegie died in 1919, sad to have seen a world ravaged by war. Louise
Carnegie survived her husband by several decades. She continued to keep
his spirit of philanthropy alive, donating money and land to deserving
institutions. She died in 1946.[31]

Finally, there was Walter Damrosch. He was a key individual in the
entire process. Without his perseverance and dedication, the Music Hall
might never have become a reality—nor would the performing groups his
father originally created have had the potential to survive as they did. The
Oratorio Society went on to become the city's second oldest cultural institution, their annual performance of Handel's *Messiah* an unbroken tradition. Over the ensuing years, they received many awards—including New
York's Handel Medallion and UNESCO's Commemorative Medal—and
became the first group of its kind to broadcast a choral concert from
Carnegie Hall.[32] The Symphony Society—eventually known as the New
York Symphony Orchestra—performed successfully in concert series, on
tour, and in radio broadcasts. In 1928, they merged with onetime rival,
the New York Philharmonic, also still in existence.[33] Walter Damrosch
was a strong force in the life of both of these groups.

In perpetual motion as always, the Tuesday following the May 10 dinner at the Carnegie mansion, Damrosch conducted an orchestra at Chickering Hall on the occasion of the graduation ceremonies for the New-York
College of Music. Student soloists performed.[34] The next day he and his
wife set sail for Europe with the Carnegies. While on this trip, Damrosch
headed for Germany, this time it was to find a new concertmaster for the
Symphony Society as well as to spend one month in Bayreuth, studying
both rehearsals and performances of Wagnerian operas there.[35] Damrosch
was never idle, and his schedule continued in a similar pattern for years
to come. He continually thrived in the musical world, premiering new
compositions, leading the Oratorio and Symphony societies, giving
concert-lectures, presenting radio programs, composing, traveling—the
list was exhaustive. He was his father's son. Music and musicians always
filled Damrosch's home—rehearsals, singing, the sounds of a piano—just
as he had once known as a youth in Breslau.

Walter Damrosch outlived the other major players in the Music Hall's
story—Carnegie, Tchaikovsky, Reno, Tuthill. He was energized by the work
that he loved—always rehearsing, always preparing for the next perform-

Evening outside the Music Hall.

ance. Throughout future years, he also continued to be a part of Carnegie Hall—particularly at the conductor's podium. This was his life.

Later, his daughter shared an indelible memory of her father, a scene that occurred time and again on the night of a concert and one that captured the essence of the man and the musician. There would be Walter Damrosch, dressed in formal, elegant concert attire, complete with "high silk hat."[36] Leaving home at the appointed time, he would walk down the street, his dignified figure fading into the shades of twilight. Secured firmly beneath his arm was the musical score for the evening's performance[37]—something that was always a part of him.

Epilogue

Progress has many definitions. In 1891, it signified the inauguration of a new Music Hall for New York with its promise of expanded cultural horizons. In 1957, though, it meant a wrecker's ball and a red skyscraper in a city-wide trend toward modernization. Carnegie Hall was in danger of vanishing, and its historical richness and quintessential inspiration along with it. This was no idle threat. In a startling article in *Life* magazine that year—with an all-too-graphic depiction of the prospective red replacement building—demolition plans for the venerable old hall were announced for 1959.[1]

The New York Philharmonic, a long-time resident group at Carnegie Hall, was scheduled to move in a few short years to another home at Lincoln Center, the expansive arts complex about to be built a short distance away. It would not only be new, but it was also designed to revitalize a significant portion of its West Side neighborhood. The orchestra would eventually be joined by the Metropolitan Opera and the Juilliard School of Music, among other organizations.

Still, could anything really replace Carnegie Hall? This was not some dusty relic but, instead, a symbol to the world—a place of proven historical significance and one of aspirations and dreams. Its stage had seen a wide variety of legendary performers—from Vladimir Horowitz to Judy Garland, from Yo-Yo Ma to Johnny Cash, and from Sissieretta Jones to the Beatles. It had been the site of unforgettable events—Benny Goodman's classic 1938 *Sing, Sing, Sing* concert, Irving Berlin's 100th birthday tribute—the list was exhaustive.[2] There had been lectures, suffrage rallies, and political speeches. And countless individuals who were not at all famous still had the joy of appearing there—in a debut recital or as a member of a student or touring group. There was nothing that could compare with performing at Carnegie Hall.

Although the building might have needed some refurbishment, no one could deny its intrinsic value—a place known globally, even by those with no interest in the arts. Its interior was still one of acoustical perfection, and it also carried inspiring echoes from its history—reflecting its creators, performers, and audiences.

Fortunately, through heroic efforts led by renowned violinist Isaac Stern[3]; his wife Vera[4]; Nelson Rockefeller, then governor of New York State; and a host of other individuals—from Eleanor Roosevelt to Pablo Casals—Carnegie Hall was saved.[5] There was no wrecker's ball. No red skyscraper. There was room for both the old hall and the new arts complex—precious links between the inspiring pages of history and the as-yet unwritten ones.

A resilient spirit is at the heart of what has always made Carnegie Hall so important—from its earliest days to the present. I chose to focus on the former time—one of improbability as well as promise. Hopefully, the stories of the people and events that were a part of the creation and opening of Carnegie Hall will inspire readers to discover more about it—both then and now.

Carnegie Hall continues to reflect and honor the past—through its ongoing tradition of eclectic performances and events, the collections in its wonderful museum and archives, and its careful preservation of the edifice itself. It also looks to the future with fresh plans for education, outreach, expanded performance opportunities, and more—all of it honoring the original visions of its creators and constantly building upon them.

During his speech at cornerstone laying ceremony in 1890, Andrew Carnegie was emphatic that this building should never be silent but always be vitally alive with fine events for the enjoyment and benefit of everyone. This has always been so, making Carnegie Hall—in its founder's words more than a century ago—"no ordinary structure."[6]

Appendix I:
Books for Further Study

Carnegie Hall

Cron, Theodore O., and Burt Goldblatt. *Portrait of Carnegie Hall.* New York: Macmillan, 1966.

Page, Tim, and Carnegie Hall. *Carnegie Hall Treasures.* Collins Design/Harper Collins, 2010.

Peyser, Ethel. *The House That Music Built: Carnegie Hall.* New York: Robert M. McBride, 1936.

Schickel, Richard. *The World of Carnegie Hall.* New York: Julian Messner, 1960.

Schickel, Richard, and Michael Walsh. *Carnegie Hall: The First One Hundred Years.* New York: Harry N. Abrams, 1987.

Andrew Carnegie

Carnegie, Andrew. *The Autobiography of Andrew Carnegie and His Essay "The Gospel of Wealth."* Mineola, NY: Dover, 2014.

Nasaw, David. *Andrew Carnegie.* New York: Penguin, 2006.

Louise Carnegie

Hendrick, Burton J., and Daniel Henderson. *Louise Whitfield Carnegie: The Life of Mrs. Andrew Carnegie.* New York: Hastings House, 1950.

Walter Damrosch/Damrosch Family

Damrosch, Walter. *My Musical Life.* New York: Scribner's, 1930.

Martin, George. *The Damrosch Dynasty: America's First Family of Music.* Boston: Houghton Mifflin, 1983.

Tchaikovsky's Trip to New York

The Diaries of Tchaikovsky. Translated from the Russian, with notes, by Wladimir Lakond. New York: W. W. Norton, 1945.

Sidelnikov, Leonid, and Galina Pribegina. *25 Days in America: For the Centenary of Peter Tchaikovsky's Concert Tour.* Moscow: "Muzyka," 1991.

Yoffe, Elkhonon, with translations from Russian by Lidya Yoffe. *Tchaikovsky in America: The Composer's Visit in 1891.* New York: Oxford University Press, 1986.

Appendix II:
Online Resources

Organizations

Carnegie Hall
http://www.carnegiehall.org/
Extensive historical and biographical resources; information on archival and museum collections; educational and special community offerings; and details on current schedules and performers. Video presentations, slideshows, blogs on a variety of topics, and absorbing digital materials enhance this comprehensive experience.

Metropolitan Opera
www.metopera.org/
In-depth performance notes, biographies, histories, extensive educational guides, plot synopses, video and audio resources, and many additional features well complement information on the current season.

New York Philharmonic
http://nyphil.org/
Broad historical descriptions, educational and community resources, playlists, on-line exhibits, biographical and musical overviews, and numerous digital collections offer a fine supplement to concert details.

Oratorio Society of New York
http://www.oratoriosocietyofny.org/
Historical background, performance news, details on educational and community resources, membership information, and video and recording presentations provide a good overview of this well-established organization.

Online Books and Resources

The Library of Congress Performing Arts Encyclopedia
http://www.loc.gov/performingarts/
A wealth of information and resources on many branches of the performing arts.

Music Festival Under the Direction of Walter Damrosch for the Inauguration of "Music Hall," Founded by Anderew Carnegie. May 5th, 6th, 7th, 8th, and 9th. New York: The Cherouny Printing & Publishing Company, 1891. Cornell University Library, Digital Collection. https://archive.org/details/cu31924018549836
The program for the Music Hall's opening week Festival. A helpful introduction, repertoire listings, and notes/texts, where applicable, are included.

William Steinway Diary: 1861–1896, The. Steinway & Sons Records and Family Papers. Smithsonian Institution. National Museum of American History. Archives Center. http://americanhistory.si.edu/steinwaydiary/

A reproduction of the piano manufacturer's diary with supplemental biographical information, notes, and historical details pertaining to the entries.

Chapter Notes

Chapter One

1. "Mr. Carnegie's Wedding," *The New York Times*, April 23, 1887, 1, http://timesmachine.nytimes.com/timesmachine/1887/04/23/100908391.html?pageNumber=1.

2. *Ibid.*

3. *Ibid.*

4. Herman Rossberg, "Wedding Ensemble" from "The Collection Online," The Metropolitan Museum of Art, www.metmuseum.org/collection/the-collection-online/search/81137.

5. *Ibid.*

6. David Nasaw, *Andrew Carnegie* (New York: Penguin, 2006), 296.

7. "Mr. Carnegie's Wedding," *The New York Times*.

8. *Ibid.*

9. "The New Steam-Ship Fulda," *The New York Times*, March 24, 1883, 5, http://timesmachine.nytimes.com/timesmachine/1883/03/24/102807358.html?pageNumber=5.

10. Burton J. Hendrick and Daniel Henderson, *Louise Whitfield Carnegie: The Life of Mrs. Andrew Carnegie* (New York: Hastings House, 1950), 87.

11. *Ibid.*

12. Walter Damrosch, *My Musical Life* (New York: Charles Scribner's Sons, 1930), 77.

13. *Ibid.*, 78.

14. George Martin, *The Damrosch Dynasty: America's First Family of Music* (Boston: Houghton Mifflin, 1983), 97.

15. Walter Damrosch, "Recollections of Andrew Carnegie," in *Andrew Carnegie Centenary* (Carnegie Corporation of New York, 1935), 26.

16. Damrosch, *My Musical Life*, 90.

17. Walter Damrosch, letter to Dr. Franz W. Beidler, December 14, 1936, in *Walter Damrosch Papers 1862–1950*, New York Public Library for the Performing Arts, Music Division, Special Collections, Box 8.

18. Damrosch, *My Musical Life*, 2.

19. Gretchen Finletter, *From the Top of the Stairs* (Boston: Little, Brown, 1946), 199.

20. Damrosch, *My Musical Life*, 9.

21. Irving Kolodin, Francis D. Perkins, Susan Thiemann Sommer, "Choral Societies," in *The New Grove Dictionary of American Music*, Volume Three, edited by H. Wiley Hitchcock and Stanley Sadie (New York: Grove's Dictionaries of Music, Inc., 1986), 359.

22. James G. Smith, Thomas Brawley, "Choral Music," in *The New Grove Dictionary of American Music*, Volume One, edited by H. Wiley Hitchcock and Stanley Sadie (New York: Grove's Dictionaries of Music, Inc., 1986), 431–32.

23. Martin, *Damrosch Dynasty*, 11.

24. Smith and Brawley, "Choral Music," *New Grove Dictionary*, 432.

25. H. E. Krehbiel, Richard Aldrich, H. C. Colles, R. Allen Lott, "Leopold Damrosch," in *The New Grove Dictionary of American Music*, Volume One, edited by H. Wiley Hitchcock and Stanley Sadie (New York: Grove's Dictionaries of Music, Inc., 1986), 565.

26. James Chute, "Van der Stucken, Frank (Valentine)," in *The New Grove Dictionary*, Volume Four, edited by H. Wiley Hitchcock and Stanley Sadie (New York: Grove's Dictionaries of Music, Inc., 1986), 444.

27. Damrosch, *My Musical Life*, 10.

28. Damrosch to Beidler, December 14, 1936.

29. Damrosch, *My Musical Life*, 23.

30. "Walter W. Naumberg 1867–1959, Founder of the Walter W. Naumburg Memorial Funds in The New York Community Trust," pamphlet, http://www.nycommunitytrust.org/Portals/0/Uploads/Documents/BioBrochures/Walter%20W.%20Naumburg.pdf.

31. Ethel Peyser, *The House That Music Built: Carnegie Hall* (New York: Robert M. McBride & Company, 1936), 26.

32. Martin, *Damrosch Dynasty*, 31–32.

33. H. E. Krehbiel, *Choral Music in New York: Notes on the Cultivation of Choral Music and the Oratorio Society of New York* (H. E. Krehbiel, 1884), 59.

34. "A New Concert Room," *The Sun* (New York), March 13, 1891, 3, Library of Congress, Chronicling America: Historic American Newspapers, http://chroniclingamerica.loc.gov/lccn/sn83030272/1891–03–13/ed-1/seq-3/.

35. "The History of the Society," *Oratorio Society of New York*, www.oratoriosocietyofny.org/about-history.html.

36. Martin, *Damrosch Dynasty*, 33.

37. *Ibid.*

38. Damrosch, *My Musical Life*, 23.

39. *Ibid.*, 169.

40. Kolodin et al., "Choral Societies," *New Grove Dictionary*, 359.

41. Damrosch, *My Musical Life*, 23.

42. *The New Music Review and Church Music Review, Volume 4* (New York: Novello, Ewer & Company, 1904), 54.

43. Damrosch, *My Musical Life*, 23.

44. Hendrick and Henderson, *Louise Whitfield Carnegie*, 40.

45. *Ibid.*

46. Damrosch, *My Musical Life*, 170.

47. Oratorio Society of New York, *The Oratorio Society Minutes, 1889–99*. Used with the permission of the Oratorio Society of New York.

48. Damrosch, *My Musical Life*, 170.

49. Irving Kolodin, Francis D. Perkins, Susan Thiemann Sommer, "Orchestras and Bands," in *The New Grove Dictionary of American Music*, Volume Three, edited by H. Wiley Hitchcock & Stanley Sadie (New York: Grove's Dictionaries of Music, Inc., 1986), 356.

50. Damrosch, *My Musical Life*, 32.

51. *Ibid.*, 171.

52. *Ibid.*, 36.

53. *Ibid.*

54. *Ibid.*, 47.

55. *Ibid.*, 49.

56. *Ibid.*, 42.

57. *Ibid.*, 36, 44.

58. *Ibid.*, 42–43.

59. Martin, *Damrosch Dynasty*, 77.

60. Katie Agocs, "Introduction," *Leopold Damrosch: Symphony in A Major*, by Leopold Damrosch and edited by Katie Agocs, *Recent Researches in American Music*, Volume 54 (Middleton, WI: A-R Editions, Inc., 2005), xiii, https://books.google.com/books?id=4fgJawIYjHwC&printsec=frontcover&source=gbs_ge_summary_r&cad=0#v=onepage&q&f=false.

61. "Metropolitan Opera House," *The New York Times*, February 18, 1885, 5, http://timesmachine.nytimes.com/timesmachine/1885/02/18/103627922.html?pageNumber=5.

62. Olin Downes, "Evangel of Music," *The New York Times*, December 31, 1950, 117, http://timesmachine.nytimes.com/timesmachine/1950/12/31/118433686.html?pageNumber=117.

63. Henry T. Finck, *My Adventures in the Golden Age of Music* (New York: Funk & Wagnalls, 1926), 252.

64. Richard Schickel, *The World of Carnegie Hall* (New York: Julian Messner, Inc., 1960), 21.

65. Russel Crouse, "That Was New York: Opera through Glasses-II," *The New Yorker*, November 24, 1928, 38, 40.

66. Edward Robb Ellis, *The Epic of New York City: A Narrative History* (New York: Old Town Books, 1966), 380.

67. Crouse, "That Was New York," *New Yorker*.

68. "Amusements," *The New York Times*, April, 22, 1887, 7, http://timesmachine.nytimes.com/timesmachine/1887/04/22/issue.html.

69. Damrosch, *My Musical Life*, 186.

70. Andrew Carnegie, "The Gospel of Wealth," in *The Autobiography of Andrew Carnegie and His Essay "The Gospel of Wealth"* (Mineola, NY: Dover, 2014, 1920, 1889), 277.

71. Schickel, *World of Carnegie Hall*, 25.

72. Carnegie, *Autobiography*, 2–3.

73. *Ibid.*

74. Hendrick and Henderson, *Louise Whitfield Carnegie*, 52.

75. *Ibid.*, 54.

76. *Ibid.*, 41.

77. *Ibid.*

78. Carnegie, *Autobiography*, 155.

79. Nasaw, *Andrew Carnegie*, 297.

80. "Mr. Carnegie's Wedding," *The New York Times*.

81. Hendrick and Henderson, *Louise Whitfield Carnegie*, 90–91.

82. *Ibid.*, 90.

83. *Ibid.*, 103.

84. Martin, *Damrosch Dynasty*, 95.

85. Hendrick and Henderson, *Louise Whitfield Carnegie*, 92–103.

86. Carnegie, *Autobiography*, 251.

87. Damrosch, *My Musical Life*, 91.

88. *Ibid.*, 93.

89. Carnegie, *Autobiography*, 33–34.

90. Damrosch, *My Musical Life*, 4.

91. Finletter, *From the Top of the Stairs*, 141.

92. Damrosch, *My Musical Life*, 92.

93. Finck, *My Adventures*, 256.

94. Carnegie, *Autobiography*, 37.

95. *Ibid.*, 38.

96. Damrosch, *My Musical Life*, 92.

97. Nasaw, *Andrew Carnegie*, 608.

98. *Ibid.*

99. Schickel, *World of Carnegie Hall*, 28.

100. "New Music for Plymouth Church," *The New York Times*, February 14, 1885, 5, http://timesmachine.nytimes.com/timesmachine/1885/02/14/106299095.html?pageNumber=5.

101. Damrosch, *My Musical Life*, 94.

102. *Ibid.*, 92.

103. Damrosch, "Recollections of Andrew Carnegie," 27.

104. *Ibid.*

105. Hendrick and Henderson, *Louise Whitfield Carnegie*, 116–118.

106. Damrosch, *My Musical Life*, 98.

107. Hendrick and Henderson, *Louise Whitfield Carnegie*, 119–120.

108. *Ibid.*, 122.

109. *Ibid.*, 123.

110. *Ibid.*, 121–22.

111. Damrosch, *My Musical Life*, 98.

112. *Ibid.*

113. Hendrick and Henderson, *Louise Whitfield Carnegie*, 125.

114. *Ibid.*, 123.

115. *Ibid.*, 125.

116. Damrosch, *My Musical Life*, 99.

117. Hendrick and Henderson, *Louise Whitfield Carnegie*, 131.

118 Damrosch, *My Musical Life*, 99.

119. Martin, *Damrosch Dynasty*, 103.

120. Damrosch, *My Musical Life*, 95.

121. Martin, *Damrosch Dynasty*, 99.

Chapter Two

1. Jeffery S. McMillan, "Grail Crazy," *Opera News*, March 2013, www.operanews.com/Opera_News_Magazine/2013/3/Features/Grail_Crazy.html.

2. *Ibid.*

3. *Ibid.*

4. *Ibid.*

5. "Amusements: The Oratorio Society," *The Sun* (New York), March 5, 1886, 2, Library of Congress, Chronicling America: Historic American Newspapers, http://chroniclingamerica.loc.gov/lccn/sn83030272/1886–03–05/ed-1/seq-2/.

6. "William B. Tuthill, Architect, Is Dead," *The New York Times*, August 27, 1929, 21, http://timesmachine.nytimes.com/timesmachine/1929/08/27/94174740.html?pageNumber=21.

7. Jean Lee Raines, *Burnet C. Tuthill: His Life and Music* (Ph.D. dissertation, Michigan State University, Department of Music, 1979), 2–3.

8. *Ibid.*, 3.

9. "William B. Tuthill Dead," *The New York Times*.

10. Sarah Eldridge, *Burnet Corwin Tuthill: The Unique Life of an Educator* (Memphis, Rhodes College, Institute for Regional Studies), 2, http://hdl.handle.net/10267/2417.

11. Raines, *Burnet C. Tuthill*, 2.

12. *Ibid.*

13. *Ibid.*, 2–3.

14. United States Federal Census 1900, Manhattan, New York, New York; Roll 1103; Page 14A; Enumeration District: 0481; FHL microfilm 1241103 (William Z. [sic] Tuthill).

15. Eldridge, *Burnet Corwin Tuthill*, 1.

16. "William B. Tuthill Dead," *The New York Times*.

17. *Ibid.*

18. Paul Goldberger, "Architecture: Two Richard Morris Hunt Shows," *The New York Times*, May 22, 1986, http://www.nytimes.com/1986/05/22/arts/architecture-two-richard-morris-hunt-shows.html.

19. Richard Plunz, "Apartments," in *The Encyclopedia of New York City*, edited by Kenneth T. Jackson (New Haven: Yale University Press & New York: The New-York Historical Society, 1995), 39.

20. Goldberger, "Two Richard Morris Hunt Shows," *The New York Times*.

21. Rosalie Genevro, "Architectural League of New York," in *Encyclopedia of New York City*, edited by Kenneth T. Jackson (New Haven: Yale University Press & New York: The New-York Historical Society, 1995), 44.

22. Plunz, "Apartments," *Encyclopedia of New York City*, 39.

23. "Death of Richard M. Hunt," *The New York Times*, August 1, 1895, http://timesmachine.nytimes.com/timesmachine/1895/08/01/106066243.html?pageNumber=5.

24. "William B. Tuthill," *New York, New York, City Directory 1883*, 884, in ancestry.com U.S. City Directories 1821–1989 (database online), Provo, UT, USA. Ancestry.com Operations, Inc., 2011.

25. Goldberger, "Two Richard Morris Hunt Shows," *The New York Times*.

26. "William B. Tuthill Dead," *The New York Times*.

27. "History," *The Architectural League of New York*, http://archleague.org/about/history/.

28. "1886: League Holds Its First Annual Exhibition," *The Architectural League of New York*, http://archleague.org/2010/12league-holds-its-first-annual-exhibition/.

29. Burnet C. Tuthill, Letter to Music Editor in "Mail Pouch: Carnegie," *The New York Times*, January 31, 1960, 337, http://timesmachine.nytimes.com/timesmachine/1960/01/31/99473690.html?pageNumber=337.

30. Emily Thompson, *The Soundscape of Modernity: Architectural Acoustics and the Culture of Listening in America, 1900–1933* (Cambridge: MIT Press, 2002), 26–27.

31. *Ibid.*, 28.

32. William Burnet Tuthill, *Practial Acoustics: A Study of the Diagrammatic Preparation of a Hall of Audience* (completed in 1928 and published posthumously by Burnet C. Tuthill in 1946), Hathi Trust Digital Library, www.catalog.hathitrust.org/Record/000929291, 3–27.

33. Tuthill, "Letter to Music Editor," *The New York Times*.

34. "The New Music Hall," *The New York Times*, March 24, 1889, 3, http://timesmach

ine.nytimes.com/timesmachine/1889/03/24/106205968.html?pageNumber=3.

35. *Ibid.*

36. Ethel Peyser, *The House That Music Built: Carnegie Hall* (New York: Robert M. McBride & Company, 1936), 33.

37. "Sherman W. Knevals," *Biographical Directory of the State of New York, 1900* (New York: Biographical Directory Company, 1899), http://www.archive.org/details/biographicaldire00biog.

38. George Martin, *The Damrosch Dynasty: America's First Family of Music* (Boston: Houghton Mifflin, 1983), 38.

39. United States Federal Census 1880; New York City, New York, New York; Roll: 894; Family History Film: 1254894; Page: 201D; Enumeration District: 571; Image: 0397 (Morris Reno).

40. "Real Estate: 'The N.J. Land and Improvement Building Company,'" *The Sun* (New York), June 15, 1872, 4, Library of Congress, Chronicling America: Historic American Newspapers, http://chroniclingamerica.loc.gov/lccn/sn83030272/1872-06-15/ed-1/seq-4/.

41. "Real Estate: Justus M. Phelps, Auctioneer," *The Sun* (New York), July 4, 1872, 4, Library of Congress, Chronicling America: Historic American Newspapers, http://chroniclingamerica.loc.gov/lccn/sn83030272/1872-07-04/ed-1/seq-4/.

42. "Real Estate: O.H. Pierson, Auctioneer," *The Sun* (New York), October 11, 1872, 4, Library of Congress, Chronicling America: Historic American Newspapers, http://chroniclingamerica.loc.gov/lccn/sn83030272/1872-10-11/ed-1/seq-4/.

43. H. E. Krehbiel, *Choral Music in New York: Notes on the Cultivation of Choral Music and the Oratorio Society of New York* (H.E. Krehbiel, 1884), 61.

44. "Amusements: Oratorio Society of New-York," *The New-York Tribune*, November 4, 1883, 15, Library of Congress, Chronicling America: Historic American Newspapers, http://chroniclingamerica.loc.gov/lccn/sn83030214/1883-11-04/ed-1/seq-15/.

45. "Amusements: Symphony Society of New-York," *The New-York Tribune*, November 4, 1883, 15, Library of Congress, Chronicling America: Historic American Newspapers, http://chroniclingamerica.loc.gov/lccn/sn83030214/1883-11/04/ed-1/seq-15/.

46. "Morris Reno Dies at 83," *The New York Times*, June 12, 1917, 13, http://timesmachine.nytimes.com/timesmachine/1917/06/12/102552940.html?pageNumber=13.

47. Krehbiel, *Choral Music in New York*, 59.

48. "Death of G. F. W. Holls," *The New York Times*, July 24, 1903, 3, http://timesmachine.nytimes.com/timesmachine/1903/07/24/105055810.html?pageNumber=3.

49. *Ibid.*

50. "Off for Europe," *The New York Times*, April 24, 1887, 3, http://timesmachine.nytimes.com/timesmachine/1887/04/24/103141709.html?pageNumber=3.

51. "Symphony Society," clippings files, The New York Public Library for the Performing Arts, Music Division, Special Collections.

52. Abram Wakeman, *History and Reminiscences of Lower Wall Street and Vicinity* (New York: The Spice Mill Publishing Co., 1914), 107. http://catalog.hathitrust.org/Record/008587463.

53. Martin, *Damrosch Dynasty*, 54.

54. Wakeman, *History and Reminiscences*, 107.

55. "John W. Aitken Dead," *The New York Times*, September 4, 1915, 7, http://timesmachine.nytimes.com/timesmachine/1915/09/04/100175625.html?pageNumber=7.

56. "William S. Hawk Was Retired Hotel Owner," *The Kingston Daily Freeman*, March 15, 1935, http://fultonhistory.com/newspaper%2010/Kingston%20NY%20Daily%20Freeman/Kingston%20NY%20Daily%20Freeman%201935%20Grayscale/Kingston%20NY%20Daily%20Freeman%201935%20-%201090.pdf.

57. Peyser, *House That Music Built*, 43.

58. *Carnegie Hall: Collections of Ledgers and Cash Books Covering the Period 1891–1925*, The New York Public Library for the Performing Arts, Music Division, Special Collections.

59. Cyril Ehrlich, "Steinway," in *The New Grove Dictionary of American Music*, Volume Four, edited by H. Wiley Hitchcock and Stanley Sadie (New York: Grove's Dictionaries of Music, Inc., 1986), 303–4.

60. *Ibid.*

61. Cynthia Adams Hoover, "Steinway, William," in *The New Grove Dictionary of American Music*, Volume Four, edited by H. Wiley Hitchcock and Stanley Sadie (New York: Grove's Dictionaries of Music, Inc., 1986), 304–5.

62. Marc Ferris, "Steinway Hall," in *The Encyclopedia of New York City*, edited by Kenneth T. Jackson (New Haven: Yale University Press & New York: The New-York Historical Society, 1995), 1121.

63. Michael and Ariane Batterberry, *On the Town in New York: From 1776 to the Present* (New York: Charles Scribner's Sons, 1973), 132.

64. Arthur Loesser, *Men, Women and Pianos: A Social History* (Mineola, NY: Dover, 1990), 531–32.

65. Marc H. Aronson, "Booksellers," in *The Encyclopedia of New York City*, edited by Kenneth T. Jackson (New Haven: Yale University Press & New York: The New-York Historical Society, 1995), 127–28.

66. Gale Harris and Jay Shockley, "East 17th Street/Irving Place Historic Designation Report," NYC Landmarks Preservation Commis-

sion, 1998, http://www.nyc.gov/html/lpc/down
loads/pdf/reports/EAST_17TH_STREET_-_
IRVING_PLACE_-_HISTORIC_DISTRICT.
pdf.
    67. Theodore O. Cron and Burt Goldblatt,
Portrait of Carnegie Hall (New York: Macmillan, 1966), 12.
    68. Richard Schickel, *The World of Carnegie
Hall* (New York: Julian Messner, Inc., 1960),
33.
    69. *Appleton's Dictionary of Greater New
York and Its Vicinity* (New York: D. Appleton,
1892), 222, www.catalog.hathitrust.org/Rec
ord/002129722.
    70. Schickel, *World of Carnegie Hall*, 31.
    71. "A New Music Hall," *Musical Courier*,
March 20, 1889, 2 (222), University of Michigan Library, Hathi Trust Digital Library, http://
babel.hathitrust.org/cgi/pt?id=mdp.39015025
410013;view=1up;seq=230.
    72. *Ibid.*
    73. *Ibid.*, 3 (223).
    74. "Some Fine New Buildings," *The New
York Times*, December 15, 1889, 11, http://
timesmachine.nytimes.com/timesmachine/
1889/12/15/100981377.html?pageNumber=11.
    75. Christopher Gray, "Streetscapes: 57th
Street Between Avenue of the Americas and
Seventh Avenue; High and Low Notes of a
Block with a Musical Bent," *The New York
Times*, May 9, 1999, http://www.nytimes.com/
1999/05/09/realestate/streetscapes-57th-
street-between-avenue-americas-seventh-ave
nue-high-low-notes.html.
    76. Christopher Gray, *New York Street-
scapes: Tales of Manhattan's Significant Buildings and Landmarks* (New York: Harry N.
Abrams, 2003), 192.
    77. Cron and Goldblatt, *Portrait of Carnegie
Hall*, 14.
    78. Oratorio Society of New York, *A Record
of the Sixteenth Season, 1888–1889, of the Oratorio Society of New York–Musical Director,
Walter J. Damrosch*. Used with the permission
of the Oratorio Society of New York.
    79. *Carnegie Hall: Collections of Ledgers and
Cash Books.*
    80. Peyser, *House That Music Built*, 35.
    81. *Carnegie Hall: Collections of Ledgers and
Cash Books.*
    82. "Carnegie Music Hall: The Work of
Construction Is Expected to Begin Soon," *The
New York Times*, July 19, 1889, http://times
machine.nytimes.com/timesmachine/1889/
07/19/106356928.html?pageNumber=8.
    83. *Carnegie Hall: Collections of Ledgers and
Cash Books.*
    84. Peyser, *House That Music Built*, 35.
    85. Donal Henahan, "Music View; The
Sound of Carnegie Hall," *The New York Times*,
May 3, 1981, http://www.nytimes.com/1981/
05/03/arts/music-view-the-sound-of-carne
gie-hall.html.

    86. Thompson, *Soundscape of Modernity*,
29.
    87. Henahan, "Music View," *The New York
Times.*
    88. *Carnegie Hall: Collections of Ledgers
and Cash Books.*
    89. Thompson, *Soundscape of Modernity*,
335 (note 59).
    90. *Ibid.*, 336 (note 60).
    91. Peyser, *House That Music Built*, 35.
    92. Thompson, *Soundscape of Modernity*,
338 (note 60).
    93. Peyser, *House That Music Built*, 35.
    94. Richard Schickel, *Carnegie Hall: The
First One Hundred Years* (New York: Harry N.
Abrams, 1987), 12.
    95. Schickel, *World of Carnegie Hall*, 34.
    96. "Isaac A. Hopper's Record," *The New
York Times*, January 1, 1893, 9, http://times
machine.nytimes.com/timesmachine/1893/01/
01/106858697.html?pageNumber=9.
    97. *Ibid.*
    98. Isaac A. Hopper scrapbook/clippings,
Carnegie Hall Archives.
    99. *Carnegie Hall: Collections of Ledgers
and Cash Books.*
    100. *Engineering News-record*, Volume 40,
December 29, 1898, p. xxv, https://books.
google.com/books?id=WN82AQAAMAAJ
&pg=PR25&lpg=PR25&dq=john+j.+hopper,+
building+contractor&source=bl&ots=6rr
f1RzoO9&sig=a-l1_bSI7xrS6Z9CG-pKGMP
bVzk&hl=en&sa=X&ei=sYd4VMORMI6Rs
QTnmYE4&ved=0CCQQ6AEwAQ#v=one
page&q=john%20j.%20hopper%2C%20build
ing%20contractor&f=false.
    101. "Annual   Exhibition—Architectural
League of New York 1898," p. lxxxiii, http://
archleague.org/.
    102. Isaac Hopper scrapbook/clippings,
Carnegie Hall Archives.
    103. "Alfred R. Wolff 1855–1909,"ASHRAE
Pioneers of Industry Award, American Society
of Heating, Refrigerating and Air-Conditioning Engineers, ASHRAE website, https://www.
ashraeorg/membership—conferences/
honors—awards/ashrae-pioneers-of-industry.
    104. *Carnegie Hall: Collections of Ledgers
and Cash Books.*
    105. *Real Estate Record and Builders' Guide*,
Volume 51, ads following p. 652, https://books.
google.com/books?id=4rlRAAAAYAAJ&pg=
PA653-IA1&lpg=PA653-IA1&dq=%22Johnson
+%26+Morris%22+—+1890&source=bl&ots=
7SLtCh1823&sig=20cMrbT33XG0Gsle2SY
4a51gVB8&hl=en&sa=X&ei=Qt93VPr6KLe
QsQT9sYHgAQ&ved=0CEYQ6AEwCQ#v=
onepage&q=%22Johnson%20%26%20Mor
ris%22%20—%201890&f=false
    106. *The Heating and Ventilating Magazine*,
Volume 11, January 1914, Volume XL, No. 1, p.
78, https://books.google.com/books?id=acU7
AQAAMAAJ&pg=RA8-PA78&lpg=RA8-PA

78&dq=%22Johnson+%26+Morris%22+new+
york&source=bl&ots=M3tQH9yImP&sig=
KgjBrys6IPPR7y_NFsHd2-yEDYE&hl=en&
sa=X&ei=OX94VI73Hrj-sASV-4CABQ&ved=
0CDAQ6AEwBA#v=onepage&q=%22John
son%20%26%20Morris%22%20new%20york&
f=false

107. Johnson & Morris (Series II. Construction Notes and Correspondence, Box 8, Folder 5, 1913–1914), www.frick.org/sites/default/files/FindingAids/OneEast70thStreetPapers.html/.

108. "The Electric Light Plant," Souvenir Booklet, Carnegie Hall Archives.

109. "Charles Henry Davis—Chronology of the Life of Charles Henry Davis," U.S. Department of Transportation—Federal Highway Administration website, www.fhwa.dot.gov/infrastructure/davis2.cfm.

110. Mary C. Henderson, *The City & the Theatre: New York Playhouses from Bowling Green to Times Square* (Clifton, NJ: James T. White & Company, 1973), 152.

111. *Ibid.*, 137–138.

112. *Palaces for the People*, The Museum of the City of New York, exhibit, March 26 through September 7, 2014, www.mcny.org/palaces-for-the-people-guastavino.

113. John Ochsendorf, *Guastavino Vaulting: The Art of Structural Tile* (New York: Princeton Architectural Press, 2010), 20.

114. "Fire-Proof Construction," Souvenir Booklet, Carnegie Hall Archives.

115. Ochsendorf, *Guastavino Vaulting*, 59.

116. "Other Details of Construction," Souvenir Booklet, Carnegie Hall Archives.

117. *Carnegie Hall: Collections of Ledgers and Cash Books.*

118. "Root's Patent Spiral Pipe: Made of Sheet-Iron, Either Black Galvanized or Asphalted for Water Works and Hydraulic Mininc," *The Chace Catalog*, http://chace.athm.org/singleDisplay.php?kv=58341.

119. Deborah Dependahl Waters, "Herter Brothers," in *Encyclopedia of New York City*, edited by Kenneth T. Jackson (New Haven: Yale University Press & New York: The New-York Historical Society, 1995), 541.

120. *Carnegie Hall: Collections of Ledgers and Cash Books.*

121. *Ibid.*

122. "Superior Seating," Souvenir Booklet, Carnegie Hall Archives.

123. *Carnegie Hall: Collections of Ledgers and Cash Books.*

124. Peyser, *House That Music Built*, 36.

125. *Carnegie Hall: Collections of Ledgers and Cash Books.*

126. "Amusements: Sarasate and D'Albert," *The New York Times*, May 14, 1890, 4, http://timesmachine.nytimes.com/timesmachine/1890/05/14/103242881.html?pageNumber=4.

127. "Amusements This Evening," *The New York Times*, May 13, 1890, 4, http://timesmachine.nytimes.com/timesmachine/1890/05/13/issue.html.

128. "New-York College of Music," *The New York Times*, May 14, 1890, 4, http://timesmachine.nytimes.com/timesmachine/1890/05/14/103242881.html?pageNumber=4.

129. "A New Home for Music," *The Sun* (New York), May 14, 1890, 7, Library of Congress, Chronicling America: Historic American Newspapers, http://chroniclingamerica.loc.gov/lccn/sn83030272/1890-05-14/ed-1/seq-7/.

130. *Ibid.*

131. "Music's Promised Home," *The New York Times*, May 14, 1890, http://timesmachine.nytimes.com/timesmachine/1890/05/14/103242914.html?pageNumber=8.

132. *Ibid.*

133. "History of the Hall," Carnegie Hall, http://www.carnegiehall.org/History/.

134. "Music's Promised Home," *The New York Times*.

135. "New Home for Music," *The Sun*.

136. Oratorio Society of New York, *The Oratorio Society Minutes, 1889–99*, May 13, 1890. Used with the permission of the Oratorio Society of New York.

137. "New Home for Music," *The Sun*.

138. "Music's Promised Home," *The New York Times*.

139. *Ibid.*

140. *Ibid.*

141. "Wedded in Washington," *The New York Times*, May 18, 1890, 1, http://timesmachine.nytimes.com/timesmachine/1890/05/18/103243355.html?pageNumber=1.

142. *Ibid.*

Chapter Three

1. Elkhonon Yoffe, with translations from Russian by Lidya Yoffe, *Tchaikovsky in America: The Composer's Visit in 1891* (New York: Oxford University Press, 1986), 10.

2. *Ibid.*, 10–11.

3. "Walter Damrosch, 1862–1950," in *Performing Arts Encyclopedia*, Library of Congress, http://lcweb2.loc.gov/diglib/ihas/loc.natlib.ihas.200035728/default.html.

4. Yoffe, *Tchaikovsky in America*, 11.

5. "Hermann Wolff," *Tchaikovsky Research*, http://en.tchaikovsky-research.net/pages/Hermann_Wolff.

6. Yoffe, *Tchaikovsky in America*, 12.

7. *Ibid.*, 18.

8. *Ibid.*, 13.

9. *Ibid.*

10. *Ibid.*

11. *Ibid.*, 21–23.

12. Tim Page and Carnegie Hall, *Carnegie Hall Treasures* (New York: Collins Design, 2010), Opening Night Souvenir Booklet, 1891.

13. Oratorio Society of New York, *The Oratorio Society Minutes 1888–1899*, March 12, 1891. Used with the permission of the Oratorio Society of New York.

14. "A New Concert Room," *The Sun* (New York), March 13, 1891, 3, Library of Congress, Chronicling America: Historic American Newspapers, http://chroniclingamerica.loc.gov/lccn/sn83030272/1891–03–13/ed-1/seq-3/.

15. *Ibid.*

16. "In Favor of One Pitch," *The New York Times*, April 1, 1891, 5, http://timesmachine.nytimes.com/timesmachine/1891/04/01/103300684.html?pageNumber=5.

17. "Amusements," *The Sun* (New York), March 29, 1891, 9, Library of Congress, Chronicling America: Historic American Newspapers, http://chroniclingamerica.loc.gov/lccn/sn83030272/1891–03–29/ed-1/seq-2/.

18. "Mr. Rummel's Recital," *The New York Times*, April 2, 1891, 4, http://timesmachine.nytimes.com/timesmachine/1891/04/02/103300806.html?pageNumber=4.

19. *Ibid.*

20. *Harper's New Monthly Magazine*, May 1891.

21. *Ibid.*

22. "Death List of a Day: Franz Rummel," *The New York Times*, May 5, 1901, 9, http://timesmachine.nytimes.com/timesmachine/1901/05/05/101072570.html?pageNumber=9.

23. "Mr. Franz Rummel," Pittsburgh May Music Festival Programme, in *Andreas Dippel Concert Programs*, The New York Public Library for the Performing Arts, Music Division, Special Collections.

24. *Ibid.*

25. *Ibid.*

26. "Mr. Franz Rummel's Recital," *The New York Times*, May 9, 1879, p. 5, http://timesmachine.nytimes.com/timesmachine/1879/05/09/80751936.html?pageNumber=5.

27. "Musical Notes," *The New-York Tribune*, April 3, 1880, p. 4, Library of Congress, Chronicling America: Historic American Newspapers, http://chroniclingamerica.loc.gov/lccn/sn83030214/1880–04–03/ed-1/seq-4/.

28. "Franz Rummel's Bride: The Pianist Married to Miss Leila Morse at Poughkeepsie," *The New York Times*, April 5, 1881, 1, http://timesmachine.nytimes.com/timesmachine/1881/04/05/98552452.html?pageNumber=1.

29. "Leila Rummel, 87, Morse's Daughter," *The New York Times*, December 10, 1937, 25, http://timesmachine.nytimes.com/timesmachine/1937/12/10/101016062.html?pageNumber=25.

30. "Franz Rummel's Bride," *The New York Times*.

31. "Mr. Rummel's Piano Recitals," *The New York Times*, February 25, 1881, p. 5, http://timesmachine.nytimes.com/timesmachine/1881/02/25/98912925.html?pageNumber=5.

32. "Amusements: General Mention," *The New York Times*, June 19, 1881, 7, http://timesmachine.nytimes.com/timesmachine/1881/06/19/98561851.html?pageNumber=7.

33. "Musical Notes," *The New York Times*, October 26, 1890, 13, http://timesmachine.nytimes.com/timesmachine/1890/10/26/103273963.html?pageNumber=13.

34. "Mr. Rummel's Recitals," *The New York Times*, December 5, 1890, 4, http://timesmachine.nytimes.com/timesmachine/1890/12/05/103284570.html?pageNumber=4.

35. "Live Musical Topics," *The New York Times*, March 8, 1891, p. 12 (quoting from the Milwaukee *Daily Journal*), http://timesmachine.nytimes.com/timesmachine/1891/03/08/103298123.html?pageNumber=12.

36. J. Bradford Young, "Schuberth, E.," in *The New Grove Dictionary of American Music*, Volume Four, edited by H. Wiley Hitchcock & Stanley Sadie (New York: Grove's Dictionaries of Music, Inc., 1986), 164.

37. George Martin, *The Damrosch Dynasty: America's First Family of Music* (Boston: Houghton Mifflin, 1983), 11.

38. "Musical Notes," *The New York Times*, March 22, 1891, 13, http://timesmachine.nytimes.com/timesmachine/1891/03/22/106048064.html?pageNumber=13.

39. "Live Musical Topics," *The New York Times*, June 7, 1891, 12, http://timesmachine.nytimes.com/timesmachine/1891/06/07/106049790.html?pageNumber=12.

40. "Amusements," *The Sun* (New York), April 1, 1891, 10, Library of Congress, Chronicling America: Historic American Newspapers, http://chroniclingamerica.loc.gov/lccn/sn83030272/1891–04–01/ed-1/seq-10/.

41. "Franz Rummel," Performance History, Carnegie Hall, www.carnegiehall.org/PerformanceHistorySearch/#!

42. "Amusements: Mr. Rummel's Recital," *The New York Times*, April 2, 1891, 4, http://timesmachine.nytimes.com/timesmachine/1891/04/02/103300806.html?pageNumber=4.

43. Harold C. Schonberg, *The Great Pianists from Mozart to the Present* (New York: Simon & Schuster, 1963), 289. (Emil Liebling was said to be the source of this comment.)

44. "Death List of a Day: Franz Rummel," *The New York Times*.

45. "Floersheim, Otto," in *Appleton's Cyclopaedia of American Biography, Volume 7*, edited by James Grant Wilson and John Fiske (New York: D. Appleton & Company, 1901), 105.

46. E. Douglas Bomberger, *A Tidal Wave of Encouragement* (Westport, CT: Praeger, 2002), 6.

47. "Rummel," Performance History, Carnegie Hall.

48. "Amusements: Mr. Rummel's Recital," *The New York Times.*

49. *Ibid.*

50. Ethel Peyser, *The House That Music Built: Carnegie Hall* (New York: Robert M. McBride & Company, 1936), 186.

51. "Jadassohn, Salomon," in *Baker's Biographical Dictionary of Musicians, Seventh Edition*, Revised by Nicolas Slonimsky (New York: Schirmer Books, 1984), 1100–1101.

52. "Outline of Raff's Life," *Joachim Raff*, www.raff.org/life/outline.htm.

53. "Rummel," Performance History, Carnegie Hall.

54. "Amusements: Mr. Rummel's Recital," *The New York Times.*

55. *Ibid.*

56. "Musical Notes," *The New York Times*, April 5, 1891, 13, http://timesmachine.nytimes.com/timesmachine/1891/04/05/103301272.html?pageNumber=13.

57. "The Grand Army of the Republic and Kindred Societies," Introduction, in Library of Congress, General Collections, http://www.loc.gov/rr/main/gar/.

58. "Grand Army Celebration," *The New York Times*, April 1, 1891, 3, http://timesmachine.nytimes.com/timesmachine/1891/04/01/103300640.html?pageNumber=3.

59. "Grand Army of the Republic Celebration," Performance History, Carnegie Hall, www.carnegiehall.org/PerformanceHistory Search/#!

60. Peyser, *House That Music Built*, 186.

61. "Ingersoll Biography," *Council for Secular Humanism*, www.secularhumanism.org/index.php/1172, also see "Robert Green Ingersoll: Colonel, United States Army," Arlington National Cemetery, www.arlingtoncemetery.net/rgingersoll.htm.

62. "Notes of the Stage," *The New York Times*, April 5, 1891, 13, http://timesmachine.nytimes.com/timesmachine/1891/04/05/103301272.html?pageNumber=13.

63. "Grand Army Celebration," Performance History, Carnegie Hall.

64. "Celebrated in this City," *The New York Times*, April 7, 1891, 5, http://timesmachine.nytimes.com/timesmachine/1891/04/07/103301596.html?pageNumber=5.

65. *Ibid.*

66. "Notes of the Stage," *The New York Times*, June 5, 1885, 4, http://timesmachine.nytimes.com/timesmachine/1885/06/05/103021833.html?pageNumber=4.

67. "General Mention," *The New York Times*, May 22, 1885, 4, http://timesmachine.nytimes.com/timesmachine/1885/05/22/103017008.html?pageNumber=4.

68. "Bill Nye Well Received," *Daily Alta California*, March 14, 1890, p. 4, California Digital Newspaper Collection, www.cdnc.ucr.edu/cgi-bin/cdnc?a=d&d=DAC18900314.2.50#.

69. Richard Schickel, *The World of Carnegie Hall* (New York: Jullian Messner, 1960), 37; and also in "Celebrated in This City," *The New York Times.*

70. Schonberg, Harold C., *The Great Pianists from Mozart to the Present* (New York: Simon & Schuster, 1963), 303–305.

71. Arthur Friedheim, *Life & Liszt: The Recollections of a Concert Pianist*, edited by Theodore L. Bullock (Mineola, NY: Dover, 2012), 8.

72. *Ibid.*, 9.

73. *Ibid.*

74. *Ibid.*, 196.

75. *Ibid.*, 10, 199.

76. *Ibid.*, 212.

77. "Amusements," *The Sun* (New York), March 29, 1891, 9, Library of Congress, Chronicling America: Historic American Newspapers, http://chroniclingamerica.loc.gov/lccn/sn83030272/1891-03-29/ed-1/seq-9/.

78. "Herr Friedheim's Debut," *The New-York Tribune*, Library of Congress, Chronicling America: Historic American Newspapers, April 1, 1891, 6, http://chroniclingamerica.loc.gov/lccn/sn83030214/1891-04-01/ed-1/seq-6/.

79. "Amusements," *The Sun.*

80. Friedheim, *Life & Liszt*, 212.

81. *Ibid.*, 213.

82. *Ibid.*, 12.

83. "Charles F. Tretbar," *The William Steinway Diary, 1861–1896*, Smithsonian Institution, National Museum of American History, http://americanhistory.si.edu/steinwaydiary/search/?keyword=charles+tretbar&type=annotation&date=&edate=.

84. Friedheim, *Life & Liszt*, 12.

85. *Ibid.*, illustration.

86. "Amusements: "Mr. Friedheim's Recital," *The New York Times*, April 8, 1891, 4, http://timesmachine.nytimes.com/timesmachine/1891/04/08/issue.html.

87. "Music: Arthur Friedheim's Recital," *The New-York Tribune*, April 8, 1891, 6, Library of Congress, Chronicling America: Historic American Newspapers, http://chroniclingamerica.loc.gov/lccn/sn83030214/1891-04-08/ed-1/seq-6/.

88. "Amusements: Mr. Friedheim's Recitals," *The New York Times*, April 15, 1891, 4, http://timesmachine.nytimes.com/timesmachine/1891/04/15/103302439.html?pageNumber=4.

89. Peyser, *House That Music Built*, 187.

90. "Graduation: University of the City of New York Women's Law Class," Performance History, Carnegie Hall, www.carnegiehall.org/PerformanceHistorySearch/#!

91. "Graduation: University of the City of New York Women's Law Class," program, Carnegie Hall Archives.

92. "These Women Know Law," *The New York Times*, April 11, 1891, 4, http://timesmachine.nytimes.com/timesmachine/1891/04/11/103302026.html?pageNumber=4.

93. "Graduation," Performance History, Carnegie Hall.
94. "Miss Titus to Become a Wife," *The New York Times*, June 3, 1896, 4, http://times machine.nytimes.com/timesmachine/1896/06/03/503156782.html?pageNumber=4.
95. "Graduation," Performance History, Carnegie Hall.
96. "Mrs. Theodore Sutro Dead," *The New York Times*, April 28, 1906, 11, http://times machine.nytimes.com/timesmachine/1906/04/28/101839400.html?pageNumber=11.
97. "Eden Musee Faces Bankruptcy Court," *The New York Times*, June 8, 1915, 17, http://timesmachine.nytimes.com/timesmachine/1915/06/08/99437228.html?pageNumber=17.
98. "Ferenc Erkel," in *Encyclopaedia Britannica*, www.britannica.com/biography/Ferenc-Erkel.
99. Margaret William McCarthy, "Fay, Amy," in *The New Grove Dictionary of American Music*, Volume Two, edited by H. Wiley Hitchcock & Stanley Sadie (New York: Grove's Dictionaries of Music, Inc., 1986), 105.
100. "Musical Correspondence," *Dwight's Journal of Music*, April 12, 1879, 63.
101. "The Social World," *The New York Times*, April 17, 1894, 5, http://timesmachine.nytimes.com/timesmachine/1894/04/17/104109000.html?pageNumber=5.
102. "Graduation," Performance History, Carnegie Hall.
103. Claire Ashley Wolford, "Archivist's Angle: The NYU Glee Club," *NYU Alumni Connect*, www.alumni.nyu.edu/s/1068/2col_scripts.aspx?sid=1068&gid=1&pgid=2568.
104. "Lecture by Frank Damrosch," Performance History, Carnegie Hall, www.carnegiehall.org/PerformanceHistorySearch/#!
105. H.E. Krehbiel, Richard Aldrich, H.C. Colles, R. Allen Lott, "Frank (Heino) Damrosch," in *The New Grove Dictionary of American Music*, Volume One, edited by H. Wiley Hitchcock & Stanley Sadie (New York: Grove's Dictionaries of Music, Inc., 1986), 565.
106. "A. Victor Benham with Orchestra," Performance History, Carnegie Hall, www.carnegiehall.org/PerformanceHistorySearch/#!
107. Peyser, *House That Music Built*, 187.
108. *Ibid.*
109. "A. Victor Benham,"Performance History," Carnegie Hall.
110. "Musical Notes," *The New York Times*, April 5, 1891, 13, http://timesmachine.nytimes.com/timesmachine/1891/04/05/issue.html.
111. "Amusements: Mr. Benham's concert," *The New York Times*, April 22, 1891, 4, http://timesmachine.nytimes.com/timesmachine/1891/04/22/issue.html.
112. A. Victor Benham clippings files, New York Public Library for the Performing Arts, Music Division, Special Collections, NBC press release, November 20, 1931.
113. *Ibid.*, from *Musical Courier*, November 27, 1912.
114. *Ibid.*, from Bureau of Musical America, December 26, 1913.
115. *Ibid.*, untitled, August, 28, 1909.
116. *Ibid.*, from *Musical Courier*, October 7, 1914.
117. James Chute, "Van der Stucken, Frank (Valentine)," in *The New Grove Dictionary of American Music*, Volume Four, edited by H. Wiley Hitchcock & Stanley Sadie (New York: Grove's Dictionaries of Music, Inc., 1986), 444–445.
118. Rupert Hughes, *American Contemporary Composers* (Boston: L.C. Page and Company, 1900), 190–191.
119. "The New Music Hall," *The New York Daily Tribune*, May 3, 1891, 5, Library of Congress, Chronicling America: Historic American Newspapers, http://chroniclingamerica.loc.gov/lccn/sn83030272/1891–05–03/ed-1/seq-5/.
120. Schonberg, *Great Pianists*, 317.
121. *Ibid.*, 319.
122. *Ibid.*, 319–320.
123. *Ibid.*, 319.
124. "Amusements: Notes of the Stage," *The New York Times*, September 7, 1890, 13, http://timesmachine.nytimes.com/timesmachine/1890/09/07/106042481.html?pageNumber=13.
125. "Leopold Godowsky," Performance History, Carnegie Hall, www.carnegiehall.org/PerformanceHistorySearch/#!
126. *Ibid.*
127. University Musical Society: "A History of Great Performance," UMS Concert Program, December 9, 1881: Haydn's Oratorio of 'the Creation'—The Choral Union, www.ums.aadl.org/ums/programs_18811209.
128. "Manhattan Beach's Jubilee," *The New York Times*, August 18, 1887, 13, http://timesmachine.nytimes.com/timesmachine/1887/08/18/100929422.html?pageNumber=3.
129. "Musical Notes," *The New York Times*, February 22, 1891, 13, http://timesmachine.nytimes.com/timesmachine/1891/02/22/106047138.html?pageNumber=13.
130. "Miss Lillie Berg," brochure, clippings files, New York Public Library for the Performing Arts, Music Division, Special Collections.
131. *Ibid.*, 2.
132. *Ibid.*
133. *Ibid.*, 4.
134. *Ibid.*, 5.
135. *Ibid.*, 7–8.
136. *Ibid.*, 9–12.
137. "Women in Music: 1850–1900," Oxford Music Online, http://www.oxfordmusiconline.com/public/page/Women_in_music.
138. Peyser, *House That Music Built*, 187.
139. "Lillie P. Berg," Performance History, Carnegie Hall, www.carnegiehall.org/PerformanceHistorySearch/#!

140. "Musical Notes," *The New York Times*, April 19, 1891, 13, http://timesmachine.nytimes.com/timesmachine/1891/04/19/103303113.html?pageNumber=13.

141. *Ibid.*

142. "Miss Lillie Berg's Benefit," *The New York Times*, February 9, 1893, 5, http://timesmachine.nytimes.com/timesmachine/1893/02/09/106813332.html?pageNumber=5.

Chapter Four

1. "The New Music Hall," *The New-York Tribune*, May 3, 1891, 5, Library of Congress, Chronicling America: Historic American Newspapers, http://chroniclingamerica.loc.gov/lccn/sn83030214/1891-05-03/ed-1/seq-5.

2. Oratorio Society of New York, *The Oratorio Society Minutes 1889–99*, January 8, 1891. Used with the permission of the Oratorio Society of New York.

3. George Martin, *The Damrosch Dynasty: America's First Family of Music* (Boston: Houghton Mifflin, 1983), 115.

4. Elkhonon Yoffe, with translations from Russian by Lidya Yoffe, *Tchaikovsky in America: The Composer's Visit in 1891* (New York: Oxford University Press, 1986), 22–23.

5. "Musical Notes," *The New York Times*, January 4, 1891, 13, http://timesmachine.nytimes.com/timesmachine/1891/01/04/103289441.html?pageNumber=13.

6. "Musical Notes," *The New York Times*, December 21, 1890, 13, http://timesmachine.nytimes.com/timesmachine/1890/12/21/103287545.html?pageNumber=13.

7. "Society Topics of the Week," *The New York Times*, January 11, 1891, 12, http://timesmachine.nytimes.com/timesmachine/1890/12/21/103287540.html?pageNumber=12.

8. *Ibid.*

9. *Gilded New York*, ongoing exhibition, Museum of the City of New York, www.mcny.org/content/gilded-new-york.

10. "Music for the Masses," *The New York Times*, February 3, 1890, 8, http://timesmachine.nytimes.com/timesmachine/1890/02/03/103227282.html?pageNumber=8.

11. "A Popular Free Concert," *The New York Times*, March 2, 1891, 3, http://timesmachine.nytimes.com/timesmachine/1891/03/02/106047552.html?pageNumber=3.

12. Martin, *The Damrosch Dynasty*, 112.

13. *Ibid.*, 109.

14. *Ibid.*, 110.

15. *Ibid.*, 112.

16. *Ibid.*

17. Kimberly Chou, "Opening Night, Before It Was Carnegie Hall," *The Wall Street Journal*, September 30, 2011, http://www.wsj.com/articles/SB10001424052970204226204576601010452872084.

18. *Ibid.*

19. *Ibid.*

20. "Amusements," *The New York Times*, May 5, 1891, 7, http://timesmachine.nytimes.com/timesmachine/1891/05/05/issue.html.

21. "This is an Explanation: The Music Hall Managers and Ticket Speculators," *The New York Times*, April 27, 1891, 5, http://timesmachine.nytimes.com/timesmachine/1891/04/27/103304393.html?pageNumber=5.

22. "Amusements," *The Sun* (New York), March 31, 1891, 10, Library of Congress, Chronicling America: Historic American Newspapers, http://chroniclingamerica.loc.gov/lccn/sn83030272/1891-03-31/ed-1/seq-10 .

23. "Premiums for the Boxes," *The New York Times*, April 1, 1891, 3, http://timesmachine.nytimes.com/timesmachine/1891/04/01/103300633.html?pageNumber=3.

24. *Ibid.*

25. "A Rare Musical Event," *The Sun* (New York), May 6, 1891, 1, Library of Congress, Chronicling America: Historic American Newspapers, http://chroniclingamerica.loc.gov/lccn/83030272/1891-05-06/ed-1/seq-1.

26. "Four New French Steamers," *The New York Times*, March 25, 1885, 8, http://timesmachine.nytimes.com/timesmachine/1885/03/25/102963618.html?pageNumber=8.

27. Anthony Holden, *Tchaikovsky: A Biography* (New York: Random House, 1995), 298–299.

28. Richard Schickel, *The World of Carnegie Hall* (New York: Julian Messner, Inc., 1960), 39.

29. Martin, *Damrosch Dynasty*, 113–114.

30. "Isaac A. Hopper's Record," *The New York Times*, January 1, 1893, 9, http://timesmachine.nytimes.com/timesmachine/1893/01/01/106858697.html?pageNumber=9.

31. "City and Suburban News," *The New York Times*, October 5, 1884, 7, http://timesmachine.nytimes.com/timesmachine/1884/10/05/106160367.html?pageNumber=7.

32. "Von Bulow Is Here," *The New York Times*, March 24, 1889, 9, http://timesmachine.nytimes.com/timesmachine/1889/03/24/106206070.html?pageNumber=9.

33. "Xavier Scharwenka Arrives," *The New York Times*, January 5, 1891, 8, http://timesmachine.nytimes.com/timesmachine/1891/01/05/103289642.html?pageNumber=8.

34. "Bartholdi Well Pleased," *The New York Times*, October 26, 1886, 2, http://timesmachine.nytimes.com/timesmachine/1884/05/08/106278328.html?pageNumber=4.

35. "Decoration Day Celebration," *The New York Times*, May 9, 1885, 3, http://timesmachine.nytimes.com/timesmachine/1885/05/09/121573074.html?pageNumber=3.

36. Yoffe, *Tchaikovsky in America*, 71.

37. Holden, *Tchaikovsky*, 300.

38. "History," *Wm Knabe & Co.*, http://www.knabepianos.com/history.php.

39. *Ibid.*
40. Yoffe, *Tchaikovsky in America*, 56.
41. Schickel, *World of Carnegie Hall*, 40.
42. Yoffe, *Tchaikovsky in America*, 57.
43. *Ibid.*
44. *Ibid.*
45. "William-Adolphe Bouguereau: *Nymphs and Satyr* 1873," The Clark Museum, www.clarkart.edu/Art-Pieces/6158.
46. "John Drew to Become a Star," *The New York Times*, May 5, 1891, 2, http://timesmachine.nytimes.com/timesmachine/1891/05/05/103305408.html?pageNumber=2.
47. Michael and Ariane Batterberry, *On the Town in New York: From 1776 to the Present* (New York: Charles Scribner's Sons, 1973), 144–145.
48. Martin, *Damrosch Dynasty*, 115.
49. Yoffe, *Tchaikovsky in America*, 57.
50. *Ibid.*
51. *Ibid.*, 75.
52. Schickel, *World of Carnegie Hall*, 41.
53. "Napoleon Sarony (1821–1896)," National Portrait Gallery, www.npg.org.uk/collections/search/person.php?LinkID=mp07523&wPage=1.
54. "Napoleon Sarony (1821–1896)," Broadway Photographs, http://broadway.cas.sc.edu/content/napoleon-sarony.
55. Yoffe, *Tchaikovsky in America*, 59.
56. *Ibid.*
57. *Ibid.*
58. "Max Wilhelm Karl Vogrich," *The William Steinway Diary, 1861–1896*, Smithsonian Institution, National Museum of American History, http://americanhistory.si.edu/steinwaydiary/annotations/?id=743.
59. Yoffe, *Tchaikovsky in America*, 59.
60. Batterberry, *On the Town*, 162.
61. Yoffe, *Tchaikovsky in America*, 60.
62. "E. Francis Hyde," in *New York State's Prominent and Progressive Men: An Encyclopaedia of Contemporaneous Biography, Volume 3*, compiled by Mitchell C. Harrison (New York: New York Tribune, 1902), 171–172, https://archive.org/stream/newyorkstatespro02harr/newyorkstatespro02harr_djvu.txt.
63. Yoffe, *Tchaikovsky in America*, 60.
64. *Ibid.*
65. *Ibid.*, 61.
66. *Ibid.*, 65.
67. "The Raconteur," *Musical Courier*, Volume 18–19, March 13, 1889, 203, http://babel.hathitrust.org/cgi/pt?id=mdp.39015025410013;view=1up;seq=211.
68. Yoffe, *Tchaikovsky in America*, 60.
69. "Raconteur," *Musical Courier*.
70. "Ivy Maud Ross, NewsWriter, Dies," *The New York Times*, March 5, 1933, 62, http://timesmachine.nytimes.com/timesmachine/1933/03/05/99297023.html?pageNumber=62.
71. Yoffe, *Tchaikovsky in America*, 71–72, quoting the *New York Morning Journal*.
72. "Helen Hopekirk," Scottish Music Centre, http://www.scottishmusiccentre.com/members/helen_hopekirk/home/full_biography/.
73. "Helen Hopekirk Collection," in *Performing Arts Encyclopedia*, Library of Congress, Music Division, http://lcweb2.loc.gov/diglib/ihas/loc.natlib.scdb.200033628/default.html.
74. "Helen Hopekirk," Scottish Music Centre.
75. *Ibid.*, 62.
76. Yoffe, *Tchaikovsky in America*, 62.
77. Moses Rischin, *The Promised City: New York's Jews, 1870–1914* (Cambridge: Harvard University Press, 1962, 1977), 129.
78. Yoffe, *Tchaikovsky in America*, 64–65.
79. "Amusements," *The New-York Daily Tribune*, May 4, 1891, 11, Library of Congress, Chronicling America: Historic American Newspapers, http://chroniclingamerica.loc.gov/lccn/sn83030214/1891–05–04/ed-1/seq-11/.
80. "Mr. Santley Once More," *The New York Times*, May 5, 1891, 5, http://timesmachine.nytimes.com/timesmachine/1891/05/05/103305477.html?pageNumber=5.
81. Yoffe, *Tchaikovsky in America*, 79.
82. *Ibid.*, 68.
83. *Ibid.*, 79.

Chapter Five

1. "Music Crowned in Its New Home," *The New York Herald*, May 6, 1891, 7, http://fultonhistory.com/my%20photo%20albums/All%20Newspapers/New%20York%20NY%20Herald/index.html.
2. Elkhonon Yoffe, with translations from Russian by Lidya Yoffe, *Tchaikovsky in America: The Composer's Visit in 1891* (New York: Oxford University Press, 1986), 82.
3. *Ibid.*
4. *Ibid.*
5. *Ibid.*
6. "Anton Seidl," The New York Philharmonic, https://nyphil.org/about-us/artists/anton-seidl.
7. Yoffe, 82.
8. *Ibid.*, 209, note 34. *Tchaikovsky in America* spells the name "Margulis," yet news accounts and numerous other sources cite it as "Margulies," which is used in this narrative.
9. Ancestry.com. New York, New York, Marriage index 1866–1937. Provo, UT, USA: Ancestry.com Operations, Inc., 2014. Leo Margulies to Anna Reno. Manhattan, New York, USA. Marriage Date: 27 Oct. 1886. Certificate Number: 62361. (Margulies is occasionally referred to as "Leo," although most sources refer his first name as "Leon," which is used in this narrative.).
10. Yoffe, *Tchaikovsky in America*, 209, note 34.

11. *Ibid.*, 83.
12. "The Music Hall Opened," *The New-York Tribune*, May 6, 1891, 1, Library of America, Chronicling America: Historic American Newspapers, http://chroniclingamerica.loc.gov/lccn/sn83030214/1891–05–06/ed-1/seq-1/.
13. Yoffe, *Tchaikovsky in America*, 83.
14. "Amusements," *The New York Times*, May 5, 1891, 7, http://timesmachine.nytimes.com/timesmachine/1891/05/05/issue.html.
15. "Theatrical Gossip," *The New York Times*, May 5, 1891, 8, http://timesmachine.nytimes.com/timesmachine/1891/05/05/103305515.html?pageNumber=8.
16. "Music Crowned," *The New York Herald*.
17. "A Rare Musical Event," *The Sun* (New York), May 6, 1891, 1, Library of Congress, Chronicling America: Historic American Newspapers, http://chroniclingamerica.loc.gov/lccn/sn83030272/1891–05–06/ed-1/seq-1/.
18. Kimberly Chou, "Opening Night, Before It Was Carnegie Hall," *The Wall Street Journal*, September 30, 2011, www.wsj.com/articles/SB10001424052970204226204576601010452872084.
19. "Rare Musical Event," *The Sun*.
20. *Ibid.*
21. "Rare Musical Event," *The Sun*.
22. Tim Page and Carnegie Hall, *Carnegie Hall Treasures* (New York: Collins Design/HarperCollins, 2010), Opening Night Souvenir Booklet 1891.
23. "It Stood the Test Well," *The New York Times*, May 6, 1891, 5, http://timesmachine.nytimes.com/timesmachine/1891/05/06/103305634.html?pageNumber=5.
24. "Rare Musical Event," *The Sun*.
25. David Nasaw, *Andrew Carnegie* (New York: Penguin, 2006), 280.
26. "Carnegie Music Hall," *Pittsburgh Dispatch*, May 6, 1891, 1, Library of Congress, Chronicling America: Historic American Newspapers, http://chroniclingamerica.loc.gov/lccn/sn84024546/1891–05–06/ed-1/seq-1/.
27. "Rare Musical Event," *The Sun*.
28. *Ibid.*
29. Richard Schickel and Michael Walsh, *Carnegie Hall: The First One Hundred Years* (New York: Harry N. Abrams, 1987), 14.
30. "Music Hall Opened," *The New-York Tribune*.
31. "Music Crowned," *The New York Herald*.
32. "Music Hall Opened," *The New-York Tribune*.
33. "Music Crowned," *The New York Herald*.
34. Page, *Carnegie Hall Treasures*, Opening Night Souvenir Booklet.
35. *The William Steinway Diary, 1861–1896*, Smithsonian Institution, National Museum of American History, May 5, 1891 entry, http://americanhistory.si.edu/steinwaydiary/diary/?date=may+5%2C+1891&x=31&y=7.

36. Page, *Carnegie Hall Treasures*, Souvenir Booklet.
37. "History," *Wm. Knabe & Co.*, www.knabepianos.com/history.php.
38. George Martin, *The Damrosch Dynasty: America's First Family of Music* (Boston: Houghton Mifflin, 1983), 116.
39. H. E. Krehbiel, *Choral Music in New York: Notes on the Cultivation of Choral Music and the Oratorio Society of New York* (H. E. Krehbiel, 1884), 91–92.
40. "Rare Musical Event," *The Sun*.
41. *Ibid.*
42. "Music Hall Opened," *The New-York Tribune*.
43. "Rare Musical Event," *The Sun*.
44. Oratorio Society of New York, *The Oratorio Society Minutes 1888–1899*, addendum to May 13, 1891, letter from Andrew Carnegie to William Burnet Tuthill. Used with the permission of the Oratorio Society of New York.
45. "Rare Musical Event," *The Sun*.
46. "Her Point of View," *The New York Times*, May 10, 1891, 12, http://timesmachine.nytimes.com/timesmachine/1891/05/10/103306454.html?pageNumber=12.
47. "Rare Musical Event," *The Sun*.
48. Martin, *Damrosch Dynasty*, 116.
49. "Rare Musical Event," *The Sun*.
50. Yoffe, *Tchaikovsky in America*, 83.
51. "Rare Musical Event," *The Sun*.
52. Jane Allen, "Potter, Henry Codman," in *The Encyclopedia of New York City*, edited by Kenneth T. Jackson (New Haven: Yale University Press & New York: The New-York Historical Society, 1995), 931.
53. Edwin G. Burrows and Mike Wallace, *Gotham: A History of New York City to 1898* (New York: Oxford University Press, 1999), 1087.
54. Edward Robb Ellis, *The Epic of New York City: A Narrative History* (New York: Old Town Books, 1966), 391, 417.
55. "The Washington Arch," *The New York Times*, May 28, 1890, 5, http://timesmachine.nytimes.com/timesmachine/1890/05/28/103245170.html?pageNumber=5.
56. "Pastor Weds the Soprano," *The Evening World, Extra 2:00 O'Clock*, May 8, 1891, 1, Library of Congress, Chronicling America: Historic American Newspapers, http://chroniclingamerica.loc.gov/lccn/sn83030193/1891-05-08/ed-1/seq-1/.
57. "It Stood Test," *The New York Times*.
58. "Music Hall Opened," *The New-York Tribune*.
59. *Ibid.*
60. *Ibid.*
61. "Rare Musical Event," *The Sun*.
62. Vera Brodsky Lawrence, *Music for Patriots, Politicians, and Presidents: Harmonies and Discords of the First Hundred Years* (New York: Macmillan, 1975), 262.

63. Ellis, *Epic of New York City*, 391.
64. Phillip Huscher, "Leonore Overture No. 3," Chicago Symphony Orchestra, program notes,https://cso.org/uploadedFiles/1_Tickets_and_Events/Program_Notes/061510_ProgramNotes_Beethoven_LeonoOverture3.pdf.
65. "Ludwig van Beethoven," in *Composers on Music: Eight Centuries of Writings*, edited by Josiah Fisk (Boston: Northeastern University Press, 1997), 58.
66. Michael Steinberg, "Beethoven: Leonore Overture No. 3, Opus 72A," San Francisco Symphony, program notes, http://www.sfsymphony.org/Watch-Listen-Learn/Read-Program-Notes/Program-Notes/BEETHOVEN-Leonore-Overture-No-3,-Opus-72a.aspx.
67. "Trumpet Call from the Overture Leonore No. 3 by Ludwig van Beethoven," MFiles, http://www.mfiles.co.uk/scores/trumpet-call-from-beethoven-overture-leonore-no3.htm.
68. Huscher, "Leonore Overture."
69. "Music Crowned," *The New York Herald*.
70. "Peace on the Steinway Road," *The New York Times*, May 6, 1891, 8, http://timesmachine.nytimes.com/timesmachine/1891/05/06/103305674.html?pageNumber=8.
71. "Music Crowned," *The New York Herald*.
72. Yoffe, *Tchaikovsky in America*, 83.
73. "Music Crowned," *The New York Herald*.
74. *Ibid.*
75. "It Stood Test," *The New York Times*.
76. Page, *Carnegie Hall Treasures*, Souvenir Booklet.
77. Emanuel Rubin, "Jeannette Meyers Thurber and the National Conservatory of Music," *American Music*, Volume 8, Number 3, Fall 1990, 294–298.
78. "Music Crowned," *The New York Herald*.
79. Jeanne Rogers, "Festival Coronation March" (Coronation March for Alexander III), The Austin Symphony, October 19–20, program notes, http://www.austinsymphony.org/events/washington-garcia-piano/.
80. "It Stood Test," *The New York Times*.
81. Vivien Schweitzer, "No, Not That Concerto: New York Philharmonic Plays Tchaikovsky at Avery Tisher Hall," *The New York Times*, July 8, 2012, http://www.nytimes.com/2012/07/09/arts/music/new-york-philharmonic-plays-tchaikovsky-at-avery-fisher-hall.html?_r=0.
82. Burton J. Hendrick and Daniel Henderson, *Louise Whitfield Carnegie: The Life of Mrs. Andrew Carnegie* (New York: Hastings House, 1950), 103.
83. Rogers, "Festival Coronation March," notes.
84. "Rare Musical Event," *The Sun*.
85. *Ibid.*
86. "Music Crowned," *The New York Herald*.
87. Schickel and Walsh, *Carnegie Hall: First Hundred*, 15.
88. Yoffe, *Tchaikovsky in America*, 83–84.

89. "Carnegie Music Hall," *Pittsburgh Dispatch*.
90. Ora Frishberg Saloman, "Presenting Berlioz's Music in New York, 1846–1890: Carl Bergmann, Theodore Thomas, Leopold Damrosch," in *European Music and Musicians in New York City, 1840–1900*, edited by John Graziano (Rochester: University of Rochester Press, 2006), 37–39.
91. James M. Keller, "Berlioz: Te Deum, Opus 22," San Francisco Symphony, program notes, www.sfsymphony.org/Watch-Listen-Learn/Read-Program-Notes/Program-Notes/BERLIOZ-Te-Deum,-Opus-22.aspx.
92. "It Stood Test," *The New York Times*.
93. "Music Crowned," *The New York Herald*.
94. Keller, "Berlioz: Te Deum."
95. Milton Goldin, *The Music Merchants* (London: Collier-Macmillan, 1969), 94.
96. "Amusements: Notes of the Week," *The New York Times*, June 8, 1890, 13, http://timesmachine.nytimes.com/timesmachine/1890/06/08/103247171.html?pageNumber=13.
97. "Amusements," *The New-York Tribune*, May 3, 1891, 11, Library of Congress, Chronicling America: Historic American Newspapers, http://chroniclingamerica.loc.gov/lccn/sn83030214/1891/05–03/ed-1/seq-11/.
98. "Gilmore at Coney Island," *The New York Times*, June 29, 1889, 2, http://timesmachine.nytimes.com/timesmachine/1889/06/29/106354245.html?pageNumber=2.
99. "Music Hall Opened," *The New-York Tribune*.
100. *Ibid.*
101. "Troubadour Song," *The World's Best Music: Famous Songs and Those who Made Them Famous, Volume I*, editors/special contributors, Helen Kendrick Johnson, Frederic Dean, Reginald De Koven, Gerrit Smith (New York: The University Society, 1904; The University of Michigan, digitized October 2, 2009), 29, https://books.google.com/books?id=Vk3kAAAAMAAJ&pg=PA29&lpg=PA29&dq=st.+chrysostom%27s+chapel—wenzel+a.+raboch&source=bl&ots=NCB3V_NrVN&sig=-6Afg-2l_IICajGEX1zQDLXg_7k&hl=en&sa=X&ei=UTlpVPTMD6GLsQTbwIKwAQ&ved=0CB4Q6AEwAA#v=onepage&q=st.%20chrysostom's%20chapel—wenzel%20a.%20raboch&f=false.
102. *Nickerson's Illustrated Church Musical and School Directory of New-York and Brooklyn* (New York: Nickerson & Young Publishers, 1895), 117.
103. "Ascension Day Services," *The New York Times*, May 5, 1891, 9, http://timesmachine.nytimes.com/timesmachine/1891/05/05/103305524.html?pageNumber=9.
104. "Music Crowned," *The New York Herald*.
105. Richard Schickel, *The World of Carnegie*

Hall (New York: Julian Messner, Inc., 1960), 46–47.

106. "The Cleaner," *Evening World*, May 6, 1891, 2, Chronicling America: Historic American Newspapers. Library of Congress, http://chroniclingamerica.loc.gov/lccn/sn83030193/1891–05–06/ed-1/seq-2/.

107. "Rare Musical Event," *The Sun*.

108. "Music Crowned," *The New York Herald*.

109. "Rare Musical Event," *The Sun*.

110. "Music Crowned," *The New York Herald*.

Chapter Six

1. "It Was Cold Yesterday," *The New York Times*, May 7, 1891, 1, http://timesmachine.nytimes.com/timesmachine/1891/05/07/103305762.html?pageNumber=2.

2. Elkhonon Yoffe, with translations from Russian by Lidya Yoffe *Tchaikovsky in America: The Composer's Visit in 1891* (New York: Oxford University Press, 1986), 99. Note: Yoffe refers to the name as "Romaiko," but the correct spelling is "Romeike" as included in *The Diaries of Tchaikovsky*, translated from the Russian, with notes, by Wladimir Lakond (New York: W. W. Norton, 1945), 315.

3. "New York City Signs—14th to 42nd Street," www.14to42.net/17street4.5.html.

4. "The Press: Clipping Business," *Time*, May 30, 1932, http://content.time.com/time/magazine/article/0,9171,769604,00.html. Also, "Death of Henry Romeike," *The New York Times*, June 4, 1903, 9, http://timesmachine.nytimes.com/timesmachine/1903/06/04/102005146.html?pageNumber=9.

5. "A Rare Musical Event," *The Sun* (New York), May 6, 1891, 1, Library of Congress, Chronicling America: Historic American Newspapers, http://chroniclingamerica.loc.gov/lccn/sn83030272/1891–05–06/ed-1/seq-1/pdf.

6. "It Stood the Test Well," *The New York Times*, May 6, 1891, 5, http://timesmachine.nytimes.com/timesmachine/1891/05/06/103305634.html?pageNumber=5.

7. Yoffe, *Tchaikovsky in America*, quoting the *Morning Journal*, 86–87.

8. "Music Crowned in Its New Home," *The New-York Herald*, May 6, 1891, 7, Library ofCongress, Chronicling America: Historic American Newspapers, http://fultonhistory.com/my%20photo%20albums/All%20Newspapers/New%20York%20NY%20Herald/index.html.

9. Yoffe, *Tchaikovsky in America*, 91.

10. "Music Crowned," *The New York Herald*.

11. "Rare Musical Event," *The Sun*.

12. Yoffe, *Tchaikovsky in America*, quoting *The Press*, 91.

13. *Ibid.*, quoting the *Morning Journal*, 87.

14. *Ibid.*, quoting letter to Alexey Sofronov, 81.

15. James Trager, *The New York Chronology* (New York: Harper Resource, 2003), 226.

16. Yoffe, *Tchaikovsky in America*, 92.

17. *Ibid.*, 91–92.

18. *Ibid.*, 92 and 208 (note).

19. *Ibid.*, 92.

20. "Amusements," *The New York Times*, April 30, 1858, 5, http://timesmachine.nytimes.com/timesmachine/1858/04/30/78943019.html?pageNumber=5.

21. "Amusements: Steinway Hall," *The New York Times*, June 8, 1867, 5, http://timesmachine.nytimes.com/timesmachine/1867/06/08/87581432.html?pageNumber=5.

22. "Amusements: Musical. Festival Week Performances," *The New York Times*, April 23, 1873, 7, http://timesmachine.nytimes.com/timesmachine/1873/04/23/90124931.html?pageNumber=7.

23. H.E. Krehbiel, *Choral Music in New York: Notes on the Cultivation of Choral Music and the Oratorio Society of New York* (H.E. Krehbiel, 1884), 91, 94, 97, 99, 103.

24. George Martin, *The Damrosch Dynasty: America's First Family of Music* (Boston: Houghton Mifflin, 1983), 69.

25. "The Oratorio Society," *The New York Times*, November 16, 1888, 5, http://timesmachine.nytimes.com/timesmachine/1888/11/16/100951689.html?pageNumber=5.

26. Howard D. McKinney and W. R. Anderson, *Music in History: The Evolution of an Art*, 3d ed. (New York: American Book Company, 1966), 475–6.

27. Michael Moore, "Elijah," The Mendelssohn Club of Philadelphia, program notes, April 21, 2007, www.mcchorus.org/program_notes/elijah042007.pdf.

28. *Ibid.*

29. *Ibid.*

30. Thomas May, "Mendelssohn's Elijah," Nashville Symphony, program notes, http://www.nashvillesymphony.org.

31. Moore, "Elijah," Mendelssohn Club.

32. Milton Goldin, *The Music Merchants* (London: Collier-Macmillan, 1969), 25.

33. F. G. Edwards, *The History of Mendelssohn's "Elijah"* (London: Novello and Company Limited; New York: Novello, Ewer and Co., 1896), 35–37, Project Gutenberg, released 12/5/2011, E Book #38223.

34. *Ibid.*, 135.

35. May, "Elijah," Nashville Symphony.

36. Moore, "Elijah," Mendelssohn Club.

37. May, "Elijah," Nashville Symphony.

38. James M. Keller, "Elijah, Oratorio on Words of the Old Testament, Op. 70, Felix Mendelssohn," The New York Philharmonic, program notes, http://nyphil.org/~media/pdfs/watch-listen/commercial-recordings/1011/release5.pdf.

39. May, "Elijah," Nashville.
40. Krehbiel, *Choral Music in New York*, 85–106.
41. Moore, "Elijah," Mendelssohn Club.
42. May, "Elijah," Nashville.
43. "Music: Mendelssohn's 'Elijah,'" *The New-York Daily Tribune*, May 7, 1891, 6, Library of Congress, Chronicling America: Historic American Newspapers, http://chronicl ingamerica.loc.gov/lccn/sn83030214/1891–05–07/ed-1/seq-6/.
44. "Amusements: The Music Hall Concerts," *The New York Times*, May 7, 1891, 4, http://timesmachine.nytimes.com/timesmach ine/1891/05/07/103305805.html?pageNum ber=4.
45. Irving Kolodin, *The Story of the Metropolitan Opera* (New York: Alfred A. Knopf, 1953), 9.
46. Walter Damrosch, *My Musical Life* (New York, Charles Scribner's Sons, 1930), 134.
47. "Emil Fischer" (Pittsburgh concert program) in *Andreas Dippel Concert Programs 1890–1892*, New York Public Library for the Performing Arts, Music Division, Special Collections.
48. "In Focus: *Seigfried*," The Metropolitan Opera, http://www.metopera.org/metopera/ news/festivals/infocus-siegfried.aspx?src= prodpg.
49. "In Focus: *Die Meistersinger*," The Metropolitan Opera, http://www.metopera.org/ Search/?q=in%20focus%20—%20emil%20fisc her.
50. Damrosch, *My Musical Life*, 134.
51. *Ibid.*, 67.
52. *Ibid.*, 136–137.
53. "Rather Disappointing: Were Some of the Artists in the Carnegie Concert Last Night," *The Pittsburgh Dispatch*, May 7, 1891, 1, Library of Congress, Chronicling America: Historic American Newspapers, http://chron iclingamerica.loc.gov/lccn/sn84024546/1891–05–07/ed-1/seq-1.
54. "Antonia Mielke" (Cincinnati concert program) in *Andreas Dippel Concert Programs 1890–1892*, New York Public Library for the Performing Arts, Music Division, Special Collections.
55. "Antonia Mielke" (Pittsburgh concert program) in *Andreas Dippel Concert Programs 1890–1892*, New York Public Library for the Performing Arts, Music Division, Special Collections.
56. "Mielke" (Cincinnati program) in *Dippel*.
57. "Amusements: The Damrosch Festival," *The Sun* (New York), May 7, 1891, 2, Library of Congress, Chronicling America: Historic American Newspapers, http://chronicling america.loc.gov/lccn/sn83030272/1891–05–07/ed-1/seq-2/.
58. "Antonia Mielke Dead," *The New York Times*, November 21, 1907, 9, http://times machine.nytimes.com/timesmachine/1907/11/ 21/104712214.html?pageNumber=9.
59. "Amusements: Music Hall Concerts," *The New York Times.*
60. "Marie Ritter-Goetze" (Cinncinnati concert program) in *Andreas Dippel Concert Programs 1890–1892*, New York Public Library for the Performing Arts, Music Division, Special Collections.
61. *Ibid.*
62. "Dippel, Tenor, Dies in Want on Coast," *The New York Times*, May 14, 1932, 15, http:// timesmachine.nytimes.com/timesmachine/ 1932/05/14/100738696.html?pageNumber= 15.
63. "Andreas Dippel" (Pittsburg concert program) in *Adreas Dippel Concert Programs 1890–1892*, New York Public Library for the Performing Arts, Music Division, Special Collections.
64. "Dippel, Tenor, Dies," *The New York Times.*
65. "Amusements: The Damrosch Festival," *The Sun.*
66. "Amusements," *The Evening World*, March 27, 1889, 3, Library of Congress, Chronicling America: Historic American Newspapers, http://chroniclingamerica.loc. gov/lccn/sn83030193/1889–03–27/ed-1/seq-3/.
67. "Amusements: Benefit Concert," *The New York Times*, May 8, 1884, 4, http://times machine.nytimes.com/timesmachine/1884/ 05/08/106278328.html?pageNumber=4.
68. "The Oratorio Society," *The New York Times*, March 16, 1890, 3, http://timesmachine. nytimes.com/timesmachine/1890/03/16/1032 34059.html?pageNumber=3.
69. "The World of Music," *The Musical Record & Review*, July 1893, 5.
70. "Woes of the Beth-El Choir," *The Sun* (New York), November 6, 1891, 3, Library of Congress, Chronicling America: Historic American Newspapers, http://chronicling america.loc.gov/lccn/sn83030193/1893–07–27/ed-1/seq-5/.
71. "Amusements," *The New-York Tribune*, November 20, 1890, 9, Library of Congress, Chronicling America: Historic American Newspapers, http://chroniclingamerica.loc.gov/lc cn/sn83030214/1890–11–20/ed-1/seq-9/.
72. "Changes in Plays," *The New York Tribune*, November 9, 1890, 24, Library of Congress, Chronicling America: Historic American Newspapers, http://chroniclingamerica. loc.gov/lccn/sn83030214/1890–11–09/ed-1/ seq-24/.
73. "New-York City," *The New-York Tribune*, March 7, 1895, 12, Library of Congress, Chronicling America: Historic American Newspapers, http://chroniclingamerica.loc.gov/lccn/ sn83030214/1895–03–07/ed-1/seq-12/.

74. "Amusements: The Damrosch Festival," *The Sun* (New York), May 7, 1891, 2, Library of Congress, Chronicling America: Historic American Newspapers, http://chronicling america.loc.gov/lccn/sn83030272/1891–05–07/ed-1/seq-2/.
75. "Amusements: Music Hall Concerts," *The New York Times.*
76. "Music: Mendelssohn's 'Elijah,'" *The New York Daily Tribune*, May 7, 1891, 6, Library of Congress, Chronicling America: Historic American Newspapers, http://chroniclingamerica. loc.gov/lccn/sn83030214/1891-05-07/ed-1/ seq-6.
77. Damrosch, *My Musical Life*, 355.
78. "Amusements: The Damrosch Festival," *The Sun.*
79. *Ibid.*
80. Yoffe, *Tchaikovsky in America*, 92·

Chapter Seven

1. Elkhonon Yoffe, with translations from Russian by Lidya Yoffe, *Tchaikovsky in America: The Composer's Visit in 1891* (New York: Oxford University Press, 1986), 93.
2. *Ibid.*, 99.
3. *Ibid.*, 90.
4. *Ibid.*, 91.
5. *Ibid.*, 86.
6. *Ibid.*, 92.
7. *Ibid.*
8. "Blaine Is Stricken," *The Evening World* (New York), May 11, 1891, 1, Library of Congress, Chronicling America: Historic American Newspapers, http://chroniclingamerica. loc.gov/lccn/sn83030193/1891–05–11/ed-1/ seq-1/.
9. Burton J. Hendrick and Daniel Henderson, *Louise Whitfield Carnegie: The Life of Mrs. Andrew Carnegie* (New York: Hastings House, 1950), 79–81.
10. "Mr. Carnegie's Wedding," April 23, 1887, 1, *The New York Times*, http://times machine.nytimes.com/timesmachine/1887/ 04/23/100908391.html?pageNumber=1.
11. "A Rare Musical Event," *The Sun* (New York), May 6, 1891, 1, Library of Congress, Chronicling America: Historic American Newspapers, http://chroniclingamerica.loc. gov/lccn/sn83030272/1891-05-06/ed-1/seq-1/.
12. "Diploma Day at Bellevue," *The New York Times*, March 31, 1891, 3, http://times machine.nytimes.com/timesmachine/1891/03/ 31/106048797.html?pageNumber=3.
13. "Dr. E. G. Janeway, Diagnostician, Dead," *The New York Times*, February 11, 1911, 11, http://timesmachine.nytimes.com/timesmac hine/1911/02/11/104779187.html?pageNum ber=11.
14. "Death of General Sherman," *Donahoe's Monthly Magazine*, Volume 25, April 1891,

375; also cited in "Gen. Sherman Sorely Ill," *The New York Times*, February 12, 1891, 1, http://timesmachine.nytimes.com/timesmachine/ 1891/02/12/106046782.html?pageNumber=1.
15. "Sherman's Memory Honored," *The Evening World, 5 O'Clock Special*, May 7, 1891, 1, Library of Congress, Chronicling America: Historic American Newspapers, http://chron iclingamerica.loc.gov/lccn/sn83030193/1891/ 05/07/ed-3/seq-1/.
16. "In Memory of Sherman," *The Sun* (New York), May 8, 1891, 3, Library of Congress, Chronicling America: Historic American Newspapers, http://chroniclingamerica.loc.gov/lccn/ sn83030272/1891–05–08/ed-1/seq-3/.
17. "Blaine Is Stricken," *The Evening World.*
18. "Amusements," *The Sun*, May 7, 1891, 10, Library of Congress, Chronicling America: Historic American Newspapers, http://chron iclingamerica.loc.gov/lccn/sn83030272/1891– 05–07/ed-1/seq-10/.
19. Richard B. Sylvester, *Tchaikovsky's Complete Songs: A Companion with Texts and Translations* (Bloomington: Indiana University Press, 2002), 17.
20. "About the Piece: The Marriage of Figaro," LA Phil, http://www.laphil.com/philpe dia/music/marriage-of-figaro-wolfgang-ama deus-mozart.
21. Jacques De Loustal, "Nights at the Opera," *The New Yorker*, January 8, 2007.
22. *Ibid.*
23. Mary C. Henderson, *The City & the Theatre: New York Playhouses from Bowling Green to Times Square* (Clifton, NJ: James T. White & Company, 1973), 74.
24. *Ibid.*, 75.
25. Henry Edward Krehbiel, *Chapters of Opera* (New York: Henry Holt & Co., 1911), 20, http://www.gutenberg.org/cache/epub/5995/ pg5995-images.html.
26. *Ibid.*, 21 quoting from the diary of Philip Hone.
27. De Loustal, "Nights at the Opera."
28. Henderson, *City & the Theatre*, 75.
29. "The Concerts," *The New York Times*, October 5, 1852, 1, http://timesmachine.ny times.com/timesmachine/1852/10/05/751181 37.html?pageNumber=1.
30. Vera Brodsky Lawrence, *Strong on Music: The New York Music Scene in the Days of George Templeton Strong, Volume III Repercussions 1857–1862* (Chicago: University of Chicago Press, 1999), 166.
31. "Amusements: Academy of Music," *The New York Times*, November 25, 1858, 4, http:// timesmachine.nytimes.com/timesmachine/ 1858/11/25/78880196.html?pageNumber=4.
32. "Amusements. Operatic: 'The Marriage of Figaro' at the Academy," *The New York Times*, March 15, 1870, 5, http://timesmachine. nytimes.com/timesmachine/1870/03/15/ 80219782.html?pageNumber=5.

33. "The Damrosch Festival," *The Sun* (New York), May 8, 1891, 7, Library of Congress, Chronicling America: Historic American Newspapers, http://chroniclingamerica.loc.gov/lccn/sn83030272/1891-05-08/ed-1/seq-7/.

34. "Richard Strauss 1864–1949," in *Composers on Music: Eight Centuries of Writings*, edited by Josiah Fisk (Boston: Northwestern University Press, 1997), 212.

35. Donald Jay Grout, *A Short History of Opera* (New York: Columbia University Press, 1965), 284–285.

36. *Ibid.*, 283–285.

37. "Clementine De Vere" (Pittsburgh concert program) in *Adreas Dippel Concert Programs 1890–1892*, New York Public Library for the Performing Arts, Music Division, Special Collections.

38. "Changes in Dr. Paxton's Choir," *The New York Times*, February 12, 1893, 10, http://timesmachine.nytimes.com/timesmachine/1893/02/12/106813929.html?pageNumber=10.

39. "Music of the Week: Personal Gossip of Musicians, By One of Them," *Music and Drama: A Journal Devoted to Sport, Music and the Drama*, April 8, 1893, 17.

40. "Conrad Behrens," clippings files, New York Public Library for the Performing Arts, Music Division, Special Collections.

41. "Theodor Reichmann" (Pittsburgh concert program) in *Adreas Dippel Concert Programs 1890–1892*, New York Public Library for the Performing Arts, Music Division, Special Collections.

42. "Amusements: The Music Hall Concerts," *The New York Times*, May 8, 1891, 4, http://timesmachine.nytimes.com/timesmachine/1891/05/08/103306020.html?pageNumber=4.

43. "Georges Bizet 1838–1875," in *Composers on Music: Eight Centuries of Writings*, edited by Josiah Fisk (Boston: Northwestern University Press, 1997), 146.

44. "Amusements: Music Hall Concerts," *The New York Times*.

45. "Damrosch Festival," *The Sun*.

46. Michael Fleming, "Suite No. 3," *Tchaikovsky: Complete Suites*, recording, Detroit Symphony Orchestra, Neeme Jarvi, conductor, Chandos Records Ltd., recorded March 10–12, 1995, liner notes, 8–9.

47. Herbert Glass, "About the Piece: Suite No. 3, Peter Ilyich Tchaikovsky," LA Phil, http://www.laphil.com/philpedia/music/suite-no-3-peter-ilyich-tchaikovsky.

48. "Suite No. 3 in G major, Op. 55, Pyotr Ilyich Tchaikovsky," NY Phil, http://nyphil.org/~/media/pdfs/program-notes/1314/TchaikovskySuite%20No%203%20in%20G%20major.pdf.

49. David Brown, *Tchaikovsky: The Man and His Music* (New York: Pegasus Books, 2007), 276.

50. *Ibid.*, 277.

51. Lawrence and Elisabeth Hanson, *Tchaikovsky: The Man Behind the Music* (New York: Dodd, Mead & Company, 1966), 267.

52. Glass, "About the Piece: Suite No. 3," LA Phil.

53. "Suite No. 3 in G major," NY Phil.

54. "Amusements: Music Hall Concerts," *The New York Times*.

55. *Ibid.*

56. "The Damrosch Festival," *The Sun*.

57. Demar Irvine, *Massenet: A Chronicle of His Life and Times* (Portland, OR: Amadeus Press, 1994), 163–164.

58. Steven Huebner, *French Opera at the Fin de Siecle* (New York: Oxford University Press, 2006), 80.

59. Tim Page, "Demanding 'Esclarmonde' Gets Vigorous, If Dubious, Workout," *The Washington Post* online, April 11, 2005, http://www.washingtonpost.com/wp-dyn/articles/A42725-2005Apr10.html.

60. "Amusements: Music Hall Concerts," *The New York Times*.

61. "The Damrosch Festival," *The Sun*.

62. "Making a Case for Massenet, The Misunderstood Sentimentalist," *Deceptive Cadence* from NPR Classical, Tom Huizenga, August 14, 2012, http://www.npr.org/sections/deceptivecadence/2012/08/14/158750921/making-a-case-for-massenet-the-misunderstood-sentimentalist.

63. "The Music Hall Concerts," *The New York Times*.

64. New York Philharmonic Digital Archives, February 8, 1890, November 21, 22, 1890, http://archives.nypil.org/.

65. "Heinrich August Marschner," in *Encyclopaedia Britannica online*, http://www.britannica.com/EBchecked/topic/366447/Heinrich-August-Marschner.

66. "Heinrich Marschner," Opera Glass, Stanford University, http://opera.stanford.edu/Marschner/.

67. "Ralph Vaughan Williams 1872–1958," in *Composers on Music: Eight Centuries of Writings*, edited by Josiah Fisk (Boston: Northwestern University Press, 1997), 230.

68. "Amusements: Music Hall Concerts," *New York Times*.

69. Marc Mandel, "Wagner: Prelude and Liebestod from Tristan and Isolde," San Francisco Symphony, http://www.sfsymphony.org/Watch-Listen-Learn/Read-Program-Notes/Program-Notes/WAGNER-Prelude-and-Liebestod-from-Tristan-und-Isol.aspx.

70. Fred Plotkin, "In the Footsteps of Richard Wagner: Zurich (Part II)," WQXR, http://www.wqxr.org/#!/story/309018-footsteps-richard-wagner-zurich-part-ii/.

71. *Ibid.*

72. Mandel, "Wagner: Prelude and Liebestod," San Francisco Symphony.

73. Phillip Huscher, "Richard Wagner—Prelude and 'Liebestod' from Tristan and Isolde," Rockford Symphony Orchestra, program notes, http://www.rockfordsymphony.com/wagner-prelude-and-liebestod-notes/.

74. "Amusements," *The New York Times*, February 12, 1866, 5, http://timesmachine.nytimes.com/timesmachine/1866/02/12/83449873.html?pageNumber=5.

75. "Amusements: Philharmonic Society," *The New York Times*, March 12, 1866, 4, http://timesmachine.nytimes.com/timesmachine/1866/03/12/83451693.html?pageNumber=4.

76. "Amusements: Musical. Mr. Thomas' Symphony Concerts, *The New York Times*, January 9, 1872, 5, http://timesmachine.nytimes.com/timesmachine/1872/01/09/79011155.html?pageNumber=5.

77. "Tristan and Isolde," *Music Festival Under the Direction of Walter Damrosch for the Inauguration of "Music Hall," Founded by Anderew Carnegie. May 5th, 6th, 7th, 8th, and 9th* (New York: The Cherouny Printing & Publishing Company, 1891), 31–32, Cornell University Library, Digital Collection, https://archive.org/details/cu31924018549836.

78. "The Damrosch Festival," *The Sun*.

79. "Amusements: Music Hall Concerts, *New York Times*.

80. "Another Comic Opera," *The New York Times*, May 8, 1891, 4, http://timesmachine.nytimes.com/timesmachine/1891/05/08/103306020.html?pageNumber=4.

81. "Rather Disappointing," *The Pittsburgh Dispatch*, May 7, 1891, 1, Library of Congress, Chronicling America: Historic American Newspapers, http://chroniclingamerica.loc.gov/lccn/sn84024546/1891-05-07/ed-1/seq-1/.

82. Yoffe, *Tchaikovsky in America*, 93.

Chapter Eight

1. Oratorio Society of New York. *The Oratorio Society Minutes 1888–1899*, addendum to May 13, 1891, letter from Andrew Carnegie to William Burnet Tuthill. Used with the permission of the Oratorio Society of New York.

2. Elkhonon Yoffe, with translations from Russian by Lidya Yoffe, *Tchaikovsky in America: The Composer's Visit in 1891* (New York: Oxford University Press, 1986), 99.

3. "Individual Mention," *The Critic and Record* (Washington D.C.), May 8, 1891, 4, Library of Congress, Chronicling America: Historic American Newspapers, http://chroniclingamerica.loc.gov/lccn/sn87062228/1891-05-08/ed-1/seq-4/.

4. "Armor Tests at Annapolis," *The New York Times*, May 9, 1891, 1, http://timesmachine.nytimes.com/timesmachine/1891/05/09/103306107.html?pageNumber=1.

5. Untitled, *Chariton Courier* (Keytesville,

Missouri), May 7, 1891, 1, Library of Congress, Chronicling America: Historic American Newspapers, http://chroniclingamerica.loc.gov/lccn/sn88068010/1891-05-07/ed-1/seq-1/.

6. "The News of the World," *The Indiana State Sentinel*, May 6, 1891, 6, Library of Congress, Chronicling America: Historic American Newspapers, http://chroniclingamerica.loc.gov/lccn/sn87056600/1891-05-06/ed-1/seq-6/; and also "Notes and Comments," *The Iola Register* (Iola, Kansas), May 88, 1891, 6, Library of Congress, Chronicling America: Historic American Newspapers, http://chroniclingamerica.loc.gov/lccn/sn83040340/1891-05-08/ed-1/seq-6/.

7. "Miscellaneous Items," *Brenam Weekly Banner* (Brenham, Texas), May 7, 1891, 6, Library of Congress, Chronicling America: Historic American Newspapers, http://chroniclingamerica.loc.gov/lccn/sn86089443/1891-05/07/ed-1/seq-6/.

8. "Off for Europe," *The Pittsburgh Dispatch*, May 9, 1891, 1, Library of Congress, Chronicling America: Historic American Newspapers, http://chroniclingamerica.loc.gov/lccn/sn84024546/1891-05-09/ed-1/seq-1/.

9. Gretchen Finletter, *From the Top of the Stairs* (Boston: Little, Brown, 1946), 176.

10. Yoffe, *Tchaikovsky in America*, 98.

11. *Ibid.*

12. Leonid Sidelnikov & Galina Pribegina, *25 Days in America: For the Centenary of Peter Tchaikovsky's Concert* (Moscow: "Muzyka," 1991), photo inset.

13. Yoffe, *Tchaikovsky in America*, 98.

14. Edwin G. Burrows and Mike Wallace, *Gotham: A History of New York City to 1898* (New York: Oxford University Press, 1999), 1153.

15. Barbara Blumberg, "Statue of Liberty," in *The Encyclopedia of New York City*, edited by Kenneth T. Jackson (New Haven: Yale University Press & New York: The New-York Historical Society, 1995), 1119.

16. Edward Robb Ellis, *The Epic of New York City: A Narrative History* (New York: Old Town Books, 1966), 384–392.

17. "Her Maiden Voyage," *The New York Times*, August 23, 1886, 8, http://timesmachine.nytimes.com/timesmachine/1886/08/23/103973937.html?pageNumber=8.

18. "Four New French Steamers," *The New York Times*, March 25, 1885, 6, http://timesmachine.nytimes.com/timesmachine/1885/03/25/102963618.html?pageNumber=8.

19. Yoffe, *Tchaikovsky in America*, 40.

20. "Bartholdi Well Pleased," *The New York Times*, October 26, 1886, 1–2, http://timesmachine.nytimes.com/timesmachine/1886/10/26/106304259.html?pageNumber=1.

21. "French Guests Welcomed," *The New York Times*, October 27, 1886, 3, http://times

machine.nytimes.com/timesmachine/1886/10/27/106304559.html?pageNumber=5.

22. "The Great Celebration," *The New York Times*, October 27, 1886, 1–2, http://timesmachine.nytimes.com/timesmachine/1886/10/27/106304465.html?pageNumber=1.

23. Jeffrey A. Kroessler, *New York Year by Year: A Chronology of the Great Metropolis* (New York: New York University Press, 2002), 136.

24. "France's Gift Accepted: Liberty's Statue Unveiled on Bedlow's Island," *The New York Times*, October 29, 1886, 1, http://timesmachine.nytimes.com/timesmachine/1886/10/29/103989753.html?pageNumber=1.

25. "Bartholdi Well Pleased," *The New York Times*.

26. *Ibid.*

27. *Ibid.*

28. Yoffe, *Tchaikovsky in America*, 98 (Note: Although cited as "Martelli's" in Yoffe, it is referenced as "Martinelli's in Sidelnikov and Pribegina).

29. Yoffe, *Tchaikovsky in America*, 98.

30. "MacGahan, Barbara (nee Varvara Elagina) 1850–1904," *Historical Dictionary of United States-Russian/Soviet Relations*, 236, https://books.google.com/books?id=Lf4lAAAAQBAJ&pg=PA236&lpg=PA236&dq=MacGahan,+Barbara+(nee+Varvara+Elagina)+1850–1904,+Historical+Dictionary+of+United+States-Russian/Soviet+Relations,&source=bl&ots=KfSIfUmrra&sig=BQzk8IYwTTkof8L6SHkHuR7bsFg&hl=en&sa=X&ved=0CCAQ6AEwAGoVChMIjvaMhaisxwIVlBOSCh1uLQqM#v=onepage&q&f=false.

31. *Yoffe, Tchaikovsky* in America, 98.

32. *Ibid.*

33. *Ibid.*, 98–99.

34. Charles Tuttle Howe, *All About the Flute ... Containing a History of the Flute from Ancient Times* (Columbus: Charles T. Howe, 1898), 28.

35. Nancy Toff, *The Flute Book: A Complete Guide for Students and Performers* (New York: Oxford University Press, 1996), 245–246.

36. Yoffe, *Tchaikovsky in America*, 98.

37. Howard D. McKinney & W. R. Anderson, *Music in History: The Evolution of an Art* (New York: American Book Company, 1966), 306.

38. "Here on a Sunday Morning," (HOASN), WBAI, http://www.hoasm.org/.

39. McKinney and Anderson, *Music in History*, 306–307.

40. "Here on a Sunday Morning," WBAI.

41. "The Seven Words," *Music Festival Under the Direction of Walter Damrosch for the Inauguration of "Music Hall," Founded by Andrew Carnegie. May 5th, 6th, 7th, 8th, and 9th* (New York: The Cherouny Printing & Publishing Company, 1891), 35, Cornell University Library, Digital Collection, https://archive.org/details/cu31924018549836.

42. *Ibid.*, 36.

43. "Amusements: The Music Hall Concerts," *The New York Times*, May 9, 1891, 4, http://timesmachine.nytimes.com/timesmachine/1891/05/09/103306224.html?pageNumber=4.

44. "Seven Words," *Music Festival*, 36.

45. "Amusements: Music Hall Concerts," *The New York Times*.

46. "Music: Third Night of the Festival," *The New-York Tribune*, May, 1891, 6, Library of Congress, Chronicling America: Historic American Newspapers, http://chroniclingamerica.loc.gov/lccn/sn83030214/1891-05-09/ed-1/seq-6/.

47. "Frank L. Sealy, 80, A Leading Organist," *The New York Times*, December 14, 1938, 25, http://timesmachine.nytimes.com/timesmachine/1938/12/14/98873427.html?pageNumber=25.

48. Henry Mason Baum, *The Church Review*, Volumes 58–59 (New York: Macmillan, 1890), 320.

49. "Frank L. Sealy," *The New York Times*.

50. "The Frank Roosevelt Organ, Opus #433," Church of the Angels, www.coa-pasadena.org/organ-music.

51. "Wedded in Washington," *The New York Times*, May 18, 1890, 1, http://timesmachine.nytimes.com/timesmachine/1890/05/18/103243355.html?pageNumber=1.

52. "Carnegie Hall: Frank Roosevelt, Opus #486–1891," American Guild of Organists, http://www.nycago.org/Organs/NYC/html/CarnegieHall.html#Roosevelt.

53. "The Frank Roosevelt Organ, Opus #433."

54. "The Organ," Souvenir Booklet, Carnegie Hall Archives.

55. Yoffe, *Tchaikovsky in America*, quoting the *Morning Journal*, 100–101.

56. Richard D. Sylvester, *Tchaikovsky's Complete Songs* (Bloomington: University of Indiana Press, 2002) 163–165.

57. "Amusements: Music Hall Concerts," *The New York Times*.

58. "Music: The Oratorio Society," *The Critic*, Volume 2, May 6, 1882, 134, Google.

59. "Amusements: Music Hall Concerts," *The New York Times*.

60. "Sulamith," in *Music Festival Under the Direction of Walter Damrosch for the Inauguration of "Music Hall," Founded by Anderew Carnegie. May 5th, 6th, 7th, 8th, and 9th* (New York: The Cherouny Printing & Publishing Company, 1891), 39, Cornell University Library, Digital Collection, https://archive.org/details/cu31924018549836.

61. *Ibid.*

62. "Music: Oratorio Society," *The Critic*.

63. Wayne D. Shirley, "Leopold Damrosch as Composer," *European Music and Musicians in New York City, 1840–1900*, edited by John

Graziano (Rochester: University of Rochester Press, 2006), 105–106.

64. "Music: Third Night of Festival," *The New-York Tribune.*

65. H. E. Krehbiel, *Choral Music in New York: Notes on the Cultivation of Choral Music and the Oratorio Society of New York* (H. E. Krehbiel, 1884), 94.

66. "Music: Third Night of Festival," *The New-York Tribune.*

67. Yoffe, *Tchaikovsky in* America, 99.

68. "Music: Third Night of Festival," *The New-York Tribune.*

69. "Amusements: Music Hall Concerts," *The New York Times.*

70. *Ibid.*

71. "Gustav Dannreuther Dies of Pneumonia," *Vassar Miscellany News*, Volume VIII, Number 21, January 12, 1924, 2, http://news paperarchives.vassar.edu/cgi-bin/vassar?a= d&d=miscellany19240112–01.2.14.

72. Jeremy Dibble, "Edward George Dannreuther (1844–1905), pianist and writer," *Oxford Dictionary of National Biography*, Oxford University Press, 2004, www.oxforddnb.com/ view/article/40938/accessed.

73. "Frits Hartvigson," Tchaikovsky Research, http://en.tchaikovsky-research.net/ pages/Frits_Hartvigson.

74. Yoffe, *Tchaikovsky in America*, 99.

75. *Ibid.*

76. "Music: Third Night of Festival," *The New-York Tribune.*

Chapter Nine

1. "Music Hall's Fire Baptism," *The Evening World (Baseball Extra)*, May 9, 1891, 3, Library of Congress, Chronicling America: Historic American Newspapers, http://chronicling america.loc.gov/lccn/sn83030193/1891–05– 09/ed-4/seq-3/.

2. "Fierce Fire in Gotham," *The Chicago Daily Tribune*, January 3, 1891, 1, www.ar chives.chicagotribune.com/1891/01/03/page/ 1/article/fierce-fire-in-gotham.

3. "Music Hall's Fire Baptism," *Evening World.*

4. Different newspaper accounts spell his name "Chesebro or Cheseborough. The Carnegie Corporation's ledger books and city directories of the era indicate the first spelling.

5. "Music Hall's Fire Baptism," *Evening World.*

6. "The Fire in the Carnegie Music Hall," *The Sun* (New York), May 10, 1891, 21, Library of Congress, Chronicling America: Historic American Newspapers, http://chronicling america.loc.gov/lccn/sn83030272/1891–05– 10/ed-1/seq-21/.

7. *Ibid.*

8. "Losses by Fire," *The New York Times*, May 10, 1891, 2, http://timesmachine.nytimes.

com/timesmachine/1891/05/10/103306326. html?pageNumber=2.

9. Elkhonon Yoffe, translations from Russian by Lidya Yoffe, *Tchaikovsky in America: The Composer's Visit in 1891* (New York: Oxford University Press, 1986), 102.

10. *Ibid.*

11. "The Damrosch Festival," *The Sun* (New York), May 8, 1891, 7, Library of Congress, Chronicling America: Historic American Newspapers. http://chroniclingamerica.loc.gov/lc cn/sn83030272/1891–05–08/ed-1/seq-7/.

12. Yoffe, *Tchaikovsky in America*, 102; this refers to "Howson."

13. "Frank A. Howson, Composer, Dead," *The New York Times*, June 30, 1926, 25, http:// timesmachine.nytimes.com/timesmachine/ 1926/06/30/98384963.html?pageNumber=25.

14. "Manuscript Society's Dinner," *The New York Times*, April 21, 1893, 2, http://timesmac hine.nytimes.com/timesmachine/1893/04/21/ 109698147.html?pageNumber=2.

15. "Dr. Gerrit Smith," *The New York Times*, July 22, 1912, 7, http://timesmachine.nytimes. com/timesmachine/1912/07/22/104901838. html?pageNumber=7.

16. Yoffe, *Tchaikovsky in America*, 102.

17. "Music Hall Perquisites," *The New York Times*, May 10, 1891, 8, http://timesmachine. nytimes.com/timesmachine/1891/05/10/ 103306404.html?pageNumber=8.

18. *Ibid.*

19. "Beethoven's Fifth Symphony," *Music Festival Under the Direction of Walter Damrosch for the Inauguration of "Music Hall," Founded by Anderew Carnegie. May 5th, 6th, 7th, 8th, and 9th* (New York: The Cherouny Printing & Publishing Company, 1891), 45, Cornell University Library, Digital Collection, https://archive.org/details/cu31924018549836.

20. Walter Damrosch, *My Musical Life* (New York: Charles Scribner's Sons, 1930), 9.

21. *Ibid.*, 32–33.

22. George Martin, *The Damrosch Dynasty: America's First Family of Music* (Boston: Houghton Mifflin, 1983), 97.

23. *Ibid.*, 96.

24. Damrosch, *My Musical Life*, 366.

25. Jan Swafford, *Beethoven: Anguish and Triumph* (Boston: Houghton Mifflin Harcourt, 2014), 495.

26. Adrienne Fried Block, "Thinking About Serious Music in New York," in *American Orchestras in the Nineteenth Century,* ed. John Spitzer (Chicago: University of Chicago Press, 2012), 440.

27. *Ibid.*, 439.

28. "Beethoven," *Music Festival Under Direction of Walter Damrosch*, 46.

29. *Ibid.*

30. Damrosch, *My Musical Life*, 376.

31. "Beethoven," *Music Festival Under Direction of Walter Damrosch*, 48.

32. "The Music Hall Concerts," *The New York Times*, May 10, 1891, 5, http://timesmach ine.nytimes.com/timesmachine/1891/05/10/103306374.html?pageNumber=5.

33. "Mrs. Carl Alves," clippings files, New York Public Library for the Performing Arts, Music Division, Special Collections.

34. Yoffe, *Tchaikovsky in America*, 102.

35. John H. Chandler, "Robin Hood: Development of a Popular Hero," *The Robin Hood Project*, University of Rochester, http://d.lib.rochester.edu/robin-hood/text/chandler-robin-hood-development-of-a-popular-hero.

36. Walter Damrosch, *To Sleep*, manuscript score, New York Public Library for the Performing Arts, Music Division, Special Collections.

37. Alfred, Lord Tennyson, *The Foresters: Robin Hood and Maid Marian*, Act I, Scene III, *The Robin Hood Project*, University of Rochester, http://d.lib.rochester.edu/robin-hood/text/tennyson-foresters.

38. Damrosch, *To Sleep*.

39. "Musical Notes," *The New York Times*, April 5, 1891, 13, http://timesmachine.nytimes.com/timesmachine/1891/04/05/103301272.html?pageNumber=13.

40. "By Way of Diversion," *The New York Times*, December 7, 1890, 4, http://timesmach ine.nytimes.com/timesmachine/1890/12/07/103284911.html?pageNumber=4.

41. "The Manuscript Society," *The New York Times*, December 11, 1890, 1890, 4, http://timesmachine.nytimes.com/timesmachine/1890/12/11/103285681.html?pageNumber=4.

42. Richard Aldrich, "Peter Ilyitch Tchaikovsky: A Critical Note," in *Peter Ilyitch Tchaikovsky: Twelve Songs for Voice and Piano* (New York: G. Schirmer, Inc., 1902), iv.

43. *Ibid.*, v.

44. Richard D. Sylvester, *Tchaikovsky's Complete Songs* (Bloomington: Indiana University Press, 2002), 17–18.

45. "Music Hall Concerts," *The New York Times*.

46. "Piotr Ilyich Tchaikovsky, 1840–1893" in *Composers on Music*, edited by Josiah Fisk (Boston: Northeastern University Press, 1997), 159.

47. LaWayne Leno, *The Untold Story of Adele aus der Ohe: From a Liszt Student to a Virtuoso* (Edina, MN: Beaver's Pond Press, Inc., 2012), 76–79.

48. Abram Chasins, *Speaking of Pianists* (New York: Knopf, 1957), 249.

49. "Piano Concerto No. 1," *Tchaikovsky Research*, http://en.tchaikovsky-research.net/pages/Piano_Concerto_No._1.

50. Martin, *Damrosch Dynasty*, 40.

51. Leno, *Untold Story of Adele aus der Ohe*, 3.

52. *Ibid.*, 21.

53. *Ibid.*, 22.

54. *Ibid.*, 200, 227.

55. *Ibid.*, 32–33.

56. *Ibid.*, 21.

57. *Ibid.*, 36–39.

58. "Musical Notes," *The New York Times*, January 4, 1891, 13, http://timesmachine.ny times.com/timesmachine/1891/01/04/103289441.html?pageNumber=13.

59. Yoffe, *Tchaikovsky in America*, 79.

60. Elizabeth Schwartz, "Pyotr Ilyich Tchaikovsky: Piano Concerto No. 1 in B-flat minor, Op. 23," The Oregon Symphony, *Tchaikovsky Spectacular*, program notes, http://www.or symphony.org/concerts/1415/programnotes/sc4.aspx.

61. Chasins, *Speaking of Pianists*, 249.

62. "Music: Last of the Festival Concerts," *The New-York Tribune*, May 10, 1891, 7, Library of Congress, Chronicling America: Historic American Newspapers, http://chronicling america.loc.gov/lccn/sn83030214/1891–05–10/ed-1/seq-7/.

63. David Brown, *Tchaikovsky: The Final Years (1885–1893)*, Volume IV (New York: W. W. Norton, 1991), 322.

64. Yoffe, *Tchaikovsky in America*, 102.

65. *Ibid.*, 109.

66. "Music Hall Concerts," *The New York Times*.

67. *Ibid.*, 102.

68. Yoffe, *Tchaikovsky in America*, 106.

69. "In Focus: Richard Wagner, *Parsifal*," http://www.metopera.org/PageFiles/41061/Mar%202%20Parsifal.pdf.

70. "Home News," *The Musical Courier*, Vol. 23, July 1, 1891, 8.

71. "German Opera Once Again," *The New York Times*, February 14, 1894, 4, http://times machine.nytimes.com/timesmachine/1894/02/14/106898189.html?pageNumber=4.

72. "Kronold Leaves Opera to Live Near Convent," *The New York Times*, October 3, 1904, 1, http://timesmachine.nytimes.com/timesmachine/1904/10/03/100475760.html?pageNumber=1.

73. "Chickering Hall," *The New York Times*, January 24, 1886, 6, http://timesmachine.ny times.com/timesmachine/1886/01/24/106179509.html?pageNumber=6.

74. *The Theatre, Volume 4*, by Deshler Welch (Theatre Publishing Co, 1889), 279.

75. "Mrs. Gerrit Smith," *The New York Times*, June 4, 1940, 23, http://timesmachine.nytimes.com/timesmachine/1940/06/04/113378333.html?pageNumber=23.

76. "Mrs. Ella A. Toedt of Juilliard School," *The New York Times*, June 14, 1939, 29, http://timesmachine.nytimes.com/timesmachine/1939/06/14/93928711.html?pageNumber=29.

77. "Mrs. Hattie Clapper Morris," *The New York Times*, January 23, 1930, 20, http://times machine.nytimes.com/timesmachine/1930/01/23/94233327.html?pageNumber=20.

78. "Music: Last of the Festival Concerts," *The New-York Tribune*, May 10, 1891, 7, http://chroniclingamerica.loc.gov/lccn/sn83030214/1891-05-10/ed-1/seq-7/.
79. *Ibid.*
80. Michael. C. Lister, "Israel in Egypt," Indianapolis Symphonic Choir, program notes, http://www.indychoir.org/wp-content/uploads/2014/07/Israel-In-Egypt-Program-Notes-Wriitten-By-Michael-Lister.pdf.
81. Mark P. Risinger, "Notes on the Concert—Israel in Egypt: A Composer Masters the Oratorio Form," The Providence Singers, http://www.providencesingers/org/Concerts06/Season02-03/Mar03Concert.html.
82. "Israel in Egypt," *Music Festival Under Direction of Walter Damrosch*, 53.
83. Nina Anne Greeley, "George Frideric Handel/Israel in Egypt," San Francisco Choral Society, program notes, www.sfchoral.org/site/george-frideric-handel-israel-in-egypt/.
84. "The Music Hall Concerts," *The New York Times*, May 10, 1891, 5, http://timesmachine.nytimes.com/timesmachine/1891/05/10/103306374.html?pageNumber=5.
85. "Music: Last of Festival," *The New-York Tribune.*
86. Yoffe, *Tchaikovsky in America*, 103.
87. Oratorio Society of New York, *The Oratorio Society Minutes 1888–99*, May 9, 1891. Used with the permission of the Oratorio Society of New York.
88. Yoffe, *Tchaikovsky in America*, 103.
89. *The Diaries of Tchaikovsky*, translated from the Russian, with notes, by Wladimir Lakond (New York: W. W. Norton, 1945), 351.
90. "Rudolph E. Schirmer 1859–1919," *The Etude*, October 1919, www.etudemagazine.com.
91. "Carl Christian Schurz," *The William Steinway Diary, 1861–1896*, Smithsonian Institution, National Museum of American History, http://americanhistory.si.edu/steinway diary/annotations/?id=802.
92. Yoffe, *Tchaikovsky in America*, 103.

Chapter Ten

1. Oratorio Society of New York, *The Oratorio Society Minutes 1889–99*, addendum to May 13, 1891, letter from Andrew Carnegie to William B. Tuthill. Used with the permission of the Oratorio Society of New York.
2. Harry P. Mawson, "Tchaikovsky and the Music Festival," *Harper's Weekly*, May 9, 1891, 347.
3. "Paderewski's Inaugural Concerts," Performance History Search, Carnegie Hall, http://www.carnegiehall.org/PerformanceHistorySearch/#!
4. *The William Steinway Diary, 1861–1896*, Smithsonian Institution, National Museum of

American History, November 17, 1891 entry, http://americanhistory.si.edu/steinwaydiary/diary/?show_anno=true&page=2075&view=transcription#dl.
5. Elkhonon Yoffe, with translations from Russian by Lidya Yoffe, *Tchaikovsky in America: The Composer's Visit in 1891* (New York: Oxford University Press, 1986), 118.
6. Leonid Sidelnikov and Galina Pribegina, *25 Days in America: For the Centenary of Peter Tchaikovsky's Concert Tour* (Moscow: "Muzyka," 1991), English translation, 73.
7. *Ibid.*
8. Yoffe, *Tchaikovsky in America*, 111.
9. *Ibid.*
10. *Ibid.*, 149.
11. *Ibid.*, 151.
12. *Ibid.*
13. Mawson, "Tchaikovsky and Music Festival," *Harper's.*
14. "A New Home for a College of Music," *The New-York Tribune*, June 26, 1891, 7, Library of Congress, Chronicling America: Historic American Newspapers, http://chroniclingamerica.loc.gov/lccn/sn83030214/1891-06-26/ed-1/seq-7/.
15. "Patents Inventions," *Music Trade Review*, October 13, 1894, 7, www.mtr.arcademuseum.com/MTR-1894-19-12/07/.
16. *Musical Courier*, advertisement, August 12, 1896, 12.
17. "Morris Reno," *Biographical Directory of the State of New York, 1900* (New York: Biographical Directory Company, 1899), 398, http://www.archive.org/details/biographicaldirec00biog.
18. *Ibid.*
19. "Morris Reno Dies at 83," *The New York Times*, June 12, 1917, 13, http://timesmachine.nytimes.com/timesmachine/1917/06/12/102352940.html?pageNumber=13.
20. "Mrs. S. Marie Reno Dead in Rome," *The New York Times*, November 14, 1915, 19, http://timesmachine.nytimes.com/timesmachine/1915/11/14/101571329.html?pageNumber=19.
21. "A New Concert Room," *The Sun* (New York), March 13, 1891, 3, Library of Congress, Chronicling America: Historic American Newspapers, http://chroniclingamerica.loc.gov/lccn/sn83030272/1891-03-13/ed-1/seq-3/.
22. "Notes of Music," *The New York Times*, March 4, 1894, 16, http://timesmachine.nytimes.com/timesmachine/1894/03/04/106898815.html?pageNumber=16.
23. "Amusements," *The New York Times*, March 4, 1896, 7, http://timesmachine.nytimes.com/timesmachine/1896/03/04/104112010.html?pageNumber=7.
24. "Nordica Thinks It Ridiculous," *The New York Times*, December 5, 1894, 8, http://timesmachine.nytimes.com/timesmachine/1894/12/05/106842508.html?pageNumber=8.
25. "The Bill Is Too Sweeping," *The New*

York Times, March 27, 1895, 8, http://times machine.nytimes.com/timesmachine/1895/ 03/27/102509402.html?pageNumber=8.

26. "Walter Damrosch Sued," *The New York Times*, September 3, 1896, 8, http://timesmac hine.nytimes.com/timesmachine/1896/09/03/ 106884597.html?pageNumber=8.

27. "Anna R. Margulies, Educator, Is Dead," *The New York Times*, July 8, 1929, 12, http:// timesmachine.nytimes.com/timesmachine/ 1929/07/08/94167817.html?pageNumber=12.

28. "William B. Tuthill, Architect, Is Dead," *The New York Times*, August 27, 1929, 21, http: //timesmachine.nytimes.com/timesmachine/ 1929/08/27/94174740.html?pageNumber=21.

29. "Virginia News," *Alexandria Gazette*, May 28, 1891, 2, Library of Congress, Chronicling America: Historic American Newspapers, http://chroniclingamerica.loc.gov/lccn sn85025007/1891–05–28/ed-1/seq-2/.

30. "Fame's Favored Ones," *Pittsburgh Dispatch*, May 15, 1891, 4, Library of Congress, Chronicling America: Historic American Newspapers, http://chroniclingamerica.loc.gov/lc cn/sn84024546/1891–05–15/ed-1/seq-4/.

31. "Mrs. Carnegie Dies," *The New York Times*, June 25, 1946, 22, http://timesmachine. nytimes.com/timesmachine/1946/06/25/ 107140095.html?pageNumber=22.

32. "Live Musical Topics," *The New York Times*, May 17, 1891, 13, http://timesmachine. nytimes.com/timesmachine/1891/05/17/ 103307706.html?pageNumber=13.

33. The Oratorio Society of New York, http: //www.oratoriosocietyofny.org/.

34. The New York Philharmonic, http://ny phil.org/.

35. "Damrosch in Germany," *The New York Times*, July 14, 1891, 4, http://timesmachine.ny times.com/timesmachine/1891/07/14/1033208 83.html?pageNumber=4.

36. Gretchen Finletter, *From the Top of the Stairs* (Boston: Little, Brown, 1946), 7.

37. *Ibid.*

Epilogue

1. "A Red Tower Replacing Carnegie Hall," *Life*, September 9, 1957, 91, https://books. google.com/books?id=UT8EAAAAMBAJ&q= carnegie+hall#v=snippet&q=carnegie%20hall &f=false.

2. Tim Page and Carnegie Hall, *Carnegie Hall Treasures* (New York: Collins Design/ HarperCollins, 2010).

3. Allan Kozinn, "Violinist Isaac Stern Dies at 81; Led Efforts to Save Carnegie Hall," *The New York Times*, September 23, 2001, http:// www.nytimes.com/2001/09/23/nyregion/vio linist-isaac-stern-dies-at-81-led-efforts-to- save-carnegie-hall.html .

4. William Grimes, "Vera Stern, Arts Advocate Who Helped Save Carnegie Hall, Dies at 88," *The New York Times*, July 22, 2015, http: //www.nytimes.com/2015/07/23/nyregion/ vera-stern-whose-efforts-helped-to-save- carnegie-hall-dies-at-88.html .

5. Page, *Carnegie Hall Treasures*, 27.

6. "Music's Promised Home," *The New York Times*, May 14, 1890, 8, http://timesmac hine.nytimes.com/timesmachine/1890/05/14/ 103242914.html?pageNumber=8.

Bibliography

Dissertations

Himmelein, Frederick Theodore, III. *Walter Damrosch: A Cultural Biography*. Ph.D. dissertation, University of Virginia, 1972.

Raines, Jean Lee. *Burnet C. Tuthill: His Life and Music*. Ph.D. dissertation, Michigan State University, Department of Music, 1979.

Books

Agocs, Katie. "Introduction" to *Leopold Damrosch: Symphony in a Major*. By Leopold Damrosch and edited by Katie Agocs. *Recent Researches in American Music*, Volume 54. Middleton, WI: A-R Editions, Inc., 2005, ix–xx. https://books.google.com/books?id=4fgJawIYjHwC&printsec=frontcover&source=gbs_ge_summary_r&cad=0#v=onepage&q&f=false.

American Orchestras in the Nineteenth Century. Edited by John Spitzer. Chicago: University of Chicago Press, 2012,

Appleton's Dictionary of Greater New York and Its Vicinity. New York: D. Appleton, 1892. www.catalog.hathitrust.org/Record/002129722.

Batterberry, Michael, and Ariane. *On the Town in New York: From 1776 to the Present*. New York: Charles Scribner's Sons, 1973.

Bomberger, E. Douglas. *A Tidal Wave of Encouragement: American Composers' Concerts in the Gilded Age*. Westport, CT: Praeger, 2002.

Brown, David. *Tchaikovsky: The Final Years (1885–1893)*, Volume IV. New York: W. W. Norton, 1991.

Brown, David. *Tchaikovsky: The Man and His Music*. New York: Pegasus Books, 2007.

Burrows, Edwin G., and Mike Wallace. *Gotham: A History of New York City to 1898*. New York: Oxford University Press, 1999.

Carnegie, Andrew. *The Autobiography of Andrew Carnegie and His Essay"The Gospel of Wealth."* Mineola, NY: Dover, 2014.

Chasins, Abram. *Speaking of Pianists*. New York: Knopf, 1957.

Cron, Theodore O., and Burt Goldblatt. *Portrait of Carnegie Hall*. New York: Macmillan, 1966.

Damrosch, Walter. *My Musical Life*. New York: Charles Scribner's Sons, 1930.

Davis, Ronald L. *A History of Music in American Life, Volume II—The Gilded Years, 1865–1920*. Huntington, New York: Robert Krieger Publishing Company, 1980.

The Diaries of Tchaikovsky. Translated from the Russian, with notes, by Wladimir Lakond. New York: W. W. Norton, 1945.

Edwards, F. G. *The History of Mendelssohn's "Elijah."* London: Novello and Company, Limited; New York: Novello, Ewer and Co., 1896. Project Gutenberg, released 12/5/2011, E Book #38223.

Ellis, Edward Robb. *The Epic of New York City: A Narrative History.* New York: Old Town Books, 1966.

The Encyclopedia of New York City. Edited by Kenneth T Jackson. New Haven: Yale University Press & New York: The New-York Historical Society, 1995.

Finck, Henry T. *My Adventures in the Golden Age of Music.* New York: Funk & Wagnalls, 1926.

Finletter, Gretchen. *From the Top of the Stairs.* Boston: Little, Brown, 1946.

Friedheim, Arthur. *Life & Liszt: The Recollections of a Concert Pianist.* Edited by Theodore L. Bullock. Mineola, NY: Dover, 2012, 1961.

Goldin, Milton. *The Music Merchants.* London: Collier-Macmillan, 1969.

Gray, Christopher. *New York Streetscapes: Tales of Manhattan's Significant Buildings and Landmarks.* New York: Harry N. Abrams, 2003.

Grout, Donald Jay. *A Short History of Opera.* Second Edition. New York: Columbia University Press, 1965.

Hanson, Lawrence, and Elisabeth. *Tchaikovsky: The Man Behind the Music.* New York: Dodd, Mead & Company, 1966.

Henderson, Mary C. *The City & the Theatre: New York Playhouses from Bowling Green to Times Square.* Clifton, NJ: James T. White & Company, 1973.

Hendrick, Burton J., and Daniel Henderson. *Louise Whitfield Carnegie: The Life of Mrs. Andrew Carnegie.* New York: Hastings House, 1950.

Holden, Anthony. *Tchaikovsky: A Biography.* New York: Random House, 1995.

Hughes, Rupert. *American Contemporary Composers.* Boston: L.C. Page and Company, 1900.

Kolodin, Irving. *The Story of the Metropolitan Opera 1883–1950: A Candid History.* New York: Alfred A. Knopf, 1953.

Howe, Charles Tuttle. *All About the Flute ... Containing a History of the Flute from Ancient Times.* Columbus: Charles T. Howe, 1898.

Huebner, Steven. *French Opera at the Fin De Siecle.* New York: Oxford University Press, 2006.

Irvine, Demar. *Massenet: A Chronicle of His Life and Times.* Portland, OR: Amadeus Press, 1994.

Krehbiel, H. E. *Choral Music in New York: Notes on the Cultivation of Choral Music and the Oratorio Society of New York.* H. E. Krehbiel, 1984.

Krehbiel, Henry Edward. *Chapters of Opera.* New York: Henry Holt & Co., 1911. http://www.gutenberg.org/cache/epub/5995/pg5995-images.html.

Kroessler, Jeffrey A. *New York Year by Year: A Chronology of the Great Metropolis.* New York: New York University Press, 2002.

Lawrence, Vera Brodsky. *Music for Patriots, Politicians, and Presidents: Harmonies and Discords of the First Hundred Years.* New York: Macmillan, 1975.

Lawrence, Vera Brodsky. *Strong on Music: The New York Music Scene in the Days of George Templeton Strong. Volume 3: Repercussions 1857–1862.* Chicago: University of Chicago Press, 1999.

Leno, LaWayne. *The Untold Story of Adele Aus Der Ohe: From a Liszt Student to a Virtuoso.* Edina, MN: Beaver's Pond Press, Inc., 2012.

Loesser, Arthur. *Men, Women and Pianos: A Social History.* Mineola, NY: Dover, 1990.

Mapleson Memoirs, The: The Career of an Operatic Impresario 1858–1888. Edited and annotated by Harold Rosenthal. New York: Appleton-Century, 1966.

Martin, George. *The Damrosch Dynasty: America's First Family of Music.* Boston: Houghton Mifflin, 1983.

McKinney, Howard D., and W. R. Anderson. *Music in History: The Evolution of an Art,* 3d ed. New York: American Book Company, 1966.

Music Festival Under the Direction of Walter Damrosch for the Inauguration of "Music Hall," Founded by Anderew Carnegie. May 5th, 6th, 7th, 8th, and 9th. New York: The Cherouny Printing & Publishing Company, 1891. Cornell University Library, Digital Collection. https://archive.org/details/cu31924018549836 .

Nasaw, David. *Andrew Carnegie.* New York: Penguin, 2006.

New York Biographical Directory 1902, American Memory. www.memory.loc.gov/master/gdc/scdser01/200401/miscellaneous/Miscellaneous_Biographical/NY%20Biograph ical%20Di.

Nickerson's Illustrated Church Musical and School Directory of New York and Brooklyn. New York: Nickerson & Young Publishers, 1895. http://hdl.handle.net/2027/njp.32 101021922842.

Nicholas, Jeremy. *Godowsky: The Pianist's Pianist.* Hexham: Appian Publications & Recordings, 1989.

Northrop, Henry Davenport. *Life and Public Services of Hon. James G. Blaine "The Plumed Knight."* Minneapolis: L. M. Ayer Publishing Company, 1893. http://hdl.handle.net/2027/uc1.a0008305906.

Ochsendorf, John. *Guastavino Vaulting: The Art of Structural Tile.* New York: Princeton Architectural Press, 2010.

Page, Tim, and Carnegie Hall. *Carnegie Hall Treasures.* New York: Collins Design/Harper-Collins, 2010.

Peyser, Ethel. *The House That Music Built: Carnegie Hall.* New York: Robert M. McBride & Company, 1936.

Rischin, Moses. *The Promised City: New York's Jews, 1870–1914.* Cambridge: Harvard University Press, 1962, 1977.

Schickel, Richard. *The World of Carnegie Hall.* New York: Julian Messner, Inc., 1960.

Schickel, Richard, and Michael Walsh. *Carnegie Hall: The First One Hundred Years.* New York: Harry N. Abrams, 1987.

Schonberg, Harold C. *The Great Pianists from Mozart to the Present.* New York: Simon & Schuster, 1963.

Sidelnikov, Leonid, and Galina Pribegina. *25 Days in America: For the Centenary of Peter Tchaikovsky's Concert Tour.* Moscow: "Muzyka," 1991.

Stebbins, Lucy Poate, and Richard Poate Stebbins. *Frank Damrosch: Let the People Sing.* Durham: Duke University Press, 1945.

Strimple, Nick. *Choral Music in the Nineteenth Century.* Milwaukee: Amadeus Press, 2008.

Swafford, Jan. *Beethoven: Anguish and Triumph.* Boston: Houghton Mifflin Harcourt, 2014.

Sylvester, Richard D. *Tchaikovsky's Complete Songs: A Companion with Text and Translations.* Bloomington: Indiana University Press, 2002.

Tennyson, Alfred, Lord. *The Foresters: Robin Hood and Maid Marian* (play). *The Robin Hood Project.* University of Rochester. http://d.lib.rochester.edu/robin-hood/text/tennyson-foresters.

Thompson, Emily. *The Soundscape of Modernity: Architectural Acoustics and the Culture of Listening in America, 1900–1933.* Cambridge: MIT Press, 2002.

Toff, Nancy. *The Flute Book: A Complete Guide for Students and Performers.* New York: Oxford University Press, 1996.

Trager, James. *The New York Chronology.* New York: Harper Resource, 2003.

Tuthill, William Burnet. *Practial Acoustics: A Study of the Diagrammatic Preparation of a Hall of Audience.* Completed in 1928 and published posthumously by Burnet C. Tuthill in 1946. Hathi Trust Digital Library. www.catalog.hathitrust.org/Record/000929291.

Wakeman, Abram. *History and Reminiscences of Lower Wall Street and Vicinity.* New York: The Spice Mill Publishing Co., 1914. http://catalog.hathitrust.org/Record/008587463.

William Steinway Diary: 1861–1896, The. Steinway & Sons Records and Family Papers. Smithsonian Institution. National Museum of American History, Archives Center. http://americanhistory.si.edu/steinwaydiary/annotations/?id=903&print=1.

Yoffe, Elkhonon, with translations from Russian by Lidya Yoffe. *Tchaikovsky in America: The Composer's Visit in 1891.* New York: Oxford University Press, 1986.

Articles

"A. Victor Benham with Orchestra." Performance History, Carnegie Hall. www.carnegie hall.org/PerformanceHistorySearch/#!

"About the Piece: The Marriage of Figaro." LA Phil. http://www.laphil.com/philpedia/music/marriage-of-figaro-wolfgang-amadeus-mozart.

Aldrich, Richard. "Peter Ilyitch Tchaikovsky: A Critical Note." In *Peter Ilyitch Tchaikovsky: Twelve Songs for Voice and Piano.* New York: G. Schirmer, Inc., 1902, iv.

"Alfred R. Wolff 1855–1909." ASHRAE Pioneers of Industry Award, American Society of Heating, Refrigerating and Air-Conditioning Engineers (ASHRAE). https://www.ashraeorg/membership—conferences/honors—awards/ashrae-pioneers-of-industry.

Allen, Jane. "Potter, Henry Codman." In *The Encyclopedia of New York City*, edited by Kenneth T. Jackson. New Haven: Yale University Press; New York: The New-York Historical Society, 1995, 931.

"Amusements." *The New York Times*, April 30, 1858, 5. http://timesmachine.nytimes.com/timesmachine/1858/04/30/78943019.html?pageNumber=5.

"Amusements." *The New York Times*, February 12, 1866, 5. http://timesmachine.nytimes.com/timesmachine/1866/02/12/83449873.html?pageNumber=5.

"Amusements." *The New York Times*, April 22, 1887, 7. http://timesmachine.nytimes.com/timesmachine/1887/04/22/issue.html.

"Amusements." *The Evening World*, March 27, 1889, 3. Library of Congress. Chronicling America: Historic American Newspapers. http://chroniclingamerica.loc.gov/lccn/sn83030193/1889–03-27/ed-1/seq-3/.

"Amusements." *New-York Tribune*, November 20, 1890, 9. Library of Congress. Chronicling America: Historic American Newspapers. http://chroniclingamerica.loc.gov/lccn/sn83030214/1890–11-20/ed-1/seq-9/.

"Amusements." *The Sun* (New York, N.Y.), March 29, 1891, 9. Library of Congress. Chronicling America: Historic American Newspapers. http://chroniclingamerica.loc.gov/lccn/sn83030272/1891–03-29/ed-1/seq-9/.

"Amusements." *The Sun* (New York, N.Y.), March 31, 1891, 10. Library of Congress. Chronicling America: Historic American Newspapers. http://chroniclingamerica.loc.gov/lccn/sn83030272/1891–03-31/ed-1/seq-10.

"Amusements." *The Sun* (New York, N.Y.), April 1, 1891, 10. Library of Congress. Chronicling America: Historic American Newspapers. http://chroniclingamerica.loc.gov/lccn/sn83030272/1891–04-01/ed-1/seq-10/.

"Amusements." *The New-York Tribune*, May 3, 1891, 11. Library of Congress. Chronicling America: Historic American Newspapers. http://chroniclingamerica.loc.gov/lccn/83030214/1891–05-03/ed-1/seq-11/.

"Amusements." *New-York Daily Tribune*, May 4, 1891, 11. Library of Congress. Chronicling America: Historic American Newspapers. http://chroniclingamerica.loc.gov/lccn/sn 83030214/1891–05–04/ed-1/seq-11.

"Amusements." *The New York Times*, May 5, 1891, 7. http://timesmachine.nytimes.com/timesmachine/1891/05/05/issue.html.

"Amusements." *The Sun*, May 7, 1891, 10. Library of Congress. Chronicling America: Historic American Newspapers. http://chroniclingamerica.loc.gov/lccn/sn83030272/1891–05-07/ed-1/seq-10/.

"Amusements." *The New York Times*, March 4, 1896, 7. http://timesmachine.nytimes.com/timesmachine/1896/03/04/104112010.html?pageNumber=7.

"Amusements: Academy of Music." *The New York Times*, November 25, 1858, 4. http://timesmachine.nytimes.com/timesmachine/1858/11/25/78880196.html?pageNumber=4.

"Amusements: Benefit Concert." *The New York Times*, May 8, 1884, 4. http://timesmachine.nytimes.com/timesmachine/1884/05/08/106278328.html?pageNumber=4.

"Amusements: General Mention." *The New York Times*, June 19, 1881, 7. http://timesmachine.nytimes.com/timesmachine/1881/06/19/98561851.html?pageNumber=7.

"Amusements: Mr. Benham's Concert." *The New York Times*, April 22, 1891, 4. http://timesmachine.nytimes.com/timesmachine/1891/04/22/issue.html.

"Amusements: "Mr. Friedheim's Recital." *The New York Times*, April 8, 1891, 4. http://timesmachine.nytimes.com/timesmachine/1891/04/08/issue.html.

"Amusements: Mr. Friedheim's Recitals." *The New York Times*, April 15, 1891, 4. http://timesmachine.nytimes.com/timesmachine/1891/04/15/103302439.html?pageNumber=4.

"Amusements: Mr. Rummel's Recital." *The New York Times*, April 2, 1891, 4. http://timesmachine.nytimes.com/timesmachine/1891/04/02/103300806.html?pageNumber=4.

"Amusements: Musical. Festival Week Performances." *The New York Times*, April 23, 1873, 7. http://timesmachine.nytimes.com/timesmachine/1873/04/23/90124931.html?pageNumber=7.

"Amusements: Musical. Mr. Thomas' Symphony Concerts." *The New York Times*, January 9, 1872, 5. http://timesmachine.nytimes.com/timesmachine/1872/01/09/79011155.html?pageNumber=5.

"Amusements: Musical Notes." *The New York Times*, December 21, 1890, 13. http://timesmachine.nytimes.com/timesmachine/1890/12/21/103287542.html?pageNumber=13.

"Amusements: Musical Notes." *The New York Times*, January 4, 1891, 13. http://timesmachine.nytimes.com/timesmachine/1891/01/04/103289441.html?pageNumber=13.

"Amusements: Musical Notes." *The New York Times*, February 22, 1891, 13. http://timesmachine.nytimes.com/timesmachine/1891/02/22/106047138.html?pageNumber=13.

"Amusements: Notes of the Stage." *The New York Times*, September 7, 1890, 13. http://timesmachine.nytimes.com/timesmachine/1890/09/07/106042481.html?pageNumber=13.

"Amusements: Notes of the Week." *The New York Times*. June 8, 1890, 13. http://timesmachine.nytimes.com/timesmachine/1890/06/08/103247171.html?pageNumber=13.

"Amusements. Operatic: 'The Marriage of Figaro' at the Academy." *The New York Times*, March 15, 1870, 5. http://timesmachine.nytimes.com/timesmachine/1870/03/15/80219782.html?pageNumber=5.

"Amusements: Oratorio Society of New-York." *The New-York Tribune*, November 4, 1883, 15. Library of Congress. Chronicling America: Historic American Newspapers. http://chroniclingamerica.loc.gov/lccn/sn83030214/1883–11-04/ed-1/seq-15/.

"Amusements: Philharmonic Society." *The New York Times*, March 12, 1866, 4. http://timesmachine.nytimes.com/timesmachine/1866/03/12/83451693.html?pageNumber=4.

"Amusements: Sarasate and D'albert." *The New York Times*, May 14, 1890, 4. http://timesmachine.nytimes.com/timesmachine/1890/05/14/103242881.html?pageNumber=4.

"Amusements: Steinway Hall." *The New York Times*, June 8, 1867, 5. http://timesmachine.nytimes.com/timesmachine/1867/06/08/87581432.html?pageNumber=5.

"Amusements: Symphony Society of New-York." *The New-York Tribune*, November 4, 1883, 15. Library of Congress. Chronicling America: Historic American Newspapers. http://chroniclingamerica.loc.gov/lccn/sn83030214/1883–11/04/ed-1/seq-15/.

"Amusements: The Damrosch Festival." *The Sun* (New York, N.Y.), May 7, 1891, 2. Library of Congress. Chronicling America: Historic American Newspapers. http://chroniclingamerica.loc.gov/lccn/sn83030272/1891–05-07/ed-1/seq-2/.

"Amusements: The Manuscript Society." *The New York Times*, December 11, 1890, 4. http://timesmachine.nytimes.com/timesmachine/1890/12/11/103285681.html?pageNumber=4.

"Amusements: The Music Hall Concerts." *The New York Times*, May 7, 1891, 4. http://timesmachine.nytimes.com/timesmachine/1891/05/07/103305805.html?pageNumber=4

"Amusements: The Music Hall Concerts." *The New York Times*, May 8, 1891, 4. http://timesmachine.nytimes.com/timesmachine/1891/05/08/103306020.html?pageNumber=4.

"Amusements: The Music Hall Concerts." *The New York Times*, May 9, 1891, 4. http://

timesmachine.nytimes.com/timesmachine/1891/05/09/103306224.html?pageNumber=4.

"Amusements: The Oratorio Society." *The Sun* (New York, N.Y.), March 5, 1886, 2. Library of Congress. Chronicling America: Historic American Newspapers. http://chroniclingamerica.loc.gov/lccn/sn83030272/1886–03-05/ed-1/seq-2/.

"Amusements This Evening." *The New York Times*, May 13, 1890, 4. http://timesmachine. nytimes.com/timesmachine/1890/05/13/issue.html.

"Amusements This Evening." *The New York Times*, May 5, 1891, 4. http://timesmachine. nytimes.com/timesmachine/1891/05/05/103305469.html?pageNumber=4.

Ancestry.com. New York, New York, Marriage index 1866–1937. Provo, UT, USA: Ancestry.com Operations, Inc., 2014. Leo Margulies to Anna Reno. Manhattan, New York, USA. Marriage Date: 27 Oct 1886. Certificate Number: 62361.

"Anna R. Margulies, Educator, Is Dead." *The New York Times*, July 8, 1929, 12. http://times machine.nytimes.com/timesmachine/1929/07/08/94167817.html?pageNumber=12.

"Annual Exhibition—Architectural League of New York 1898," p. lxxxiii, http://archleague. org/.

"Another Comic Opera." *The New York Times*, May 8, 1891, 4. http://timesmachine.ny times.com/timesmachine/1891/05/08/103306020.html?pageNumber=4.

"Antonia Mielke" (Cincinnati concert program). In *Andreas Dippel Concert Programs 1890–1892*. New York Public Library for the Performing Arts. Music Division, Special Collections.

"Antonia Mielke" (Pittsburgh concert program). In *Andreas Dippel Concert Programs 1890–1892*. New York Public Library for the Performing Arts, Music Division, Special Collections.

"Antonia Mielke Dead." *The New York Times*, November 21, 1907, 9. http://timesmachine. nytimes.com/timesmachine/1907/11/21/104712214.html?pageNumber=9

"Armor Tests at Annapolis." *The New York Times*, May 9, 1891, 1. http://timesmachine. nytimes.com/timesmachine/1891/05/09/103306107.html?pageNumber=1.

Aronson, Marc H. "Booksellers." In *Encyclopedia of New York City*, edited by Kenneth T. Jackson. New Haven: Yale University Press & New York: The New-York Historical Society, 1995, 127–128.

"Ascension Day Services." *The New York Times*, May 5, 1891, 9. http://timesmachine.ny times.com/timesmachine/1891/05/05/103305524.html?pageNumber=9.

"Bartholdi Well Pleased." *The New York Times*, October 26, 1886, 1. http://timesmachine. nytimes.com/timesmachine/1886/10/26/106304259.html?pageNumber=1.

"Benefit Concert." *The New York Times*, May 8, 1884, 4. http://timesmachine.nytimes. com/timesmachine/1884/05/08/106278328.html?pageNumber=4.

"Bill Is Too Sweeping, The." The *New York Times*, March 27, 1895, 8. http://timesmachine. nytimes.com/timesmachine/1895/03/27/102509402.html?pageNumber=8.

"Bill Nye Well Received." *Daily Alta California*, March 14, 1890, p. 4. California Digital Newspaper Collection. www.cdnc.vcr.edu/cgi-bin/cdnc?a=d&d=DAC18900314.2. 50#.

"Blaine Is Stricken." *The Evening World* (New York, N.Y.), May 11, 1891, 1. Library of Congress. Chronicling America: Historic American Newspapers. http://chronicling america.loc.gov/lccn/sn83030193/1891–05-11/ed-1/seq-1/.

Block, Adrienne Fried. "Thinking About Serious Music in New York." In *American Orchestras in the Nineteenth Century*, edited by John Spitzer. Chicago: University of Chicago Press, 2012, 435–450.

Blumberg, Barbara. "Statue of Liberty." In *The Encyclopedia of New York City*, edited by Kenneth T. Jackson. New Haven: Yale University Press; New York: The New-York Historical Society, 1995, 1119.

"By Way of Diversion." *The New York Times*, December 7, 1890, 4. http://timesmachine. nytimes.com/timesmachine/1890/12/07/103284911.html?pageNumber=4.

"Carl Christian Schurz." *The William Steinway Diary, 1861–1896*. Smithsonian Institution, National Museum of American History. http://americanhistory.si.edu/stein waydiary/annotations/?id=802.

"Carnegie Hall: Frank Roosevelt, Opus #486–1891." American Guild of Organists. http://www.nycago.org/Organs/NYC/html/CarnegieHall.html#Roosevelt.

"Carnegie Music Hall." *Pittsburgh Dispatch*, May 6, 1891, 1. Library of Congress. Chronicling America: Historic American Newspapers. http://chroniclingamerica.loc.gov/lccn/sn84024546/1891–05-06/ed-1/seq-1/.

"Carnegie Music Hall: The Work of Construction Is Expected to Begin Soon." *The New York Times*, July 19, 1889, 8. http://timesmachine.nytimes.com/timesmachine/1889/07/19/106356928.html?pageNumber=8.

"Celebrated in This City." *The New York Times*, April 7, 1891, 5. http://timesmachine.nytimes.com/timesmachine/1891/04/07/103301596.html?pageNumber=5.

Chandler, John H., "Robin Hood: Development of a Popular Hero," *The Robin Hood Project*, University of Rochester, http://d.lib.rochester.edu/robin-hood/text/chandler-robin-hood-development-of-a-popular-hero.

"Changes in Dr. Paxton's Choir." *The New York Times*, February 12, 1893, 10. http://timesmachine.nytimes.com/timesmachine/1893/02/12/106813929.html?pageNumber=10.

"Changes in Plays." *New York Tribune*, November 9, 1890, 24. Library of Congress. Chronicling America: Historic American Newspapers. http://chroniclingamerica.loc.gov/lccn/sn83030214/1890–11-09/ed-1/seq-24/

"Charles Henry Davis—Chronology of the Life of Charles Henry Davis." U.S. Dept of Transportation-Federal Highway Administration. www.fhwa.dot.gov/infastructure/davis2.cfm.

"Charles F. Tretbar." The *William Steinway Diary:1861–1896*. Smithsonian Institution. National Museum of American History. http://americanhistory.si.edu/steinway diary/search/?keyword=charles+tretbar&type=annotation&sdate=&edate=

"Chickering Hall." *The New York Times*, January 24, 1886, 6. http://timesmachine.nytimes.com/timesmachine/1886/01/24/106179509.html?pageNumber=6.

Chou, Kimberly. "Opening Night, Before It Was Carnegie Hall." *The Wall Street Journal*, September 30, 2011. www.wsj.com/articles/SB10001424052970204226204576601010452872084.

Chute, James. "Van Der Stucken, Frank (Valentine)." In *The New Grove Dictionary of American Music*, Volume Four, edited by H. Wiley Hitchcock & Stanley Sadie. New York: Grove's Dictionaries of Music, Inc., 1986, 444–445.

"City and Suburban News," *The New York Times*, October 5, 1884, 7. http://timesmachine.nytimes.com/timesmachine/1884/10/05/106160367.html?pageNumber=7.

"Concerts, The." *The New York Times*, October 5, 1852, 1. http://timesmachine.nytimes.com/timesmachine/1852/10/05/75118137.html?pageNumber=1.

"Chronology of the Life of Charles Henry Davis." U.S. Department of Transportation—Federal Highway Administration. www.fhwa.dot.gov/infrastructure/davis2.cfm.

"Cleaner, The," *The Evening World* (New York, N.Y.), May 6, 1891, 2. Library of Congress. Chronicling America: Historic American Newspapers. http://chroniclingamerica.loc.gov/lccn/sn83030193/1891–05-06/ed-1/seq-2/.

"Crouse, Russel. "That Was New York: Opera Through Glasses—II." *The New Yorker*, November 24, 1928, 38–46.

Damrosch, Walter. "Recollections of Andrew Carnegie." In *Andrew Carnegie Centenary*. New York: Carnegie Corporation of New York, 1935, 25–29.

"Damrosch Festival, The." *The Sun* (New York, N.Y.), May 7, 1891, 2. Library of Congress. Chronicling America: Historic American Newspapers. http://chroniclingamerica.loc.gov/lccn/sn83030272/1891–05-07/ed-1/seq-2.

"The Damrosch Festival." *The Sun* (New York, N.Y.), May 8, 1891, 7. Library of Congress. Chronicling America: Historic American Newspapers. http://chroniclingamerica.loc.gov/lccn/sn83030272/1891–05-08/ed-1/seq-7/.

"Damrosch in Germany." *The New York Times*, July 14, 1891, 4. http://timesmachine.nytimes.com/timesmachine/1891/07/14/103320883.html?pageNumber=4.

"Death List of a Day: Franz Rummel." *The New York Times*, May 5, 1901, 9. http://timesmachine.nytimes.com/timesmachine/1901/05/05/101072570.html?pageNumber=9.

"Death of G. F. W. Holls." *The New York Times*, July 24, 1903, 3. http://timesmachine.
nytimes.com/timesmachine/1903/07/24/105055810.html?pageNumber=3.

"Death of General Sherman." *Donahoe's Monthly Magazine*, Volume 25, April 1891, 375.
http://babel.hathitrust.org/cgi/pt?id=umn.31951000728703e;view=1up;seq=391.

Death of Henry Romeike." *The New York Times*, June 4, 1903, 9. http://timesmachine.
nytimes.com/timesmachine/1903/06/04/102005146.html?pageNumber=9.

"Death of Richard M. Hunt." *The New York Times*, August 1, 1895, 5. http://timesmachine.
nytimes.com/timesmachine/1895/08/01/106066243.html?pageNumber=5.

"Decoration Day Celebration." *The New York Times*, May 9, 1885, 3. http://timesmachine.
nytimes.com/timesmachine/1885/05/09/121573074.html?pageNumber=3.

De Loustal, Jacques. "Nights at the Opera," *The New Yorker*, January 8, 2007.

"Diploma Day at Bellevue." *The New York Times*, March 31, 1891, 3. http://timesmachine.
nytimes.com/timesmachine/1891/03/31/106048797.html?pageNumber=3.

Dibble, Jeremy. "Edward George Dannreuther (1844–1905), Pianist and Writer." In *Oxford
Dictionary of National Biography*. Oxford University Press, 2004. www.oxforddnb.
com/view/article/40938/accessed.

"Dippel, Tenor, Dies in Want on Coast." *The New York Times*, May 14, 1932, 15. http://
timesmachine.nytimes.com/timesmachine/1932/05/14/100738696.html?pageNum
ber=15.

Downes, Olin. "Evangel of Music." *The New York Times*, December 31, 1950, 117. http://
timesmachine.nytimes.com/timesmachine/1950/12/31/118433686.html?pageNum
ber=117.

"Dr. E. G. Janeway, Diagnostician, Dead." *The New York Times*, February 11, 1911, 11.
http://timesmachine.nytimes.com/timesmachine/1911/02/11/104779187.html?
pageNumber=11.

"Dr. Gerrit Smith." *The New York Times*, July 22, 1912, 7. http://timesmachine.nytimes.
com/timesmachine/1912/07/22/104901838.html?pageNumber=7.

"E. Francis Hyde." *New York State's Prominent and Progressive Men: An Encyclopaedia of
Contemporaneous Biography, Volume 3*, Compiled by Mitchell C. Harrison. New
York: New York Tribune, 1902, 171–172. https://archive.org/stream/newyorkstate
spro02harr/newyorkstatespro02harr_djvu.txt.

"Eden Musee Faces Bankruptcy Court." *The New York Times*, June 8, 1915, 17. http://
timesmachine.nytimes.com/timesmachine/1915/06/08/99437228.html?pageNum
ber=17.

"Editorial Article 5—No Title." *The New York Times*, May 7, 1891, 4. http://timesmachine.
nytimes.com/timesmachine/1891/05/07/103305796.html?pageNumber=4.

Ehrlich, Cyril. "Steinway." In *The New Grove Dictionary of American Music*, Volume Four,
edited by H. Wiley Hitchcock and Stanley Sadie. New York: Grove's Dictionaries of
Music, Inc., 1986, 303–4.

"1886: League Holds Its First Annual Exhibition." *The Architectural League of New York*.
http://archleague.org/2010/12league-holds-its-first-annual-exhibition/.

Eldridge, Sarah. *Burnet Corwin Tuthill: The Unique Life of an Educator*. Memphis, Ten-
nessee: Rhodes College, Institute for Regional Studies, 2. http://hdl.handle.net/
10267/2417.

"Emil Fischer" (Pittsburgh concert program). In *Andreas Dippel Concert Programs 1890–
1892*. New York Public Library for the Performing Arts, Music Division, Special
Collections.

Engineering News-Record, Volume 40, December 29, 1898, p. xxv, https://books.google.
com/books?id=WN82AQAAMAAJ&pg=PR25&lpg=PR25&dq=john+j.+hopper,+
building+contractor&source=bl&ots=6rrf1RzoO9&sig=a-ll_bSI7xrS6Z9CG-
pKGMPbVzk&hl=en&sa=X&ei=sYd4VMORMI6RsQTnmYE4&ved=0CCQQ
6AEwAQ#v=onepage&q=john%20j.%20hopper%2C%20building%20contractor&f=
false.

"Fame's Favored Ones," *Pittsburgh Dispatch*, May 15, 1891, 4. Library of Congress. Chronicling America: Historic American Newspapers. http://chroniclingamerica.loc.gov/
lccn/sn84024546/1891–05-15/ed-1/seq-4/.

"Ferenc Erkel: Hungarian Composer." In *Encyclopaedia Britannica*. http://www.britan nica.com/EBchecked/topic/1459262/Ferenc-Erkel.

Ferris, Marc. "Steinway Hall." In *The Encyclopedia of New York City*, edited by Kenneth T. Jackson. New Haven: Yale University Press & New York: The New-York Historical Society, 1995, 1121.

"Fierce Fire in Gotham." *The Chicago Daily Tribune*, January 3, 1891, 1. www.archives. chicagotribune.com/1891/01/03/page/1/article/fierce-fire-in-gotham.

"Fire in the Carnegie Music Hall, The." *The Sun* (New York, N.Y.), May 10, 1891, 21. Library of Congress. Chronicling America: Historic American Newspapers. http://chronicl ingamerica.loc.gov/lccn/sn83030272/1891–05-10/ed-1/seq-21.

Fleming, Michael. "Suite No. 3," *Tchaikovsky: Complete Suites*. Recording, Detroit Symphony Orchestra, Neeme Jarvi, conductor. Chandos Records Ltd, recorded March 10–12, 1995. Liner notes.

"Floersheim, Otto." In *Appleton's Cyclopaedia of American Biography*, Volume 7, edited by James Grant Wilson & John Fiske. New York: D. Appleton & Company, 1901, 105. https://books.google.com/books?id=f6oLAAAAIAAJ&q=otto+floersheim#v= snippet&q=otto%20floersheim&f=false.

"Four New French Steamers." *The New York Times*, March 25, 1885, 8. http://timesmac hine.nytimes.com/timesmachine/1885/03/25/102963618.html?pageNumber=8.

"France's Gift Accepted: Liberty's Statue Unveiled on Bedlow's Island." *The New York Times*, October 29, 1886, 1. http://timesmachine.nytimes.com/timesmachine/1886/ 10/29/103989753.html?pageNumber=1.

"Frank A. Howson, Composer, Dead." *The New York Times*, June 30, 1926, 25. http:// timesmachine.nytimes.com/timesmachine/1926/06/30/98384963.html?pageNum ber=25.

"Frank L. Sealy, 80, a Leading Organist." *The New York Times*, December 14, 1938, 25. http://timesmachine.nytimes.com/timesmachine/1938/12/14/98873427.html?page Number=25.

"Frank Roosevelt Organ, The, Opus #433." Church of the Angels. www.coa-pasadena. org/organ-music.

"Franz Rummel." Performance History, Carnegie Hall. www.carnegiehall.org/Performance HistorySearch/#!

"Franz Rummel's Bride: The Pianist Married to Miss Leila Morse at Poughkeepsie." *The New York Times*, April 5, 1881, 1. http://timesmachine.nytimes.com/timesmachine/ 1881/04/05/98552452.html?pageNumber=1.

"French Guests Welcomed." *The New York Times*, October 27, 1886, 3. http://timesmach ine.nytimes.com/timesmachine/1886/10/27/106304559.html?pageNumber=5.

"Frits Hartvigson." *Tchaikovsky Research*. http://en.tchaikovskyresearch.net/pages/Frits_ Hartvigson.

"General Mention." *The New York Times*, May 22, 1885, 4. http://timesmachine.nytimes. com/timesmachine/1885/05/22/103017008.html?pageNumber=4.

"Gen. Sherman Sorely Ill." *The New York Times*, February 12, 1891, 1. http://timesmachine. nytimes.com/timesmachine/1891/02/12/106046782.html?pageNumber=1.

Genevro, Rosalie. "Architectural League of New York." In *Encyclopedia of New York City*, edited by Kenneth T. Jackson. New Haven: Yale University Press & New York: The New-York Historical Society, 1995, 44.

"Georges Bizet 1838–1875." In *Composers on Music: Eight Centuries of Writings*, edited by Josiah Fisk. Boston: Northwestern University Press, 1997, 146.

"German Opera Once Again." *The New York Times*, February 14, 1894, 4. http://times machine.nytimes.com/timesmachine/1894/02/14/106898189.html?pageNumber=4.

Gilded New York. Ongoing exhibition. Museum of the City of New York, www.mcny.org/ content/gilded-new-york.

"Gilmore at Coney Island." *The New York Times*, June 29, 1889, 2. http://timesmachine. nytimes.com/timesmachine/1889/06/29/106354245.html?pageNumber=2.

Glass, Herbert. "About the Piece: Suite No. 3, Peter Ilyich Tchaikovsky." LA Phil. http:// www.laphil.com/philpedia/music/suite-no-3-peter-ilyich-tchaikovsky.

Goldberger, Paul. "Architecture: Two Richard Morris Hunt Shows." *The New York Times*, May 22, 1986. http://www.nytimes.com/1986/05/22/arts/architecture-two-richard-morris-hunt-shows.html.

"Graduation: University of the City of New York Women's Law Class. Performance History, Carnegie Hall. Www.Carnegiehall.Org/Performancehistorysearch/#!

"Grand Army Celebration." *The New York Times*, April 1, 1891, 3. http://timesmachine.nytimes.com/timesmachine/1891/04/01/103300640.html?pageNumber=3.

"The Grand Army of the Republic and Kindred Societies," Introduction, Library of Congress, General Collections, http://www.loc.gov/rr/main/gar/.

Gray, Christopher. "Streetscapes/57th Street Between Avenue of the Americas and Seventh; High and Low Notes of a Block with a Musical Bent." *The New York Times*, May 9, 1999. http://www.nytimes.com/1999/05/09/realestate/streetscapes-57th-street-between-avenue-americas-seventh-avenue-high-low-notes.html.

"Great Celebration, The." *The New York Times*, October 27, 1886, 1–2. http://timesmachine.nytimes.com/timesmachine/1886/10/27/106304465.html?pageNumber=1.

Greeley, Nina Anne. "George Frideric Handel/Israel in Egypt." Program notes, San Francisco Choral Society. www.sfchoral.org/site/george-frideric-handel-israel-in-egypt/.

Grimes, William. "Vera Stern, Arts Advocate Who Helped Save Carnegie Hall, Dies at 88." *The New York Times*, July 22, 2015. http://www.nytimes.com/2015/07/23/nyregion/vera-stern-whose-efforts-helped-to-save-carnegie-hall-dies-at-88.html.

"Gustav Dannreuther Dies of Pneumonia." *Vassar Miscellany News, Volume VIII, Number 21*, January 12, 1924, 2. http://newspaperarchives.vassar.edu/cgi-bin/vassar?a=d&d=miscellany19240112-01.2.14.

Harper's New Monthly Magazine, May 1891.

Harris, Gale & Jay Shockley, *East 17th Street/Irving Place Historic Designation Report*. NYC Landmarks Preservation Commission, 1998, http://www.nyc.gov/html/lpc/downloads/pdf/reports/EAST_17TH_STREET_-_IRVING_PLACE_-_HISTORIC_DISTRICT.pdf

Heating and Ventilating Magazine, The, Volume 11, January 1914, Volume XL, No. 1, p. 78. https://books.google.com/books?id=acU7AQAAMAAJ&pg=RA8-PA78&lpg=RA8-PA78&dq=%22Johnson+%26+Morris%22+new+york&source=bl&ots=M3tQH9yImP&sig=KgjBrys6IPPR7y_NFsHd2-yEDYE&hl=en&sa=X&ei=OX94VI73Hrj-sASV-4CABQ&ved=0CDAQ6AEwBA#v=onepage&q=%22Johnson%20%26%20Morris%22%20new%20york&f=false.

Heinrich August Marschner." *Encyclopaedia Britannica Online*. http://www.britannica.com/EBchecked/topic/366447/Heinrich-August-Marschner.

"Helen Hopekirk." Scottish Music Centre. http://www.scottishmusiccentre.com/members/helen_hopekirk/home/full_biography/.

"Helen Hopekirk Collection." *Performing Arts Encyclopedia*. Library of Congress, Music Division. http://lcweb2.loc.gov/diglib/ihas/loc.natlib.scdb.200033628/default.html.

Henahan, Donal. "Music View; the Sound of Carnegie Hall." *The New York Times*, May 3, 1981. http://www.nytimes.com/1981/05/03/arts/music-view-the-sound-of-carnegie-hall.html .

"Henry Wolfsohn Dies of Pneumonia." *The New York Times*, June 2, 1909, 7. http://timesmachine.nytimes.com/timesmachine/1909/06/02/101883503.html?pageNumber=7.

"Her Maiden Voyage." *The New York Times*, August 23, 1886, 8. http://timesmachine.nytimes.com/timesmachine/1886/08/23/103973937.html?pageNumber=8.

"Her Point of View." *The New York Times*, May 10, 1891, 12. http://timesmachine.nytimes.com/timesmachine/1891/05/10/103306454.html?pageNumber=12.

"Hermann Wolff," *Tchaikovsky Research*. http://en.tchaikovskyresearch.net/pages/Hermann_Wolff.

"Herr Friedheim's Debut." *New-York Tribune*, April 1, 1891, 6. Library of Congress. Chronicling America: Historic American Newspapers. http://chroniclingamerica.loc.gov/lccn/sn83030214/1891-04-01/ed-1/seq-6/.

"History." *The Architectural League of NY*. http://archleague.org/about/history/.

"History." *Wm Knabe & Co.* http://www.knabepianos.com/history.php.

"History of the Hall." *Carnegie Hall.* http://www.carnegiehall.org/History/.

"History of the Society, The." *Oratorio Society of New York.* http://www.oratoriosociety ofny.org/about-history.html.

"Home News," *The Musical Courier*, Vol. 23, July 1, 1891, 8.

"Home Notes," *Chicago Tribune*, November 30, 1884, 24. www.archives.chicagotribune. com/1 884/11/30/24/article/home-notes.

Hoover, Cynthia Adams. "Chickering." In *The New Grove Dictionary of American Music,* Volume One, edited by H. Wiley Hitchcock and Stanley Sadie. New York: Grove's Dictionaries of Music, Inc., 1986, 426–427.

Hoover, Cynthia Adams. "Steinway, William." In *The New Grove Dictionary of American Music,* Volume Four, edited by H. Wiley Hitchcock and Stanley Sadie. New York: Grove's Dictionaries of Music, Inc., 1986, 304–5.

Huscher, Phillip. "Leonore Overture No. 3," Chicago Symphony Orchestra. Program notes. https://cso.org/uploadedFiles/1_Tickets_and_Events/Program_Notes/061510_Pro gramNotes_Beethoven_LeonoOverture3.pdf.

Huscher, Phillip. Rockford Symphony Orchestra, Program Notes, "Richard Wagner— Prelude and 'Liebestod' from Tristan and Isolde," http://www.rockfordsymphony. com/wagner-prelude-and-liebestod-notes/.

"In Favor of One Pitch." *The New York Times*, April 1, 1891, 5. http://timesmachine. nytimes.com/timesmachine/1891/04/01/103300684.html?pageNumber=5.

"In Focus: *Die Meistersinger.*" The Metropolitan Opera. http://www.metopera.org/Search/ ?q=in%20focus%20—%20emil%20fischer.

"In Focus: Richard Wagner, *Parsifal.*" http://www.metopera.org/PageFiles/41061/Mar% 202%20Parsifal.pdf.

"In Focus: *Seigfried.*" The Metropolitan Opera. http://www.metopera.org/metopera/news/ festivals/infocus-siegfried.aspx?src=prodpg.

"In Memory of Sherman." *The Sun* (New York, N.Y.), May 8, 1891, 3. Library of Congress. Chronicling America: Historic American Newspapers. http://chroniclingamerica. loc.gov/lccn/sn83030272/1891–05-08/ed-1/seq-3/.

"Individual Mention." *The Critic and Record* (Washington, D.C.), May 8, 1891, 4. Library of Congress. Chronicling America: Historic American Newspapers. http://chroni clingamerica.loc.gov/lccn/sn87062228/1891–05-08/ed-1/seq-4/.

"Ingersoll Biography." *Council for Secular Humanism.* www.secularhumanism.org/index. php/1172.

"Isaac A. Hopper's Record." *The New York Times*, January 1, 1893, 9. http://timesmachine. nytimes.com/timesmachine/1893/01/01/106858697.html?pageNumber=9.

"It Stood the Test Well." *The New York Times*, May 6, 1891, 5. http://timesmachine. nytimes.com/timesmachine/1891/05/06/103305634.html?pageNumber=5.

"It Was Cold Yesterday." *The New York Times*, May 7, 1891, 1. http://timesmachine. nytimes.com/timesmachine/1891/05/07/103305762.html?pageNumber=2.

"Ivy Maud Ross, Newswriter, Dies." *The New York Times*, March 5, 1933, 62. http:// timesmachine.nytimes.com/timesmachine/1933/03/05/99297023.html?pageNum ber=62.

"Jadassohn, Salomon." In *Baker's Biographical Dictionary of Musicians, Seventh Edition,* revised by Nicolas Slonimsky. New York: Schirmer Books, 1984, 1100–1101.

"John W. Aitken Dead." *The New York Times*, September 4, 1915, 7. http://timesmachine. nytimes.com/timesmachine/1915/09/04/100175625.html?pageNumber=7.

"John Drew to Become a Star." *The New York Times*, May 5, 1891, 2. http://timesmachine. nytimes.com/timesmachine/1891/05/05/103305408.html?pageNumber=2.

Johnson & Morris. Series II. Construction Notes and Correspondence, Box 8, Folder 5, 1913–1914). www.frick.org/sites/default/files/FindingAids/OneEast70thStreetPap ers.html/.

Keller, James M. "Berlioz: Te Deum, Opus 22." San Francisco Symphony. Program notes. www.sfsymphony.org/Watch-Listen-Learn/Read-Program-Notes/Program-Notes/ BERLIOZ-Te-Deum,-Opus-22.aspx.

Keller, James M. "Elijah, Oratorio on Words of the Old Testament, Op. 70, Felix Mendelssohn." Program notes. The New York Philharmonic. http://nyphil.org/~media/pdfs/watch-listen/commercial-recordings/1011/release5.pdf.

Kolodin, Irving, Francis D. Perkins/Susan Thiemann Sommer. "Choral Societies." In *The New Grove Dictionary of American Music*, Volume Three, edited by H. Wiley Hitchcock & Stanley Sadie. New York: Grove's Dictionaries of Music, Inc., 1986, 359–360.

Kolodin, Irving, Francis D. Perkins, and Susan Thiemann Sommer. "Orchestras and Bands." In *The New Grove Dictionary of American Music*, Volume Three, edited by H. Wiley Hitchcock & Stanley Sadie. New York: Grove's Dictionaries of Music, Inc., 1986, 356–357.

Kozinn, Allan. "Violinist Isaac Stern Dies at 81; Led Efforts to Save Carnegie Hall." *The New York Times*, September 23, 2001. http://www.nytimes.com/2001/09/23/nyregion/violinist-isaac-stern-dies-at-81-led-efforts-to-save-carnegie-hall.html.

Krehbiel, H.E., Richard Aldrich, H.C. Colles/R. Allen Lott. "Damrosch Family." In *The New Grove Dictionary of American Music*, Volume One, edited by H. Wiley Hitchcock & Stanley Sadie. New York: Grove's Dictionaries of Music, Inc., 1986, 564–566.

Krehbiel, H.E., Richard Aldrich, H.C. Colles/R. Allen Lott. "Frank (Heino) Damrosch." In *The New Grove Dictionary of American Music*, Volume One, edited by H. Wiley Hitchcock & Stanley Sadie. New York: Grove's Dictionaries of Music, Inc., 1986, 565.

"Kronold Leaves Opera to Live Near Convent." *The New York Times*, October 3, 1904, 1. http://timesmachine.nytimes.com/timesmachine/1904/10/03/100475760.html?pageNumber=1.

"League Holds Its First Annual Exhibition." *Architectural League of New York*. http://archleague.org/2010/12/league-holds-its-first-annual-exhibition/.

"Lecture by Frank Damrosch." Performance History, Carnegie Hall. www.carnegiehall.org/PerformanceHistorySearch/#!

Legge, Robin H./Jerrold Northrop Moore/Katherine K. Preston. "Godowsky, Leopold." In *The New Grove Dictionary of American Music*, Volume Two, edited by H. Wiley Hitchcock & Stanley Sadie. New York: Grove's Dictionaries of Music, Inc., 1986, 235.

"Leila Rummel, 87, Morse's Daughter." *The New York Times*, December 10, 1937, 25. http://timesmachine.nytimes.com/timesmachine/1937/12/10/101016062.html?pageNumber=25.

"Leopold Godowsky." Performance History, Carnegie Hall. www.carnegiehall.org/PerformanceHistorySearch/#!

"Lillie P. Berg." Performance History, Carnegie Hall. www.carnegiehall.org/PerformanceHistorySearch/#!

Lister, Michael. C. "Israel in Egypt." Indianapolis Symphonic Choir. Program notes. http://www.indychoir.org/wp-content/uploads/2014/07/Israel-In-Egypt-Program-Notes-Wriitten-By-Michael-Lister.pdf.

"Live Musical Topics." *The New York Times*, March 8, 1891, p. 12. http://timesmachine.nytimes.com/timesmachine/1891/03/08/103298123.html?pageNumber=12.

"Live Musical Topics." *The New York Times*, May 17, 1891, 13. http://timesmachine.nytimes.com/timesmachine/1891/05/17/103307706.html?pageNumber=13.

"Live Musical Topics." *The New York Times*, June 7, 1891, 12. http://timesmachine.nytimes.com/timesmachine/1891/06/07/106049790.html?pageNumber=12.

"Losses by Fire." *The New York Times*, May 10, 1891, 2. http://timesmachine.nytimes.com/timesmachine/1891/05/10/103306326.html?pageNumber=2.

"Ludwig Van Beethoven." In *Composers on Music: Eight Centuries of Writings*, edited by Josiah Fisk. Boston: Northeastern University Press, 1997, 58.

"Macgahan, Barbara (Nee Varvara Elagina) 1850–1904." *Historical Dictionary of United States-Russian/Soviet Relations*, 236. https://books.google.com/books?id=Lf4lAAAAQBAJ&pg=PA236&lpg=PA236&dq=MacGahan,+Barbara+(nee+Varvara+Elagina)

+1850–1904,+Historical+Dictionary+of+United+States-Russian/Soviet+Relations, &source=bl&ots=KfSIfUmrra&sig=BQzk8IYwTTkof8L6SHkHuR7bsFg&hl=en&sa= X&ved=0CCAQ6AEwAGoVChMIjvaMhaisxwIVlBOSCh1uLQqM#v=onepage&q& f=false.

"Making a Case for Massenet, the Misunderstood Sentimentalist." *Deceptive Cadence* from NPR Classical, Tom Huizenga, August 14, 2012. http://www.npr.org/sections/ deceptivecadence/2012/08/14/158750921/making-a-case-for-massenet-the-misun derstood-sentimentalist

Mandel, Marc. "Wagner: Prelude and *Liebestod* from Tristan and Isolde." San Francisco Symphony. http://www.sfsymphony.org/Watch-Listen-Learn/Read-Program-Notes/ Program-Notes/WAGNER-Prelude-and-Liebestod-from-Tristan-und-Isol.aspx.

"Manhattan Beach's Jubilee." *The New York Times*, August 18, 1887, 3. http://timesmac hine.nytimes.com/timesmachine/1887/08/18/100929422.html?pageNumber=3.

"The Manuscript Society." *The New York Times*, December 11, 1890, 1890, 4. http://times machine.nytimes.com/timesmachine/1890/12/11/103285681.html?pageNumber=4.

"Manuscript Society's Dinner." *The New York Times*, April 21, 1893, 2. http://timesmach ine.nytimes.com/timesmachine/1893/04/21/109698147.html?pageNumber=2.

"Marie Ritter-Goetze" (Cinncinnati concert program). In *Andreas Dippel Concert Programs 1890–1892*. New York Public Library for the Performing Arts, Music Division, Special Collections.

Mawson, Harry P. "Tchaikovsky and the Music Festival." *Harper's Weekly*, Volume 35, May 9, 1891, 347. https://books.google.com/books?id=9kJaAAAAYAAJ&pg=PA347 &lpg=PA347&dq=thomas+ebert—oratorio+singer&source=bl&ots=VUBlHhZj Iu&sig=5GV0yhSYibHvoKQ_DkY2hZLYntU&hl=en&sa=X&ei=QBjRVMWrO ovIsATdm4LQCA&ved=0CB0Q6AEwADgK#v=onepage&q=thomas%20ebert— oratorio%20singer&f=false.

"Max Wilhelm Karl Vogrich." *The William Steinway Diary, 1861–1896*. Smithsonian Institution. National Museum of American History. http://americanhistory.si.edu/stein waydiary/annotations/?id=743.

"May Music Festival." *The Sun* (New York, N.Y.), March 7, 1891, 8. Library of Congress. Chronicling America: Historic American Newspapers. http://chroniclingamerica. loc.gov/lccn/sn83030272/1891-03-07/ed-1/seq-3.

May, Thomas. "Mendelssohn's Elijah." Nashville Symphony. Program notes. http://www. nashvillesymphony.org.

McCarthy, Margaret William. "Fay, Amy." In *The New Grove Dictionary of American Music*, Volume Two, edited by H. Wiley Hitchcock & Stanley Sadie. New York: Grove's Dictionaries of Music, Inc., 105.

McMillan, Jeffery S. "Grail Crazy." *Opera News*, March 2013. www.operanews.com/ Opera_News_Magazine/2013/3/Features/Grail_Crazy.html.

"Metropolitan Opera House." *The New York Times*, February 18, 1885, 5. http://timesmach ine.nytimes.com/timesmachine/1885/02/18/103627922.html?pageNumber=5.

"Miscellaneous Items." *Brenam Weekly Banner* (Brenham, Texas), May 7, 1891, 6. Library of Congress. Chronicling America: Historic American Newspapers. http://chroni clingamerica.loc.gov/lccn/sn86089443/1891/05/07/ed-1/seq-6/.

"Miss Berg's Concert." *The New York Times*, April 28, 1891, 4. http://timesmachine.ny times.com/timesmachine/1891/04/28/103304543.html?pageNumber=4.

"Miss Lillie Berg's Benefit." *The New York Times*, February 9, 1893, 5. http://timesmachine. nytimes.com/timesmachine/1893/02/09/106813332.html?pageNumber=5.

"Miss Titus to Become a Wife." *The New York Times*, June 3, 1896, 4. http://timesmachine. nytimes.com/timesmachine/1896/06/03/503156782.html?pageNumber=4.

Moore, Michael. "Elijah," program notes. The Mendelssohn Club of Philadelphia, April 21, 2007. www.mcchorus.org/program_notes/elijah042007.pdf.

"Morris Reno Dies at 83." *The New York Times*, June 12, 1917, 13. http://timesmachine. nytimes.com/timesmachine/1917/06/12/102352940.html?pageNumber=13.

"Mr. Carnegie's Wedding." *The New York Times*, April 23, 1887, 1. http://timesmachine. nytimes.com/timesmachine/1887/04/23/100908391.html?pageNumber=1.

"Mr. Franz Rummel's Recital." *The New York Times*, May 9, 1879, p. 5. http://timesmachine. nytimes.com/timesmachine/1879/05/09/80751936.html?pageNumber=5

"Mr. Rummel's Piano Recitals." *The New York Times*, February 25, 1881, p. 5. http:// timesmachine.nytimes.com/timesmachine/1881/02/25/98912925.html?pageNumber=5.

"Mr. Rummel's Recitals." *The New York Times*, December 5, 1890, 4. http://timesmachine. nytimes.com/timesmachine/1890/12/05/103284570.html?pageNumber=4.

"Mr. Santley Once More." *The New York Times*, May 5, 1891, 5. http://timesmachine. nytimes.com/timesmachine/1891/05/05/103305477.html?pageNumber=5.

"Mrs. Carnegie Dies." *The New York Times*, June 25, 1946, 22. http://timesmachine. nytimes.com/timesmachine/1946/06/25/107140095.html?pageNumber=22.

"Mrs. Ella A. Toedt of Juilliard School." *The New York Times*, June 14, 1939, 29. http:// timesmachine.nytimes.com/timesmachine/1939/06/14/93928711.html?pageNumber=29.

"Mrs. Gerrit Smith." *The New York Times*, June 4, 1940, 23. http://timesmachine.nytimes. com/timesmachine/1940/06/04/113378333.html?pageNumber=23.

"Mrs. Hattie Clapper Morris." *The New York Times*, January 23, 1930, 20. http://times machine.nytimes.com/timesmachine/1930/01/23/94233327.html?pageNumber=20.

"Mrs. S. Marie Reno Dead in Rome." *The New York Times*, November 14, 1915, 19. http:// timesmachine.nytimes.com/timesmachine/1915/11/14/101571329.html?pageNumber=19.

"Mrs. Theodore Sutro Dead." *The New York Times*, April 28, 1906, 11. http://timesmachine.nytimes.com/timesmachine/1906/04/28/101839400.html?pageNumber=11.

"Music: Arthur Friedheim's Recital." *New-York Tribune*, April 8, 1891, 6. Library of Congress. Chronicling America: Historic American Newspapers. http://chronicling america.loc.gov/lccn/sn83030214/1891–04-08/ed-1/seq-6/.

"Music. Mendelssohn's 'Elijah.'" *The New-York Tribune*, May 7, 1891, 6. Library of Congress. Chronicling America: Historic American Newspapers. http://chronicling america.loc.gov/lccn/sn 83030214/1891–05–07/ed-1/seq-6/.

"Music Crowned in Its New Home." *New York Herald*, May 6, 1891, 7. http://fultonhistory. com/my%20photo%20albums/All%20Newspapers/New%20York%20NY%20Herald/ index.html.

"Music for the Massses." *The New York Times*, February 3, 1890, 8. http://timesmachine. nytimes.com/timesmachine/1890/02/03/103227282.html?pageNumber=8.

"Music Hall, The." *The New-York Tribune*, May 3, 1891, 5. Library of Congress. Chronicling America: Historic American Newspapers. http://chroniclingamerica.loc.gov/lccn/ sn83030272/1891–05-03/ed-1/seq-5/

"Music Hall Concerts, The." *The New York Times*, May 10, 1891, 5. http://timesmachine. nytimes.com/timesmachine/1891/05/10/103306374.html?pageNumber=5.

"Music Hall Opened, The." *The New-York Tribune*, May 6, 1891, 1. Library of Congress. Chronicling America: Historic American Newspapers. http://chroniclingamerica. loc.gov/lccn/sn83030214/1891–05-06/ed-1/seq-1/.

"Music Hall Perquisites." *The New York Times*, May 10, 1891, 8. http://timesmachine. nytimes.com/timesmachine/1891/05/10/103306404.html?pageNumber=8.

"Music Hall's Fire Baptism." *The Evening World (Baseball Extra)*, May 9, 1891, 3. Library of Congress. Chronicling America: Historic American Newspapers. http://chroni clingamerica.loc.gov/lccn/sn83030193/1891–05-09/ed-4/seq-3/.

"Music in Boston." *The Musical Record & Review*, Issues 105–106, 1880, 149.

"Music: Last of the Festival Concerts." *New-York Tribune*, May 10, 1891, 7. Library of Congress. Chronicling America: Historic American Newspapers. http://chronicling america.loc.gov/lccn/sn83030214/1891–05-10/ed-1/seq-7/.

"Music of the Week: Personal Gossip of Musicians, by One of Them." *Music and Drama: A Journal Devoted to Sport, Music and the Drama*, April 8, 1893, 17.

"Music: The Oratorio Society." *The Critic*, Volume 2, May 6, 1882, 134.

"Music: Third Night of the Festival." *New-York Tribune*, May, 1891, 6. Library of Congress.

Chronicling America: Historic American Newspapers. http://chroniclingamerica. loc.gov/lccn/sn83030214/1891–05-09/ed-1/seq-6/.

"Music's Promised Home." *The New York Times*, May 14, 1890, 8. http://timesmachine. nytimes.com/timesmachine/1890/05/14/103242914.html?pageNumber=8.

"Musical Correspondence." *Dwight's Journal of Music*. April 12, 1879, 63.

"Musical Notes." *The New York Times*, February 15, 1880, p. 7. http://timesmachine. nytimes.com/timesmachine/1880/02/15/98887197.html?pageNumber=7.

"Musical Notes." *The New-York Tribune*, April 3, 1880, 4. Library of Congress. Chronicling America: Historic American Newspapers. http://chroniclingamerica.loc.gov/lccn. sn83030214/1880–03-ed-1/seq-4/.

"Musical Notes." *The New York Times*, October 26, 1890, p. 13. http://timesmachine. nytimes.com/timesmachine/1890/10/26/103273963.html?pageNumber=13.

"Musical Notes." *The New York Times*, December 21, 1890, 13. http://timesmachine. nytimes.com/timesmachine/1890/12/21/103287545.html?pageNumber=13.

"Musical Notes." *The New York Times*, January 4, 1891, 13. http://timesmachine.nytimes. com/timesmachine/1891/01/04/103289441.html?pageNumber=13.

"Musical Notes. the *New York Times*, February 22, 1891, 13. Http://Timesmachine.Ny times.Com/Timesmachine/1891/02/22/106047138.Html?Pagenumber=13.

"Musical Notes." *The New York Times*. March 22, 1891, 13. http://timesmachine.nytimes. com/timesmachine/1891/03/22/issue.html.

"Musical Notes." *The New York Times*, April 5, 1891, 13. http://timesmachine.nytimes. com/timesmachine/1891/04/05/103301272.html?pageNumber=13.

"Musical Notes." *The New York Times*, April 19, 1891, 13. http://timesmachine.nytimes. com/timesmachine/1891/04/19/103303113.html?pageNumber=13.

"Napoleon Sarony (1821–1896)." Broadway Photographs.http://broadway.cas.sc.edu/ content/napoleon-sarony.

"Napoleon Sarony (1821–1896)." National Portrait Gallery. www.npg.org.uk/collections/ search/person.php?LinkID=mp07523&wPage=1.

"New Concert Room, A." *The Sun* (New York, N.Y.), March 13, 1891. Library of Congress. Chronicling America: Historic American Newspapers. http://chroniclingamerica. loc.gov/lccn/sn83030272/1891–03-13/ed-1/seq-3/.

"New Home for a College of Music, A." *New-York Tribune*, June 26, 1891, 7. Library of Congress. Chronicling America: Historic American Newspapers. http://chronicling america.loc.gov/lccn/sn83030214/1891–06-26/ed-1/seq-7/.

"New Home for Music, A." *The Sun* (New York, N.Y.), May 14, 1890, 7. Library of Congress. Chronicling America: Historic American Newspapers. http://chronicling america.loc.gov/lccn/sn83030272/1890–05-14/ed-1/seq-7/.

"New Music for Plymouth Church." *The New York Times*, February 14, 1885, 5. http:// timesmachine.nytimes.com/timesmachine/1885/02/14/106299095.html?pageNum ber=5.

"New Music Hall, A." *Musical Courier*, March 20, 1889, 2 (222). University of Michigan Library, Hathi Trust Digital Library. http://babel.hathitrust.org/cgi/pt?id=mdp. 39015025410013;view=1up;seq=230.

"New Music Hall, The." *The New York Times*, March 24, 1889, 3. http://timesmachine. nytimes.com/timesmachine/1889/03/24/106205968.html?pageNumber=3.

"New Music Hall, The." *The New-York Daily Tribune*, May 3, 1891, 5. Library of Congress. Chronicling America: Historic American Newspapers. http://chroniclingamerica. loc.gov/lccn/sn83030272/1891–05-03/ed-1/seq-5/.

New Music Review and Church Music Review, The. Volume 4. New York: Novello, Ewer & Company, 1904.

"New Steam-Ship Fulda, The." *The New York Times*, March 24, 1883, 5. http://timesmach ine.nytimes.com/timesmachine/1883/03/24/102807358.html?pageNumber=5.

"News of the World, The." *The Indiana State Sentinel*, May 6, 1891, 6. Library of Congress. Chronicling America: Historic American Newspapers. http://chroniclingamerica. loc.gov/lccn/sn87056600/1891–05-06/ed-1/seq-6/.

"New-York City." *New-York Tribune*, March 7, 1895, 12. Library of Congress. Chronicling

America: Historic American Newspapers. http://chroniclingamerica.loc.gov/lccn/ sn83030214/1895–03-07/ed-1/seq-12/.

"New York City Signs—14th to 42nd Street." www.14to42.net/17street4.5.html.

"New-York College of Music." *The New York Times*, May 14, 1890, 4. http://timesmachine. nytimes.com/timesmachine/1890/05/14/103242881.html?pageNumber=4.

"Nordica Thinks It Ridiculous." *The New York Times*, December 5, 1894, 8. http://times machine.nytimes.com/timesmachine/1894/12/05/106842508.html?pageNumber =8.

"Notes and Comments." *The Iola Register* (Iola, Kansas), May 88, 1891, 6. Library of Congress. Chronicling America: Historic American Newspapers. http://chroniclingamer ica.loc.gov/lccn/sn83040340/1891–05-08/ed-1/seq-6/.

"Notes of Music." *The New York Times*, March 4, 1894, 16. http://timesmachine.nytimes. com/timesmachine/1894/03/04/106898815.html?pageNumber=16.

"Notes of the Stage." *The New York Times*, June 5, 1885, 4. http://timesmachine.nytimes. com/timesmachine/1885/06/05/103021833.html?pageNumber=4.

"Notes of the Stage." *The New York Times*, September 7, 1890, 13. http://timesmachine. nytimes.com/timesmachine/1890/09/07/106042481.html?pageNumber=13.

"Notes of the Stage." *The New York Times*, April 5, 1891, 13. http://timesmachine.nytimes. com/timesmachine/1891/04/05/103301272.html?pageNumber=13

"Off for Europe." *The New York Times*, April 24, 1887, 3. http://timesmachine.nytimes. com/timesmachine/1887/04/24/103141709.html?pageNumber=3.

"Oratorio Society, The." *The New York Times*, November 16, 1888, 5. http://timesmachine. nytimes.com/timesmachine/1888/11/16/100951689.html?pageNumber=5.

"Oratorio Society, The." *The New York Times*, March 16, 1890, 3. http://timesmachine. nytimes.com/timesmachine/1890/03/16/103234059.html?pageNumber=3.

"Outline of Raff's Life." *Joachim Raff*. www.raff.org/life/outline.htm.

Page, Tim. "Demanding 'Esclarmonde' Gets Vigorous, If Dubious, Workout. the *Washington Post* Online, April 11, 2005. Http://Www.Washingtonpost.Com/Wp-Dyn/Arti cles/A42725–2005apr10.Html.

Palaces for the People. the Museum of the City of New York. Exhibit, March 26 Through September 7, 2014. Www.Mcny.Org/Palaces-For-The-People-Guastavino.

"Pastor Weds the Soprano." *The Evening World, Extra 2:00 O'clock*, May 8, 1891, 1. Library of Congress. Chronicling America: Historic American Newspapers. http://chroni clingamerica.loc.gov/lccn/sn83030193/1891–05-08/ed-1/seq-1/.

"Peace on the Steinway Road." *The New York Times*, May 6, 1891, 8. http://timesmachine. nytimes.com/timesmachine/1891/05/06/103305674.html?pageNumber=8.

"Piano Concerto No. 1." *Tchaikovsky Research*. http://en.tchaikovskyresearch.net/pages/ Piano_Concerto_No._1.

"Piotr Ilyich Tchaikovsky, 1840–1893." In *Composers on Music*, edited by Josiah Fisk. Boston: Northeastern University Press, 1997, 159.

Plotkin, Fred. "In the Footsteps of Richard Wagner: Zurich (Part II)." WQXR. http://www. wqxr.org/#!/story/309018-footsteps-richard-wagner-zurich-part-ii/.

Plunz, Richard. "Apartments." In *The Encyclopedia of New York City*, edited by Kenneth T. Jackson. New Haven: Yale University Press & New York: The New-York Historical Society, 1995, 39.

"Popular Free Concert, A." *The New York Times*, March 2, 1891, 3. http://timesmachine. nytimes.com/timesmachine/1891/03/02/106047552.html?pageNumber=3.

"Premiums for the Boxes." *The New York Times*, April 1, 1891, 3. http://timesmachine. nytimes.com/timesmachine/1891/04/01/103300633.html?pageNumber=3.

"Preparing for 'Elijah.'" *The Saint Paul Daily Globe*, May 7, 1891, 3. Library of Congress. Chronicling America: Historic American Newspapers. http://chroniclingamerica. loc.gov/lccn/sn90059522/1891–05-07/ed-1/seq-3/.

"Press: Clipping Business, The." *Time*, May 30, 1932. http://content.time.com/time/ magazine/article/0,9171,769604,00.html.

"Raconteur, The." *Musical Courier*, Volume 18–19. March 13, 1889, 203. http://babel. hathitrust.org/cgi/pt?id=mdp.39015025410013;view=1up;seq=211.

"Ralph Vaughan Williams 1872–1958." In *Composers on Music: Eight Centuries of Writings,* edited by Josiah Fisk. Boston: Northwestern University Press, 1997, 230.

"Rare Musical Event, A." *The Sun* (New York, N.Y.), May 6, 1891, 1. Library of Congress. Chronicling America: Historic American Newspapers. http://chroniclingamerica. loc.gov/lccn/sn83030272/1891–05-06/ed-1/seq-1/.

"Rather Disappointing." *The Pittsburgh Dispatch,* May 7, 1891, 1. Library of Congress. Chronicling America: Historic American Newspapers. http://chroniclingamerica. loc.gov/lccn/sn84024546/1891–05-07/ed-1/seq-1/.

"Real Estate: Justus M. Phelps, Auctioneer." *The Sun* (New York, N.Y.), July 4, 1872, 4. Library of Congress. Chronicling America: Historic American Newspapers. http:// chroniclingamerica.loc.gov/lccn/sn83030272/1872–07-04/ed-1/seq-4/.

"Real Estate: O.H. Pierson, Auctioneer." *The Sun* (New York, N.Y.), October 11, 1872, 4. Library of Congress. Chronicling America: Historic American Newspapers. http:// chroniclingamerica.loc.gov/lccn/sn83030272/1872–10-11/ed-1/seq-4/.

Real Estate Record and Builders' Guide, Volume 51. Ads following p. 652. https://books. google.com/books?id=4rlRAAAAYAAJ&pg=PA653-IA1&lpg=PA653-IA1&dq=%22 Johnson+%26+Morris%22+—+1890&source=bl&ots=7SLtCh1823&sig=20cMrbT 33XG0Gsle2SY4a51gVB8&hl=en&sa=X&ei=Qt93VPr6KLeQsQT9sYHgAQ&ved= 0CEYQ6AEwCQ#v=onepage&q=%22Johnson%20%26%20Morris%22%20—%2018 90&f=false.

"Real Estate: The N.J. Land and Improvement Building Company." *The Sun (New York, N.Y.),* June 15, 1872, 4. Library of Congress. Chronicling America: Historic American Newspapers. http://chroniclingamerica.loc.gov/lccn/sn83030272/1872–06-15/ed-1/seq-4/.

"Red Tower Replacing Carnegie Hall, A." *Life,* September 9, 1957, 91. https://books.google. com/books?id=UT8EAAAAMBAJ&q=carnegie+hall#v=snippet&q=carnegie%20 hall&f=false.

"Richard Strauss 1864–1949." In *Composers on Music: Eight Centuries of Writings,* edited by Josiah Fisk. Boston: Northwestern University Press, 1997, 212.

Risinger, Mark P. "Notes on the Concert—Israel in Egypt: A Composer Masters the Oratorio Form." The Providence Singers. http://www.providencesingers/org/Concerts 06/Season02–03/Mar03Concert.html.

"Robert Green Ingersoll." http://www.RobertGreenIngersoll.org.

"Robert Green Ingersoll: Colonel, United States Army." Arlington National Cemetery. www.arlingtoncemetery.net/rgingersoll.htm.

"Root's Patent Spiral Pipe: Made of Sheet-Iron, Either Black Galvanized or Asphalted for Water Works and Hydraulic Mininc." *The Chace Catalog.* http://chace.athm.org/ singleDisplay.php?kv=58341.

Rossberg, Herman. "Wedding Ensemble," from "The Collection Online." The Metropolitan Museum of Art. www.metmuseum.org/collection/the-collection-online/search/ 81137.

Rubin, Emanuel. "Jeannette Meyers Thurber and the National Conservatory of Music." In *American Music,* Volume 8, Number 3, Fall 1990, 294–298.

"Rudolph E. Schirmer 1859–1919." *The Etude,* October 1919. www.etudemagazine.com.

Saloman, Ora Frishberg. "Presenting Berlioz's Music in New York, 1846–1890: Carl Bergmann, Theodore Thomas, Leopold Damrosch." In *European Music and Musicians in New York City, 1840–1900,* edited by John Graziano. Rochester: University of Rochester Press, 2006, 37–39.

Schwartz, Elizabeth. "Pyotr Ilyich Tchaikovsky: Piano Concerto No. 1 in B-Flat Minor, Op. 23." The Oregon Symphony, *Tchaikovsky Spectacular.* Program Notes. http:// www.orsymphony.org/concerts/1415/programnotes/sc4.aspx.

Schweitzer, Vivien. "No, Not That Concerto: New York Philharmonic Plays Tchaikovsky at Avery Fisher Hall." *The New York Times,* July 8, 2012. http://www.nytimes.com/ 2012/07/09/arts/music/new-york-philharmonic-plays-tchaikovsky-at-avery-fisher-hall.html?_r=0.

Shanet, Howard. "Orchestras." In *The New Grove Dictionary of American Music,* Volume

Three, edited by H. Wiley Hitchcock & Stanley Sadie. New York: Grove's Dictionaries of Music, Inc., 1986, 436–444.

"Sherman W. Knevals," *Biographical Directory of the State of New York, 1900.* New York: Biographical Directory Company, 1899. http://www.archive.org/details/biographical dire00biog.

"Sherman's Memory Honored." *The Evening World, 5 O'clock Special,* May 7, 1891, 1. Library of Congress. Chronicling America: Historic American Newspapers. http:// chroniclingamerica.loc.gov/lccn/sn83030193/1891/05/07/ed-3/seq-1/.

Shirley, Wayne D. "Leopold Damrosch as Composer." In *European Music and Musicians in New York City, 1840–1900,* edited by John Graziano. Rochester: University of Rochester Press, 2006, 105–106.

Smith, James G., Thomas Brawley. "Choral Music." In *The New Grove Dictionary of American Music,* Volume One, edited by H. Wiley Hitchcock & Stanley Sadie. New York: Grove's Dictionaries of Music, Inc., 1986, 431–432.

"The Social World." *The New York Times,* April 17, 1894, 5. http://timesmachine.nytimes. com/timesmachine/1894/04/17/104109000.html?pageNumber=5.

"Society Topics of the Week." *The New York Times,* January 11, 1891. http://timesmachine. nytimes.com/timesmachine/1890/12/21/103287540.html?pageNumber=12.

"Some Fine New Buildings." *The New York Times,* December 15, 1889, 11. http://times machine.nytimes.com/timesmachine/1889/12/15/100981377.html?pageNumber=11.

Steinberg, Michael. "Beethoven: Leonore Overture No. 3, Opus 72a." San Francisco Symphony. Program notes. http://www.sfsymphony.org/Watch-Listen-Learn/Read-Program-Notes/Program-Notes/BEETHOVEN-Leonore-Overture-No-3,-Opus-72a.aspx.

"Suite No. 3 in G Major, Op. 55, Pyotr Ilyich Tchaikovsky." NY Phil. http://nyphil.org/~/ media/pdfs/program-notes/1314/TchaikovskySuite%20No%203%20in%20G%20 major.pdf.

"Theatrical Gossip." *The New York Times,* May 5, 1891, 7. http://timesmachine.nytimes. com/timesmachine/1891/05/05/103305515.html?pageNumber=8.

"These Women Know Law." *The New York Times,* April 11, 1891, 4. http://timesmachine. nytimes.com/timesmachine/1891/04/11/103302026.html?pageNumber=4.

"This Is an Explanation: The Music Hall Managers and Ticket Speculators." *The New York Times,* April 27, 1891, 5. http://timesmachine.nytimes.com/timesmachine/1891/ 04/27/103304393.html?pageNumber=5.

"Troubadour Song." *World's Best Music, The.* Volume 1. Editors and special contributors, Helen Kendrick Johnson, Frederic Dean, Reginald deKoven, Gerrit Smith. New York: The University Society, 1904, 29. The University of Michigan, digitized October 2, 2009. https://books.google.com/books?id=Vk3kAAAAMAAJ&pg=PA29&lpg=PA 29&dq=st.+chrysostom%27s+chapel—wenzel+a.+raboch&source=bl&ots=NCB3V_ NrVN&sig=-6Afg-2l_lICajGEX1zQDLXg_7k&hl=en&sa=X&ei=UTlpVPTMD6GL sQTbwIKwAQ&ved=0CB4Q6AEwAA#v=onepage&q=st.%20chrysostom's%20cha pel—wenzel%20a.%20raboch&f=false.

"Trumpet Call from the Overture Leonore No. 3 by Ludwig Van Beethoven." MFiles. http://www.mfiles.co.uk/scores/trumpet-call-from-beethoven-overture-leonore-no3.htm.

Tuthill, Burnet C. Letter to Music Editor in "Mail Pouch: Carnegie." *The New York Times,* January 31, 1960, 337. http://timesmachine.nytimes.com/timesmachine/1960/01/ 31/99473690.html?pageNumber=337.

"UMS Concert Program, December 9, 1881: Haydn's Oratorio of 'The Creation'—The Choral Union." University Musical Society: A History of Great Performance. Ann Arbor District Library. www.ums.aadl.org/ums/programs_18811209.

University Musical Society: "A History of Great Performance." UMS Concert Program, December 9, 1881: Haydn's Oratorio of 'the Creation'—The Choral Union. www. ums.aadl.org/ums/programs_18811209.

United States Federal Census 1900, Manhattan, New York, New York; Roll 1103; Page 14A; Enumeration District: 0481; FHL microfilm 1241103 (William Z. [sic] Tuthill).

Untitled. *Chariton Courier* (Keytesville, Missouri), May 7, 1891, 1. Library of Congress. Chronicling America: Historic American Newspapers. http://chroniclingamerica. loc.gov/lccn/sn88068010/1891–05-07/ed-1/seq-1/.
"Virginia News." *Alexandria Gazette*, May 28, 1891, 2. Library of Congress. Chronicling America: Historic American Newspapers. http://chroniclingamerica.loc.gov/lccn sn85025007/1891–05–28/ed-1/seq-2/.
"Von Bulow Is Here." *The New York Times*, March 24, 1889, 9. http://timesmachine.ny times.com/timesmachine/1889/03/24/106206070.html?pageNumber=9.
"Walter Damrosch, 1862–1950)." *Performing Arts Encyclopedia*, Library of Congress. http://lcweb2.loc.gov/diglib/ihas/loc.natlib.ihas.200035728/default.html
"Walter Damrosch Sued." *The New York Times*, September 3, 1896, 8. http://timesmac hine.nytimes.com/timesmachine/1896/09/03/106884597.html?pageNumber=8.
"Walter W. Naumburg 1867–1959. Founder of the Walter W. Naumburg Memorial Funds in the New York Community Trust." 909 Third Avenue, New York, NY, 10022, pamphlet. http://www.nycommunitytrust.org/Portals/0/Uploads/Documents/BioBro chures/Walter%20W.%20Naumburg.pdf.
"The Washington Arch." *The New York Times*, May 28, 1890, 5. http://timesmachine.ny times.com/timesmachine/1890/05/28/103245170.html?pageNumber=5.
Waters, Deborah Dependahl. "Herter Brothers." In *Encyclopedia of New York City*, edited by Kenneth T. Jackson. New Haven: Yale University Press & New York: The New-York Historical Society, 1995, 541.
"Wedded in Washington." *The New York Times*, May 18, 1890, 1. http://timesmachine. nytimes.com/timesmachine/1890/05/18/103243355.html?pageNumber=1.
"William-Adolphe Bouguereau. *Nymphs and Satyr* 1873." The Clark Museum. www.clark art.edu/Art-Pieces/6158.
"William B. Tuthill." *New York, New York, City Directory 1883*, 884. In ancestry.com U.S. City Directories 1821–1989 (database on-line), Provo, UT, USA. Ancestry.com Operations, Inc., 2011.
"William B. Tuthill, Architect, Is Dead." *The New York Times*, August 27, 1929, 21. http:// timesmachine.nytimes.com/timesmachine/1929/08/27/94174740.html?pageNum ber=21.
"William S. Hawk Was Retired Hotel Owner." *The Kingston Daily Freeman*, March 15, 1935, 17. http://fultonhistory.com/newspaper%2010/Kingston%20NY%20Daily%20 Freeman/Kingston%20NY%20Daily%20Freeman%201935%20Grayscale/Kingston %20NY%20Daily%20Freeman%201935%20-%201090.pdf.
"Woes of the Beth-El Choir." *The Sun* (New York, N.Y.), November 6, 1891, 3. Library of Congress. Chronicling America: Historic American Newspapers. http://chronicling america.loc.gov/lccn/sn83030193/1893–07-27/ed-1/seq-5/.
Wolford, Claire Ashley. "Archivist's Angle: The NYU Glee Club." *NYU Alumni Connect*. www.alumni.nyu.edu/s/1068/2col_scripts.aspx?sid=1068&gid=1&pgid=2568.
Wolz, Larry. "Van Der Stucken, Frank Valentine." *Handbook of Texas Online*. Published by the Texas State Historical Association. http://www.txhaonline.org/handbook/ online/articles/fva04.
"Women in Music: 1850–1900." *Oxford Music Online*. http://www.oxfordmusiconline. com/public/page/Women_in_music.
"World of Music, The." *The Musical Record & Review*, July 1893, 5.
"Xavier Scharwenka Arrives." *The New York Times*, January 5, 1891, 8. http://timesmac hine.nytimes.com/timesmachine/1891/01/05/103289642.html?pageNumber=8.
Young, J. Bradford. "Schuberth, E." In *The New Grove Dictionary of American Music*, Volume Four, edited by H. Wiley Hitchcock & Stanley Sadie. New York: Grove's Dictionaries of Music, Inc., 1986, 164.

Archival Sources

Carnegie Hall Archives. Programs, clippings files, scrapbooks.
Library of Congress. Chronicling America: Historic American Newspapers.

Museum of the City of New York. Clippings files, programs, miscellany.

New-York Historical Society. Maps, clippings files.

New York Public Library for the Performing Arts, Music Division, Research and Special Collections.

—Clippings files: Alves, Mrs. Carl; Benham, A. Victor; Behrens, Conrad; Berg, Lillie P.; Carnegie Hall; De Vere, Clementine; Dippel, Andreas; Fischer, Emil; Mielke, Antonia; Reichmann, Theodor; Ritter-Goetze, Marie; Symphony Society.

—*Carnegie Hall: Collections of Ledgers and Cash Books Covering the Period 1891–1925.*

—*Frank Damrosch Papers 1859–1937.* Boxes 1–4.

—*Walter Damrosch Papers 1862–1950.* Boxes 1–51.

Copies of correspondence from Walter Damrosch to Dr. Franz W. Beidler (Box 8) dated December 14, 1936; May 28, 1937; and July 14, 1937.

Copy of correspondence from Walter Damrosch to Alfred A. Knopf, Esq. (Box 8) dated December 1, 1937.

New York Times, The. Online archival newspapers.

Oratorio Society of New York.

—*The Oratorio Society Minutes 1889–1899.* Entries from May 12, 1890 to May 13, 1891, including the letter from Andrew Carnegie to William Tuthill dated May 13, 1891. Used with the permission of the Oratorio Society of New York.

—*A Record of the Sixteenth Season, 1888–1889, Of the Oratorio Society of New York— Musical Director, Walter J. Damrosch.* Used with the permission of the Oratorio Society of New York.

Index

Numbers in *bold italics* indicate pages with photographs.